CHARL
MAJOR POETIC WORKS

broadview editions
series editor: Martin R. Boyne

CHARLOTTE SMITH: MAJOR POETIC WORKS

edited by
Claire Knowles and Ingrid Horrocks

broadview editions

BROADVIEW PRESS – www.broadviewpress.com
Peterborough, Ontario, Canada

Founded in 1985, Broadview Press remains a wholly independent publishing house. Broadview's focus is on academic publishing; our titles are accessible to university and college students as well as scholars and general readers. With over 600 titles in print, Broadview has become a leading international publisher in the humanities, with world-wide distribution. Broadview is committed to environmentally responsible publishing and fair business practices.

The interior of this book is printed on 100% recycled paper.

PERMANENT   100%   BIO GAS   Ancient Forest Friendly™

© 2017 Claire Knowles and Ingrid Horrocks

Library and Archives Canada Cataloguing in Publication

Smith, Charlotte, 1749–1806
[Poems. Selections]
    Charlotte Smith : major poetic works / edited by Claire Knowles and Ingrid Horrocks.

(Broadview editions)
Includes bibliographical references.
ISBN 978-1-55481-284-4 (softcover)

    I. Knowles, Claire, editor II. Horrocks, Ingrid, editor III. Title.
IV. Title: Poems. Selections. V. Series: Broadview editions

PR3688.S4A6 2017   821'.6   C2017-900397-6

Broadview Editions
The Broadview Editions series is an effort to represent the ever-evolving canon of texts in the disciplines of literary studies, history, philosophy, and political theory. A distinguishing feature of the series is the inclusion of primary source documents contemporaneous with the work.

Advisory editor for this volume: Juliet Sutcliffe

Broadview Press handles its own distribution in North America
PO Box 1243, Peterborough, Ontario K9J 7H5, Canada
555 Riverwalk Parkway, Tonawanda, NY 14150, USA
Tel: (705) 743-8990; Fax: (705) 743-8353
email: customerservice@broadviewpress.com

Distribution is handled by Eurospan Group in the UK, Europe, Central Asia, Middle East, Africa, India, Southeast Asia, Central America, South America, and the Caribbean. Distribution is handled by Footprint Books in Australia and New Zealand.

Broadview Press acknowledges the financial support of the Government of Canada through the Canada Book Fund for our publishing activities.

Canada

Typesetting and assembly: True to Type Inc., Claremont, Canada
Cover Design: Aldo Fierro

PRINTED IN CANADA

Contents

List of Illustrations

All illustrations are from Charlotte Smith, *Elegiac Sonnets; and Other Poems* (London: Printed for T. Cadell, Junior, and W. Davies, 1797), Rare Book Division, Department of Rare Books and Special Collections, Princeton University Library. Figures 1–4 and 7 first appeared in the 1789 fifth edition of the work. Figures 6 and 8 first appeared in Volume Two of the two-volume edition of 1797. Figure 5 appeared in both Volume One and Volume Two in the 1797 and 1800 editions.

List of Abbreviations

For all poems by Charlotte Smith, unless otherwise stated, line numbers referred to are to this Broadview edition.

BH   *Beachy Head.*

CL   *The Collected Letters of Charlotte Smith.* Ed. Judith Stanton. Bloomington: Indiana UP, 2003.

ES   *Elegiac Sonnets.*

Em   *The Emigrants.*

Acknowledgements

We would like to thank the Rare Book Division, Department of Rare Books and Special Collections, Princeton University Library, for permission to use the images from their copy of Charlotte Smith's *Elegiac Sonnets*; Broadview Press for permission to reproduce some of Mary Robinson's texts as presented in her *Selected Poems*, ed. Judith Pascoe (Peterborough, ON: Broadview, 2000); Cornell University Press for allowing us to reproduce lines from *The Prelude, 1798–1799*, The Cornell Wordsworth, ed. Stephen Parrish (Ithaca, NY: Cornell UP, 1977); and Indiana University Press for permission to quote from Smith, *The Collected Letters of Charlotte Smith*, ed. Judith Stanton (Bloomington: Indiana UP, 2003).

Our work on the preparation of this text has been supported by our home institutions, La Trobe University and Massey University. In particular, we would like to acknowledge the financial support of the Disciplinary Research Program in English and Theatre at La Trobe and the Massey University Research Fund Award as well as Massey's School of English and Media Studies. We are especially grateful for the support that allowed Claire to spend time in Wellington and Ingrid to spend time in Melbourne working on the text, as well as to Tessa Pratt and Robyn Walton, who provided us with invaluable research assistance and additional meticulous sets of eyes.

For reading and commenting on the Introduction we would like to thank Elizabeth Gray, Nikki Hessell, Peter Otto, and Sarah Ross. For valuable early feedback on the project we would also like to thank Harriet Guest, Stephen Behrendt, Thomas McLean, Marjorie Mather, the three anonymous readers at Broadview Press, and the contributors to the Women and Nineteenth Century Literature conference, Alexander Turnbull Library, Wellington, January 2015, who responded to our paper "Editing Charlotte Smith for the 21st Century." For her attentive copyediting we thank Juliet Sutcliffe. We would like to acknowledge Stuart Curran's ground-breaking work on Smith: all subsequent Smith scholars owe an enormous debt of gratitude to him.

We would also like to thank our families. Working on Charlotte Smith made us particularly grateful for our supportive partners, Daniel Ooi and Tim Corballis, and the material circumstances of our twenty-first-century lives. We would like to thank our children, Benjamin and Hazel, and Natasha and Lena, for being delightful and for keeping us grounded. And finally, we would like acknowledge our parents, especially Claire's father, David, who passed away unexpectedly while we were putting the finishing touches on this project.

Introduction

Politics, Poetics, and Place: Charlotte Smith's Major Works in Context

Given that the novelist and poet Charlotte Smith (1749–1806) was forced by necessity to expend so much energy on the business of simple daily survival—dealing with creditors; negotiating with lawyers and publishers; managing the fall-out from the shady dealings of a recalcitrant ex-husband; and providing for their eleven surviving children—it is remarkable that she also managed to become one of the most popular, influential, and important literary voices of the late eighteenth and early nineteenth centuries. Smith was a woman of powerful intellect, wide reading, and strongly held views, and her major poetic works are remarkable for the breadth and depth with which they engage with some of the most pressing issues of her time. In *Elegiac Sonnets*, first published in 1784 and expanded over the course of her lifetime, Smith created an autobiographical poetic persona whose melancholy musings resonated with a society keenly interested in figures of suffering and loss.[1] In *The Emigrants* (1793), a long poem in blank verse, Smith combined the personal with the political by paralleling her own experiences with those of the exiled French gentry and bourgeoisie who were forced to flee over the English Channel in the wake of the French Revolution. Her final experiment in blank verse, *Beachy Head* (1807), has long been recognized as her masterpiece. In this long poem, Smith meditates on the turbulent moment of the present (in which Britain was at war with France and feared imminent invasion) and parallel moments from England's past, all the while displaying an astonishing command of contemporaneous developments in geology, biology, and botany.

---

1   This figure of melancholy suffering had previously been exemplified in characters such as Werther, the eponymous hero of Goethe's *Die Leiden des Jungen Werthers* (1774) (translated into English in 1779 as *The Sorrows of Werter: A German Story*), and Harley, the protagonist of Henry Mackenzie's *The Man of Feeling* (1771). Smith feminized this figure and associated her with the production of poetry. For a general account of the significance of powerful feeling in this period, see Janet Todd, *Sensibility: An Introduction* (London and New York: Methuen, 1986). Claire Knowles explores Smith's poetic persona in detail in her book *Sensibility and Female Poetic Tradition, 1780–1860: The Legacy of Charlotte Smith* (Farnham: Ashgate, 2009).

The importance of Charlotte Smith's work, especially in relation to the development of a recognizably English sonnet tradition, was widely acknowledged in her own time. The sonnet had had its first flowering in English during the Renaissance, when it was imported from the Italian form by Thomas Wyatt.[1] Paula R. Feldman and Daniel Robinson note that "the sonnet became, during the English Renaissance, an experiment by which poets could prove their virtuosity and technical skill as well as their earnestness."[2] Poets like John Donne (1573–1631), John Milton (1608–74), Edmund Spenser (c. 1552–99) and William Shakespeare (1564–1616), popularized the form in the sixteenth and seventeenth centuries, but the sonnet fell out of fashion in the late 1600s until interest in the form was revived in the latter part of the eighteenth century. Samuel Taylor Coleridge (1772–1834) famously names Smith and her contemporary William Lisle Bowles (1762–1850) as key figures in this sonnet revival. Coleridge praises Smith's and Bowles's innovations in the genre, noting particularly their divergence from the strict and limited rhyme scheme characteristic of the Petrarchan (Italian) sonnet.[3] "Charlotte Smith and Bowles," he writes, "are they who first made the Sonnet popular among the present English: I am justified therefore by analogy in deducing its laws from *their* compositions."[4] The journalist and political radical John Thelwall (1764–1834) was even more fulsome in his praise, proclaiming Smith the undisputed English master of the genre. Charlotte

---

1 Paula R. Feldman and Daniel Robinson, "Introduction," *A Century of Sonnets: The Romantic Era Revival* (Oxford: Oxford UP, 1999), 5.
2 Feldman and Robinson 6.
3 There are two forms of the sonnet, the Petrarchan (or Italian) and the Shakespearean (or English), although numerous variations on these two basic forms are possible. The Italian sonnet consists of an octave (a group of eight lines) that typically rhymes abbaabba and a sestet (a group of six lines) that typically rhymes cdecde or cdcdcd. In the Petrarchan form, the octave typically develops one thought and the sestet varies this thought and completes it. This is called a "volta" or turn. The English sonnet, in contrast, typically has three quatrains (groups of four lines) rhyming abab, bcbc, cdcd and finishes with a rhyming couplet, ee. This form of the sonnet allows for the wider scope of rhymes possible in the English language.
4 Samuel Taylor Coleridge, "Introduction to the Sonnets," *Poems*, 2nd ed. (London, 1797), 71; emphasis in original. See Appendix B3. A characteristic sonnet by William Lisle Bowles and Thomas Gray's influential "Sonnet on the Death of Mr Richard West" are provided in Appendix A3 and A1, respectively.

Smith's sonnets, he writes, "display a more touching melancholy, a more poetical simplicity, nay I will venture to say, a greater vigour and correctness of genius, than any other English poems that I have ever seen, under the same denomination: and I certainly do not mean to except the sonnets of Milton."[1] Neither Coleridge nor Thelwall was prone to effusive praise, and neither was a fool. Their assessment of the poet's work and of her significance in terms of a distinctly British poetic tradition reflects more broadly the esteem in which Smith was held in her lifetime.

Smith was a prolific writer. She published ten novels in the years between 1788 and 1799, as well as two translations of French novels; five educational works; three volumes of poetry, including some ten ever-expanding editions of *Elegiac Sonnets*; and one play. But while she was a popular and critically acclaimed novelist whose works of sentimental fiction influenced writers such as Ann Radcliffe and Jane Austen, Smith believed that any subsequent literary reputation that she might enjoy would come from her poetry. In a letter to her publishers Cadell and Davies written late in her career, she writes that: "it is on the Poetry I have written that I trust for the little reputation I may hereafter have & know that it is not the <u>least</u> likely among the works of modern Poets to reach another period."[2] As it turned out, however, Smith's reputation did not fare so well in the period immediately following her death, and by the second decade of the nineteenth century she had been relegated to the position of "woman writer" and therefore "minor."[3] While Alexander Dyce still recognized her significance in his *Specimens of British Poetesses* (1827), including twelve of her poems in his anthology (more than any other poet),[4] Smith seems to have been well and truly

---

1   John Thelwall, "An essay on the ENGLISH SONNET; illustrated by a comparison between the Sonnets of MILTON and those of CHARLOTTE SMITH," *The Universal Magazine* (December 1792), 408–09. See Appendix B1. For a discussion of Smith's influence on Thelwall, see Judith Thompson (ed.), *John Thelwall: Selected Poetry and Poetics* (New York: Palgrave Macmillan, 2015).

2   Charlotte Smith to Thomas Cadell Jr. and William Davies, 18 August 1805, in *The Collected Letters of Charlotte Smith*, ed. Judith Phillips Stanton (Bloomington and Indianapolis: Indiana UP, 2003), 705–06.

3   For a more detailed account of Smith's posthumous reception see Louise Duckling, "'Tell My Name to Distant Ages': The Literary Fate of Charlotte Smith," *Charlotte Smith in British Romanticism*, ed. Jacqueline Labbe (London: Pickering and Chatto, 2008), 203–17.

4   Alexander Dyce, *Specimens of British Poetesses; Selected and Chronologically Arranged* (London: T. Rodd, 1827).

forgotten even as a female poet by the time that Elizabeth Barrett Browning made her famous lament to Henry Chorley in 1845:

> England has had many learned women, not merely readers, but writers of the learned languages in Elizabeth's time and afterwards—women of deeper acquirements than are common now on the great diffusion of letters, and yet where were the poetesses? ... How strange! And can we deny that it was so? I look everywhere for Grandmothers & see none. It is not in the filial spirit I am deficient, I do assure you—witness my reverent love of the grandfathers!—[1]

The influence of Smith's poetry, grounded as it is in the affective potential of the discourse of sensibility, can be seen in the work of some of the most popular female writers of the 1820s and 1830s. Poets that Barrett Browning read and respected, such as Felicia Hemans (1793–1835) and Letitia Landon (1802–38), were the inheritors of a tradition begun by Smith in the latter part of the eighteenth century.[2] Smith could well, then, have been the kind of poetical grandmother that Barrett Browning was looking for, but her poetry had fallen out of fashion and, as the nineteenth century wore on, it faded further and further from view. This mirrors the disappearance of numerous popular late-eighteenth-century female writers like Smith—namely Mary Robinson (1758–1800), Anna Laetitia Barbauld (1743–1825), and Anna Seward (1742–1809)—from literary history during the middle and later parts of the nineteenth century. This cultural "forgetting" of the women who dominated the poetic marketplace during Smith's heyday persisted well into the twentieth century.

After more than a century and a half in the wilderness, the re-discovery of Charlotte Smith's oeuvre and of her role in Romanticism began in the late 1980s with the emergence of what came to be regarded as "feminist Romanticism."[3] In keeping with a

---

1   Elizabeth Barrett Browning to Henry Fothergill Chorley, 7 January 1845, *The Letters of Elizabeth Barrett Browning, in Two Volumes*, ed. Frederick G. Kenyon (London: Smith, Elder and Co., 1897), 1:230.
2   Indeed, Jerome McGann places all three writers within a tradition centred upon the expression of powerful feeling and loss in *The Poetics of Sensibility: A Revolution in Literary Style* (Oxford: Oxford UP, 1996).
3   Stuart Curran's ground-breaking essay "Romantic Poetry: The I Altered" was one of the first to recognize the importance of Smith, describing her (alongside her contemporary Mary Robinson) as one of the "crucial poets" of the 1780s and 1790s. See Anne K. Mellor (ed.),

more general feminist interest in the intersections between the personal and the political, scholarship in these early decades of work on the writer (in an echo of critical responses to the poet in her own lifetime) tended to focus on *Elegiac Sonnets* and on the author's use of her own autobiography to confirm the authenticity of her powerful poetic display of sensibility. Indeed, understanding the power of the discourse of sensibility—or, "the faculty of feeling, the capacity for extremely refined emotion and a quickness to display compassion for suffering"[1]—in the late eighteenth century is central to understanding both Smith's poetry and its appeal to a broad contemporary readership. Critics such as Stuart Curran, Jacqueline Labbe, and Sarah Zimmerman played a central role both in revising conventional accounts of Romanticism, with women assuming their rightful position as central poetic voices of the 1790s, and in locating Smith at the forefront of developments in lyrical poetry in the period.[2] With Smith's position at the heart of a revised, much larger canon of Romantic writers now secure, the scene was set for an explosion of interest in her broader oeuvre.[3] In recent decades, her long

---

Romanticism and Feminism (Bloomington and Indianapolis: Indiana UP, 1988), 199.

1   Janet Todd, *Sensibility: An Introduction* (London and New York: Methuen, 1986), 7.

2   Jacqueline M. Labbe, *Charlotte Smith: Romanticism, Poetry and the Culture of Gender* (Manchester: Manchester UP, 2003); Sarah Zimmerman, *Romanticism, Lyricism, and History* (New York: SUNY P, 1999). Other important early criticism that placed Smith's poetry within a wider tradition includes dedicated chapters in Esther Schor, *Bearing the Dead: The British Culture of Mourning from the Enlightenment to Victoria* (Princeton, NJ: Princeton UP, 1994) and Adela Pinch, *Strange Fits of Passion: Epistemologies of Emotion, Hume to Austen* (Stanford, CA: Stanford UP, 1996). Important early essays on Smith include Judith Hawley, "Charlotte Smith's *Elegiac Sonnets*: Losses and Gains," in Isobel Armstrong and Virginia Blain (eds.), *Women's Poetry in the Enlightenment: The Making of a Canon, 1730–1820* (London: Macmillan, 1999), 184–98; and Daniel Robinson, "Reviving the Sonnet: Women Romantic Poets and the Sonnet Claim," *European Romantic Review* 6 (Summer 1995): 98–127. Loraine Fletcher's *Charlotte Smith: A Critical Biography* (New York: St. Martin's P, 1998) remains the definitive biography of the writer.

3   The publication of Judith Philips Stanton's *The Collected Letters of Charlotte Smith* (Bloomington and Indianapolis: Indiana UP, 2003), which brought to light many of the writer's letters for the first time, was a significant occasion in Smith studies, as was the publication of the fourteen-volume *Works of Charlotte Smith* (London: Pickering *(continued)*

poems and her ten novels, in many of which her sonnets reappear as the effusions of her characters, have attracted significant attention, while interest in her children's books and other texts is increasing steadily.

This edition presents Smith's three major works, *Elegiac Sonnets*, *The Emigrants*, and *Beachy Head*, alongside a selection of other poems useful to understanding both Smith's approach to poetic production and her popular appeal. But we want to say from the outset that *Elegiac Sonnets*, *The Emigrants*, and *Beachy Head* are not simply Smith's major poetic works; they are also major works of Romanticism. They stand alongside William Cowper's *The Task* (1785), William Wordsworth's *Prelude* (1798 and 1850), Wordsworth and Coleridge's *Lyrical Ballads* (1798), and Mary Robinson's *Sappho and Phaon* (1796) as foundational poetic texts of the period. They also remain major texts for thinking through such important issues as the relationship between public and private; the ethical treatment of refugees and other persecuted people; the position of women in a patriarchal society; and the usefulness of science as a way of making sense of a complex and ever-changing world. In this respect they are as relevant to life in a globalized twenty-first century world as they were to life in the Britain of the French-revolution era.

Smith and the Seductions of Biography: *Elegiac Sonnets*, Volume One

It remains almost impossible to separate Smith's writings from the facts of her life. Her sonnets in particular demand this type of reading, especially when viewed alongside the writer's various prefaces to the work. In the first edition of *Elegiac Sonnets and Other Essays* (1784), Smith hints at the autobiographical inspiration for her poems when she writes: "Some very melancholy moments have been beguiled by expressing in verse the sensations those moments brought." This was an understatement.

---

and Chatto, 2005) under the editorship of Stuart Curran. Jacqueline Labbe's edited collection of essays on the writer, *Charlotte Smith in British Romanticism* (London: Pickering and Chatto, 2008), perhaps best reflects the state of Smithian scholarship in the first and second decades of the twenty-first century: alongside four essays on her poetry, and five on her novels, the edition includes an essay on the comedy *What Is She?* attributed to the author, an essay on her letters, and three essays on what might broadly be termed the writer's "legacy."

Charlotte Turner was born into a landed gentry[1] family in 1749. Bignor Park, overlooking the downs in West Sussex, was the Turner family seat. Charlotte's difficulties began early in life when she was married (or in her own words sold "like a Southdown sheep"[2]) at the age of fifteen to Benjamin Smith, the son of a wealthy London merchant. Their first son was born a year later, and Smith would go on to give birth to eleven more children over the course of their marriage, often at the rate of one child per year. Only nine of these children survived to adulthood, and the death of Smith's eighth and favourite child, Anna Augusta, aged 20, was a further source of sorrow. The discomfort and danger attendant on almost constant pregnancy were compounded by the fact that Smith's marriage was an unhappy one. Her husband was a fashionable spendthrift, who appears to have treated his wife badly. He was imprisoned for debt in 1783, and as was typical of the time, Charlotte joined him in debtors' prison. Many of the 19 poems contained in the first edition of *Elegiac Sonnets* were composed during this time. In order to avoid further time in prison, Benjamin eventually moved in October 1784 to France with his family, where they stayed until the spring of 1785. In a letter to an unnamed friend, Charlotte describes the dismal journey she (heavily pregnant once again) and her children made from England to their rented French home:

> My children, fatigued almost to death, harassed by sea-sickness, and astonished at the strange noises of the French postillions, whose language they did not understand, crept close to me, while I carefully suppressed the doubts I entertained whether it were possible to reach, without some fatal accident, the place of our destination. In the situation I then was, it was little short of a miracle that my constitution resisted, not merely the fatigues of the journey, with so many little beings clinging about me (the youngest, whom I bore in my arms, scarce two years old) but the inconveniences that

---

1 The landed gentry was a social class that consisted of those landowners who could rent their land and live entirely on this income. Although the landed gentry were positioned below the aristocracy in terms of the English class system, they often had access to considerable amounts of wealth through their land holdings.

2 Charlotte Smith, letter to the Earl of Egremont, 4 February 1803, *CL* 522.

awaited my arrival at our new abode, in which no accommo-
dation was prepared for my weary charges.[1]

Her life with Benjamin eventually proved to be too much to
endure. In 1787 the writer made the very unusual move of sepa-
rating from her husband, but this left her with the responsibility for
providing for their numerous children. She did this almost entire-
ly through her literary productions: her friend, the poet William
Cowper (1731–1800), described her as "Chain'd to her desk like a
slave to his oar."[2] Long after their separation, Benjamin would
return to his wife and attempt to claim for himself the money she
earned through her writings, and he continued to be a nuisance up
until his death, some six months before Charlotte's.

After Smith's marriage, her father-in-law, Richard Smith, was
one of her few sources of consolation and support. He was as ex-
asperated by his son's exploits as was his daughter-in-law. In an
effort to protect his grandchildren from the worst of Benjamin's
excesses, Richard wrote a will that he hoped would provide an
income for Charlotte and Benjamin's children after his death.
But the elder Smith wrote his will without the benefit of legal
counsel, and he made the error of naming Benjamin co-executor.
When Richard Smith died in 1776 he had amassed a fortune of
some £36,000, and Charlotte hoped that her children's inheri-
tance from their grandfather would provide them with a measure
of financial security. However, the complicated nature of the will,
Benjamin's spendthrift ways, and the objections of various family
members to the terms of the will meant that these assets were tied
up in a legal quagmire for years. When the trust was finally settled
in 1813, seven years after Charlotte's death, the estate's value had
been reduced to about £4,000.[3] From 1785 onwards, Smith
never knew from one month to the next whether she would be
able to pay for rent and food, establish her children in marriages
or careers, or even keep her personal book collection out of the
hands of debt collectors.

These were the circumstances under which Charlotte Smith
wrote much of her poetry, and she was not backwards in bring-
ing her distress to the attention of her reading public. Jacqueline
Labbe, in an important early essay on Smith's sonnets, argues

1   Charlotte Smith to an unnamed recipient, c. September 1785, CL 6.
2   William Cowper to William Haley, 29 January 1793, in Letters and Prose
    Works of William Cowper, vol. 4, ed. James King and Charles Ryskamp
    (Oxford: Clarendon, 1984), 281.
3   Judith Stanton, "Introduction," CL xxix.

that Smith's "self-presentation as a woman stricken with loss allows her entry into the poetic market."[1] Smith asks for her reader's sympathy and understanding throughout her poetry, and the strength of her readers' responses testifies to the power of this rhetorical gesture. She was helped here by the fact that the "woman in distress" was a conventional and popular trope in the sentimental literature of the period,[2] and what Smith seemed to be presenting to her readers was a real-life version of this figure. Sonnet V, "To the South Downs," has come to be regarded as emblematically "Smithian" in the way in which it uses her own life, sketched only in vague terms, to heighten the emotional register of the poem. In this much-anthologized sonnet, Smith places her narrator in the "hills belov'd" of the Sussex countryside (and of her childhood home), and presents the unchanging beauty of the natural landscape as a counterpoint to the melancholy changes that accompany a woman's journey from childhood to adulthood (see p. 60). The Sussex landscape becomes in this poem a synecdoche for the freedom and sense of possibility that characterized Smith's own privileged upbringing. But, like the paternal family and home left behind upon marriage, the ministrations of a benevolent nature become powerless in the face of the patriarchal circumscriptions of eighteenth-century marriage. Time and time again in Smith's poetry, we see that to live as a woman in eighteenth-century England is to live without "Hope."

But while Smith clearly capitalized upon the sympathy generated by her poetical displays of personal suffering, viewing Smith's poetry through the prism offered by her own life should not blind us to the various ways in which Smith deliberately crafted a persona for public consumption.[3] Diane E. Boyd describes Smith's

1 Jacqueline M. Labbe, "Selling One's Sorrows: Charlotte Smith, Mary Robinson, and the Marketing of Poetry," *Wordsworth Circle* 25.2 (Spring 1994): 68.
2 For a detailed account of Smith's deployment of the "suffering heroine" figure in her prose, see Diane Long Hoeveler, *Gothic Feminism: The Professionalisation of Gender from Charlotte Smith to the Brontës* (University Park: Pennsylvania State UP, 1998), 27–50. Kate Ferguson Ellis also examines this type of heroine in detail in *The Contested Castle: Gothic Novels and the Subversion of Domestic Ideology* (Urbana and Chicago: U of Illinois P, 1989).
3 This aspect of Smith's poetry is explored in some detail in Kerri Andrews's "'Herself [...] Fills the Foreground': Negotiating Autobiography in the *Elegiac Sonnets* and *The Emigrants*," Labbe, *Charlotte Smith in British Romanticism* 13–27; and Zimmerman, *Romanticism, Lyricism, and History*.

authorial persona, one that Smith presents to the public primarily through her poetry but also through her prefaces, as "an uneasy amalgam of her identities as woman, mother, breadwinner, and author."[1] The "uneasiness" that Boyd identifies here should alert us to the fact that even though Smith's persona was instantly recognizable to her readers, her relationship with this persona was by no means straightforward. Perhaps most obviously, Smith exploits her own association with the landed gentry by referring, on the title page of *Elegiac Sonnets*, to her residence in "Bignor Park, Sussex." Although Smith had not lived at Bignor since she was a child, she clearly felt that it was important to assert her position as a gentlewoman in distress in order to authorize her decision to embark on a literary career. Given the complexity of Smith's performed identity, it is worth remembering that the autobiographical *always* needs to be interrogated in Smith's work: the function that her autobiographical poetic persona serves, how this persona changes, and how it is designed to be read as authentic all deserve to be closely examined.

As the sheer number and range of her in-text quotations in her poetry suggest, Smith had an impressive knowledge of English poetic tradition—from William Shakespeare, to John Milton, to Alexander Pope (1688–1744), to Thomas Gray (1716–71)—and a keen understanding of the strengths and limitations of various poetic forms. She was undoubtedly aware, for example, that "the sonnet provided an uncommonly performative—even theatrical—vehicle for the simultaneous exhibition of seemingly personal and confessional sentiment, on the one hand, and deliberate craft and technical virtuosity on the other."[2] Smith's mastery of persona and her mastery of form go hand in hand. Both come to the forefront in one of her most critically acclaimed sonnets, Sonnet XLIV, "Written in the Church Yard at Middleton in Sussex" (p. 85).

As Stephen Behrendt observes, this poem deftly combines elements of both the English and the Italian sonnet.[3] It has the octave/sestet structure characteristic of the Italian sonnet, with a volta or turn after the octave, which takes the narrator from an omniscient observation of the tide and the havoc it wreaks on the

---

1 Diane E. Boyd, "'Professing Drudge': Charlotte Smith's Negotiation of a Mother-Writer Author Function," *South Atlantic Review* 66.1 (Winter 2001): 154.

2 Stephen C. Behrendt, *British Women Poets and the Romantic Writing Community* (Baltimore: Johns Hopkins UP, 2009), 117.

3 Behrendt, *British Women Poets* 121.

coastal graveyard, first to a gloomy account of the state of the village dead whose bones are tossed in the waves, and then inwards, to the state of mind of the narrator. But superimposed on the Italian structure is the English rhyme scheme of three quatrains and a rhyming couplet. The concluding couplet is important in this poem, as it is in Smith's sonnets more generally, because it performs the speaker's final turn inwards: "While I am doom'd—by life's long storm opprest, / To gaze with envy on their gloomy rest." It is this turn inwards, toward a contemplation of the melancholy psychological state of the speaker, that helps to cement the association between the poet and her speakers.[1] This is deliberate craft, not accident, and it represents a distinctly new moment in the sonnet form in English.

The careful crafting of Smith's poetic persona is, perhaps, made most obvious in the disjunction that can be seen between the canny and altogether formidable voice glimpsed in Smith's private correspondence and the melancholy, introspective speakers of her poems. Indeed, if the various speakers of *Elegiac Sonnets* (Smith herself; the ventriloquized voices of Werther and Petrarch; the heroes and heroines of Smith's novels) are characterized by anything it is by their distinct passivity in the face of sorrow. The narrator of "To the South Downs," for example, toys with the idea of drinking from a "Lethean cup" to forget her despair, but in the end decides that "There's no oblivion—but in death alone!" (p. 60). The rage in the sonnets (and there is certainly plenty in there) tends to be sublimated into the poems' often violent imagery. Smith herself, however, was anything *but* a passive victim of her fate. Her separation from her husband was perhaps her most assertive act of defiance in the face of a deeply patriarchal marriage system, but Smith also worked tirelessly at her literary endeavours, and her letters convey her determination to secure the fortune denied to her children whatever the personal cost. In fact, there can be little doubt that Smith's dogged pursuit of her father-in-law's estate lost her friends and allies.

The fourth Earl of Egremont (George Francis Wyndham, 1786–1845) was one such ally turned enemy over the course of his trusteeship of Richard Smith's estate. The following letter,

---

1 For an extended discussion of Smith's deployment of melancholy in her sonnets, see Elizabeth Dolan, "Melancholia and the Poetics of Visibility: Charlotte Smith's *Elegiac Sonnets*," *Seeing Suffering in Women's Literature of the Romantic Era* (Aldershot: Ashgate, 2008), 21–47; for an account of Sonnet XLIV as a rewriting of the melancholy of Thomas Gray's churchyard elegy, see Schor 65–66.

written to him in 1804, shows that Smith was not afraid to share her true feelings about her estranged husband with someone who was ostensibly her social "better":

> It is very sad to have lost all credit with your Lordship, and that by the <u>Extraordinary</u> intervention of M^r B S whose total disregard of truth and every other gentleman like quality is and has been notorious to every one who has known him & felt more severely by those who have sufferd from his meanness, dishonesty, and depravity. [...] Forty years, Sir, have nearly expired since I was made over an early & unconscious victim to this half Ideot, half Madman. He has recievd with me 7000£. I have earned with my own hands upwards of 4500£ more. I wish not, My Lord, to boast of what I have done, but it is an indisputable & notorious fact, & it would be false modesty & injustice to myself not to assert that, little as I was calculated to be the slave and martyr of a man contemptible in understanding, but detestable for the corruption of his selfish heart, I have borne my fate honourably.[1]

The tone and force of this letter suggest that we are doing Smith an injustice if we straightforwardly equate her with the speakers of her sonnets. There is nothing reticent about Smith's voice here. Benjamin Smith is a "half Ideot, half Madman," while the author demonstrates a keen understanding of her own success as a writer. Benjamin Smith, she intimates, has done nothing for the £7,000 he received from her father's estate, whereas his wife earned more than half this amount through her writing. Letters such as this one remind us that Smith was a challenging and intelligent woman who displayed scant regard for social nicety in the face of social and political injustice.

Poetry and Radical Politics: *Elegiac Sonnets*, Volume Two and *The Emigrants*

Elegiac Sonnets evolved over time: Smith added to the sequence and released new editions right up until the end of the century. The first one-volume edition of *Elegiac Sonnets* had just sixteen sonnets and three other poems, but it eventually expanded to fifty-nine sonnets and eight other poems. From the fifth edition

---

1 Charlotte Smith to the Earl of Egremont, received 8 September 1804, *CL* 654.

(1789) onwards, this volume of the sonnets appeared with a series of expensively produced plates. These illustrations added to perceptions of the quality of Smith's volume, but they also represented in visual form the quiet melancholy characteristic of her early sonnets. Images such as those that accompany Sonnet IV, "To the Moon" (p. 58), and Sonnet XII, "Written on the sea shore.—October, 1784" (p. 64), are now considered iconic depictions of the female lyric poet, seen as she contemplates nature. But in 1797, Smith published a second volume of *Elegiac Sonnets* which appeared with its own set of illustrations and a new frontispiece depicting a much older (and perhaps less attractive) poet. The new frontispiece's caption—"Oh! Time has Changed me since you saw me last"—emphasized the changes, both personal and political, that had taken place since the first volume's initial publication.[1]

In the preface to Volume Two, while continuing to lament her own fate, Smith radically extends her claims for the reach of her sonnets. These later sonnets, she writes, express opinions that may be shocking even to "liberal-minded personages." In contrast to the unknown writer of 1784, the Charlotte Smith of 1797 was a literary celebrity, feted as one of her generation's best poets. She therefore writes from a position of authority and, through this warning, invites her readers to see in these poems the same radical political opinions that had begun to be widely criticized when they appeared in her novels and long poems.[2] She even warns that her sonnets may prove unpopular for daring to represent the "tragedy in real life" and for evoking "the extensive and still threatening desolation, that overspreads this country, and in some degree, every quarter of the world." These are striking claims to make for a compressed lyric form, described by Coleridge in the same year as a "small poem, in which some lonely

---

1 The final, two-volume edition of *Elegiac Sonnets, and Other Poems* appeared in 1800, taking the final number of sonnets to ninety-two. Our edition represents the complete sonnet sequence, a sample of the additional poems presented at the end of each volume, and two of the "Other Poems" from *Beachy Head, Fables, and Other Poems* (1807).

2 Her longtime publisher, Cadell, refused to take her novel *Desmond* (1792) (Fletcher 152), while William Cowper considered that *The Emigrants* should have contained less "severity" toward the emigrants and more "righteous invective against the National Convention" ("To William Hayley" [1 April 1793], *Letters and Prose Works of William Cowper* 318–19).

feeling is developed," preferably "deduced from, and associated with, the scenery of Nature."[1]

Smith was an early supporter of the French Revolution, of which the most potent symbol was the storming of the Bastille prison in Paris on 14 July 1789 and the Declaration of the Rights of Man and of the Citizen by the newly formed French National Assembly. The revolution was a reaction to profound social inequalities in France and promised to set up a whole new political order. However, like many of her contemporaries in Britain who had initially greeted the revolution with enthusiasm, including Wordsworth, Coleridge, Mary Wollstonecraft (1759–97), and many others, Smith watched with dismay from across the Channel as the revolution became bloody. In September 1792, thousands of French prisoners were summarily executed, in particular aristocrats and their suspected sympathizers, as well as clergy who had refused to accept the new laws, which included the abolition of state religion, the banning of monastic vows, and the nationalization of church property. Thousands of French were violently displaced and many more went into exile. Following the regicide of the French King Louis XVI in January 1793, war was declared between France and England in February. Smith herself directly felt the devastating personal effects of the conflict when her twenty-year-old son Charles was wounded at Dunkirk and came home with one leg amputated—"mutilated for life" as Smith put it in a letter.[2] In many of these later sonnets, the speaker seems almost paralysed by the desolation of the world she looks upon and experiences. For example, the iconic Sonnet IV, "To the Moon," is echoed in darkened form in Sonnet LXXX, "To the Invisible Moon." In the former, the speaker, in typically Smithian fashion, delights "to stray" in the light of the moon, which "sheds a soft calm" upon her "troubled breast"; in the latter, the moon itself struggles to shed its light, and is "Dark and conceal'd" from view:

> Dark and conceal'd art thou, soft Evening's Queen,
>   And Melancholy's votaries that delight
> To watch thee, gliding thro' the blue serene,
>   Now vainly seek thee on the brow of night—   (p. 116)

The narrator of this poem is not offered even the momentary, melancholy form of consolation available to the speaker of "To

---

1   Coleridge, "Introduction to the Sonnets" (Appendix B3, p. 242).
2   Charlotte Smith to Joseph Cooper Walker, 9 October 1793, *CL* 78.

the Moon." The moon becomes a solace only "for beings less accurst than I."

In poems such as Sonnet LXXXIII, "The sea view," literal images of warfare are presented to the reader, in this case a sea battle between two armed ships seen from the cliffs near Brighton. The tranquil pastoral scene described in the octave of this sonnet, reminiscent of the earlier sonnets such as "To the South Downs," is eclipsed in the sestet:

> When, like dark plague-spots by the Demons shed,
> Charged deep with death, upon the waves, far seen,
>   Move the war-freighted ships; and fierce and red,
>   Flash their destructive fires—The mangled dead
> And dying victims then pollute the flood.
> Ah! thus man spoils Heaven's glorious works with blood!

(p. 118)

In these later sonnets, Smith demonstrates that the sonnet form, and more significantly the sonnet sequence, is capacious and flexible enough to engage with a wide range of political and historical matters, and that its very reliance on a first-person lyric speaker makes it an ideal vehicle for evoking the relationships between individual experience and the historical present. Smith also includes a number of additional longer lyrics at the end of Volume Two that explicitly take up the politically charged topics evoked by a dead beggar, a female exile, and "the miseries of war."[1]

Both the location of many of these poems and the strong social and anti-war sentiments they express are also central to Smith's first long poem in blank verse, *The Emigrants* (1793). This 826-line, two-book poem is Smith's most direct contribution in poetic form to the political debates of the 1790s, which revolved around questions of rights, equality, representation, and issues of violence and warfare. Following the September massacres in France, in the autumn of 1792 French people seeking political asylum began arriving by the thousands on the stretch of British coastline from Dover to Southampton. Many arrived in need of the most basic assistance, coming in open boats with nothing but the

---

1   Both "The Female Exile, Written at Brighthelmstone in Nov. 1792" (included in this edition, pp. 200–02), and "Fragment, Descriptive of the Miseries of War; from a Poem Called 'The Emigrants' printed in 1793" (not included here), were excised and adapted from *The Emigrants*.

clothes they wore. Laws were passed in France that banished forever those who had left and declared their property to be forfeit, making emigration an automatic forfeiture of French citizenship and return to French soil punishable by death. For the next ten years, it is estimated that around 12,000 émigrés arrived in Britain every year.[1] In *The Emigrants*, Smith takes her by-then popular and recognizable persona of the displaced melancholic wanderer and uses it to explore the situation of these people displaced by wider historical forces.

Smith's poetic speaker in Book One of *The Emigrants* is imagined as walking along the cliffs near Brighton and encountering a group of emigrants. At the opening of Book Two she is out there walking again, "contemplating / Not my own wayward destiny alone, ... But in beholding the unhappy lot / Of the lorn Exiles" (2.6–7, 9–10). The poem is carefully dated: Book One November 1792, the month that saw the first great influx of arrivals on Britain's coasts; and Book Two April 1793, after the execution of the French monarch Louis XVI and the subsequent declaration of war between France and England.[2] Book Two's epigraph from Virgil ends, "*sævit toto Mars impius orbe*" (throughout the world, Impious War is raging). During the months in which Smith was writing *The Emigrants*, the British Parliament was debating the controversial Alien Bill, designed to allow the government to monitor and restrict the movements of foreign nationals. The bill, unprecedented in British legal history, was publicly opposed as breaching basic human rights by the likes of Charles James Fox (1749–1806), the leader of the Whig minority, whom Smith quotes in the Dedication to *The Emigrants* in defence of the by-then highly charged notion of "Liberty."[3] The emigrant crisis, as much as the French Revolution itself, is the immediate, urgent historical context to which Smith addresses this great poem.

The Emigrants was one of a number of responses to the situation of the emigrants, and to the questions whether Britain had a responsibility financially to support them and to what extent they were deserving of sympathy. However, Smith's ambit is exponen-

---

1 Kirsty Carpenter, *Refugees of the French Revolution: Émigrés in London, 1789–1802* (Basingstoke: Macmillan, 1999), 29–31, xix–xx, and 39–44. See also Michael Wiley, *Romantic Migrations: Local, National, and Transnational Dispositions* (New York: Palgrave, 2008), 1–23.

2 On Smith's strategic dating, see Harriet Guest, *Unbounded Attachment: Sentiment and Politics in the Age of the French Revolution* (Oxford: Oxford UP, 2013), 27–29.

3 Carpenter 36.

tially wider and more challenging than the contemporaneous responses of writers such as Hannah More (1745–1833) and Frances Burney (1752–1840), who limit their discussion to the emigrant clergy fleeing religious persecution, whom they present as uncomplicated objects of sympathy and deserving of financial assistance.[1] Smith, by contrast, dedicates lengthy passages in Book One of *The Emigrants* to different levels of clergy, from a monk (1.113–24) to a cardinal (1.125–46), to an abbot and a parish priest (1.146–53 and 169–99), as well as to an aristocratic mother with her children (1.200–32) and to the military father of this family (1.232–95). The overt aim of the poem is to develop what some critics have called a kind of "internationalist consciousness," involving the extension of universal sympathy by which, as Smith puts it in her Dedication, these images of "painful exile" "may tend to humanize both countries" and "annihilate" national (as well as class) prejudice.[2] Smith creates the experience of the "ill-starr'd Exiles," "Banish'd for ever" to "wander" "Thro' the wide World," as one to which all people could under certain circumstances be exposed, and so as the basis for the poem's call for "pure humanity!" (1.354, 97, 101, 103, 368).

Smith's depictions of the different classes of emigrants also work to identify the kinds of political situations and attitudes that she sees as causing such displacements. In her lines on the exiled monk, for example, she describes him as having previously confined himself to a "pious prison" and depicts him as surprised to encounter in Protestant England compassion from people whom "his dark creed, / Condemn'd as Heretics" (1.122–23). She annexes a lengthy endnote to her depiction of the Cardinal missing the riches of his pre-revolution life which begins: "Let it not be considered as an insult to men in fallen fortune, if these luxuries (undoubtedly inconsistent with their profession) be here

---

1 Hannah More, *Prefatory Address to the Ladies &c. of Great Britain and Ireland in Behalf of the French Clergy* (1793); [Frances Burney], *Brief Reflections Relative to the Emigrant French Clergy: Earnestly Submitted to the Humane Consideration of the Ladies of Great Britain* (1793). See Appendix A5 for an excerpt from Burney's pamphlet. Burney later went on to write a five-volume novel that took up the point of view of a female exile, *The Wanderer; or, Female Difficulties* (1814).

2 Kari Lokke uses the phrase "internationalist consciousness" in "'The Mild Dominion of the Moon': Charlotte Smith and the Politics of Transcendence," *Rebellious Hearts: British Women Writers and the French Revolution*, ed. Adriana Craciun and Kari E. Lokke (Albany: SUNY P, 2001), 92; it is picked up by Behrendt in *British Women Poets* 165.

enumerated" (1.129n). Smith also explores the outlook of various members of the now-exiled nobility and military who had dwelt in "the velvet lap of luxury" (1.238). Asylum should be offered to these various emigrants, the poem suggests, because their situation demands it; but the reasons that such asylum has become necessary should not be forgotten.[1] Smith's call for compassion is astonishingly relevant to the urgent issues of our own time, particularly in the way in which she approaches this humanitarian crisis by simultaneously holding on to the complexity of the political situation both at home and abroad, while nonetheless arguing for the extension of universal asylum to those in need: "Whate'er your errors, I lament your fate" (1.107). Smith also offers the plight of the emigrants to her readers not simply as an exercise in "pure humanity" but as a "lesson" from which Britain's more fortunate inhabitants might "learn" (1.332–33). The lesson itself is an unequivocally revolutionary one, brought home from across the channel:

... trembling, learn, that if oppress'd too long,
The raging multitude, to madness stung,
Will turn on their oppressors (1.333–35)

Much of both the political bite and the appeal of *The Emigrants* comes from Smith's representation of her female poet-wanderer persona as being, even when located in England, no less exiled and unhoused than the emigrants she observes. In her dedication to William Cowper, she describes the situation of the emigrants as having "pressed upon an heart, that has learned, perhaps from its own sufferings, to feel with acute, though unavailing compassion, the calamity of others" (p. 127). In linking herself, as Amy Garnai has observed, "socially, politically and psychologically" to the emigrants, Smith again departs from the approach taken by contemporaries, who in writing pamphlets on the emigrants' situation emphasize the authors' separate identity as members of a privileged class and nation.[2] Smith sets aside this conventional and secure hierarchical structure of sympathy,

---

1 Susan Wolfson's and Jacqueline Labbe's readings of the poem have in particular brought out what Wolfson calls the "acid," that is the class critique, in Smith's descriptions of the emigrants (Wolfson, *Romantic Interactions: Social Being and the Turns of Literary Action* [Baltimore: Johns Hopkins UP, 2010], 32; Labbe, *Charlotte Smith: Romanticism* 118).

2 Amy Garnai, *Revolutionary Imaginings in the 1790s: Charlotte Smith, Mary Robinson, Elizabeth Inchbald* (Basingstoke: Palgrave, 2009), 25–26.

introducing in its place a destabilizing and troubling engagement with displacements of all kinds.[1] Vitally, in *The Emigrants*, these matters are never simply reduced to the working out of a political position, but instead Smith tries to work out, line by line, how an individual might understand and engage with a painful world. The move into the looser and more extended form of blank verse, which demonstrates the same formal mastery that Smith shows in her sonnets, allows the poet to move easily in and out of topics, weaving together personal reflections and political analysis, vignettes and description, lyric and narrative. Her dedication to Cowper and frequent allusions to Milton place *The Emigrants* in an epic tradition. The way in which Smith places the sensations and responses of a single human subjectivity at the centre of her wide-ranging poem also develops a tradition established by Cowper and subsequently taken up by Wordsworth in *The Prelude*. *The Emigrants* is a major poem in the history of the long poem in blank verse, *the* major response to the emigrant crisis of the 1790s, and perhaps the first sustained literary attempt to think through the affective complexity of a refugee crisis of any sort. It deserves close rereading in our time.

Imagining History in *Beachy Head*

In *Beachy Head*, which appeared posthumously in *Beachy Head, Fables, and Other Poems* (1807), Smith took the long narrative poem in still new directions. Arguably her most Romantic poem, the scope of poetry to explore both the human mind and the world it inhabits is expanded still further in her last major work, which includes explorations of geology, natural history, human history, time, and individual and collective memory. The political and historical context of the 731-line *Beachy Head* is not as explicit as in *The Emigrants*. Smith herself described it as a "local poem," and in this sense it takes up the eighteenth-century tradition of the topographical poem dedicated to the description of a particular locale.[2] Beachy Head is a headland that juts out from the South Downs of Sussex and is famous for its steep chalky cliffs. Those familiar with *Elegiac Sonnets* are reminded that the surrounding area was at the centre of Smith's personal history of

---

1 For an extension of this argument on Smith's late sonnets and *The Emigrants*, see Ingrid Horrocks, *Women Wanderers and the Writing of Mobility, 1784–1814* (Cambridge: Cambridge UP, forthcoming 2017).

2 Charlotte Smith to Thomas Cadell Jr. and William Davies, 18 August 1805, *CL* 705.

loss, the place where, as she reiterates yet again in this poem, she "once was happy, when while yet a child, / I learn'd to love these upland solitudes" (282–83). But Beachy Head also held a very particular position in the national imagination. As Smith tells her reader in the first of her many footnotes, "[i]n crossing the Channel from the coast of France, Beachy-Head is the first land made" (3n). The Battle of Beachy Head in 1690 marked an English naval defeat that played a symbolic role in eighteenth-century histories of invasion, while by 1805 tensions with France had reached the point at which imminent invasion was again feared. This made Beachy Head a symbolic border location, resonant with associations of anxiety and vulnerability.[1] Rather than being the site of the arrival of French royalist émigrés seeking assistance, the south coast of Britain was by this point seen as a potential invasion point.

However, in contrast to *The Emigrants*, *Beachy Head* does not engage directly with contemporary events. Instead, Smith turns to longer, deeper histories of the earth, of peoples, and of human memory, as they have developed over time and across space, starting with an image that makes the very idea of local or national history feel short-sighted. Her speaker's first subject of contemplation revolves around the idea that Britain was once joined to France and the Continent, before being "torn from it by some convulsion of Nature" (7n). Later in the poem, the fossils of sea-shells that the speaker finds in the cliff lead her to meditate on a time before these "chalky mountains" rose out of the sea (382). Both the wide sweep of human history, told mostly in the poem as a history of invasion (of "War, and its train of horrors" [422]), and a personal history of loss such as Smith had unfolded over two decades in her poetry, are imagined as becoming insignificant in the face of the vast "lapse of Time" that Beachy Head makes visible (*BH* 434).

As Kevis Goodman has commented, Smith also uses Beachy Head in spatial terms to represent how any single place is "simultaneously local and global," evoking the location by its complex networks of connections rather than by its boundaries.[2] In line 36 of the poem, the speaker sees a "ship of commerce" on

---

1   See Lily Gurton-Wachter, "'An Enemy, I Suppose, That Nature Has Made': Charlotte Smith and the Natural Enemy," *European Romantic Review* 20.2 (2009): 200; Kevis Goodman, "Conjectures on Beachy Head: Charlotte Smith's Geological Poetics and the Ground of the Present," *ELH* 81.3 (2014): 988.

2   Goodman 986.

the horizon, and within fifteen lines the poem has mentioned the Orient, Asia, and slaves who risk their lives to secure the riches of trade. This passage is not limited to a critique of the losses and gains of global and colonial traffic, but like many parts of the poem it seeks to apprehend the sheer strangeness of all that is beyond one's sight and comprehension but to which one is nonetheless connected. "[T]he sea-snipe's cry," the passage ends, "tells that something living is abroad" (113–14). Like the image of the fossil shells embedded in the land, the travelling ship and the calling seabird make it impossible to imagine a locale that is simply local—and impossible to imagine a nation, place, or human subject in isolation, either in time or space.

Within this vast world, spread out in time and space, Smith, now in her mid-fifties, situates her poetic speaker's "reflecting mind" that guides the poem (168). In an extraordinary passage of blank verse, beginning "An early worshipper at Nature's shrine; / I loved her rudest scenes" (346–47), Smith writes of a love of nature in the kind of passionate, overflowing cadence that readers of Romanticism would come to be familiar with from Wordsworth in particular.[1] However, any direct and easy communion with nature in *Beachy Head* is ultimately confined to childhood and "fancy" (*BH* 368). If any present consolation is offered within the natural world, it is not found in "widely spreading views, mocking alike / The Poet and the Painter's utmost art" (370–71), but rather in the labour of paying attention, in the natural history endeavour of "observing objects more minute," and in the act of "Wondering" from small parts to "fathomless" wholes (372–73, 384).

In a distinct shift from *The Emigrants*, Smith's autobiographical persona recedes into the background in this poem. The poet also carefully links her exploration of natural history and geology in the body of the poem to increasingly lengthy footnotes, which in their detail claim a place for the poem in a poetic tradition made popular in particular by natural philosopher and poet Erasmus Darwin (1731–1802).[2] One of the most radical aspects

1   For the opening of the two-book *Prelude*, a passage which has distinct Smithian echoes, see Appendix A7.
2   See Appendix A9. For a more detailed discussion of Smith's engagement with botany in her poetry, see Dahlia Porter, "From Nosegay to Specimen Cabinet: Charlotte Smith and the Labour of Collecting," Labbe, *Charlotte Smith in British Romanticism* 29–44; and Donelle Ruwe, "Charlotte Smith's Sublime: Feminine Poetics, Botany and *Beachy Head*," *Prism(s): Essays in Romanticism* 7 (1999): 117–32.

of *Beachy Head* is the fact that it is spoken in many voices, and the footnotes themselves provide at least one doubling of voice, frequently speaking in the voice of what Labbe calls the poem's "well-read historian" concerned with details that the "Poet" speaker of the verse passes over.[1] Theresa Kelley has suggested that the poem's oscillation between presenting the grand narrative march of history and the "narrative description of minutiae" dramatizes an impasse in Romantic historiography between two competing models.[2] In attempting to write a history that moves between these models, Smith highlights the insufficiency of both.

There is some debate about whether, at the time of Smith's death, *Beachy Head* was complete, in part because in its final two-thirds Smith's intentions become harder to interpret.[3] In the final sections of the poem Smith brings forward a number of additional speakers: an idealized shepherd who wanders the hills (439–504); a lovelorn "stranger" who composes verses (505–670); and a hermit, with whom the poem concludes and who, in an inversion of the view from the top of Beachy Head with which the poem opens, lives in a cavern beneath the cliffs (670–730). Like the shepherd of "Poet's fancy" who also appears in *The Emigrants* (1.299–306), the shepherd in *Beachy Head* is presented as a stark contrast to the actual situation of labour and economic hardship of those living at that time in the British countryside. Here Smith directly challenges the then–still popular idealizations of pastoral poetry. In a similar way, the wandering "stranger," who is also a poet, is depicted as being enamoured of scenes of "ideal bliss" (666). Smith then disrupts the blank verse of *Beachy Head* by inserting two of this secondary poet's verses. As Melissa Richard suggests, the inserted poems, with their five- and six-line stanzas and carefully controlled rhyme schemes, "are enlightening in relationship to the poetic structure of *Beachy Head*: the poem's blank verse feels more open, as if the enjambed lines and lengthy verses literally unravel the picturesque framing of a pastoral ideal."[4]

---

1 Jacqueline Labbe, *Writing Romanticism: Charlotte Smith and William Wordsworth, 1784–1807* (Basingstoke: Palgrave, 2011), 131.

2 Theresa M. Kelley, "Romantic Histories: Charlotte Smith and Beachy Head," *Nineteenth-Century Literature* 59.3 (2004): 287–88.

3 See, for example, the Introduction to Stuart Curran's edition, *The Poems of Charlotte Smith* (Oxford: Oxford UP, 1993), xxvii.

4 Melissa Richard, "Pastoral Preoccupation and Transformation in Charlotte Smith's *The Emigrants* and *Beachy Head*," *Turning Points and Trans-*

Smith's hermit, however, is carefully denied the beauty of such pastoral scenery, living instead in a chilly cave "mined by wintry tides" (672).[1] Her final figure is not one of withdrawal, however, as one might expect, nor quite one of despair. He is a figure of continued, hazardous feeling and engagement:

> his heart
> Was feelingly alive to all that breath'd;
> And outraged as he was, in sanguine youth,
> By human crimes, he still acutely felt
> For human misery. (686–90)

The final image of Smith's final poem, which begins with an excavation of the inevitable connections between place, self, and others, is of an embrace of otherness. The hermit hazards his own life to help those shipwrecked on the rocks, and when he cannot help, he prays "For the poor helpless stranger" (715). Smith seems to be making a plea here for the power of sympathetic identification to drive positive action—it is an implicit acknowledgement of the power of her own poetic project, a project similarly based on sympathetic identification between the reader and the various suffering heroes and heroines of her poetry. At the end of the poem, Beachy Head becomes the hermit's watery grave, the poem itself imagined as "Chisel'd within the rock" (726) in honour of this man who lost his life trying to help others.

Smith's Fame, Smith's Context: Introducing This Major Works Edition

Charlotte Smith's poetry was not only critically celebrated but also incredibly popular with the reading public. It is a testament to the power of the sympathy generated by the writer's poetry, both in short and long form, that it touched its readers on a deeply visceral level. People were *moved* by Smith's work: moved to sympathize with her plight as evoked in her sonnets and their prefaces; moved to create poetry themselves as a response to her poetry; moved to support the author through subscription to her

---

formations: Essays on Language, Literature and Culture, ed. J. Page, et al. (Newcastle: Cambridge Scholars, 2011), 24. See also Kandi Tayebi, "Charlotte Smith and the Quest for the Romantic Prophetic Voice," *Women's Writing* 11.3 (2004): 421–38.

1   See Kari Lokke, "The Figure of the Hermit in Charlotte Smith's *Beachy Head*," *Wordsworth Circle* 39.1–2 (2008): 41.

volumes. In her long poems Smith found ways to extend this sympathy outward, into the world beyond her autobiographical narrator. The poet's call for compassion for the plight of disenfranchised French émigrés becomes an overtly political act in *The Emigrants*, while in *Beachy Head* sympathy has a broader sweep, working historically, chronologically, and regionally. Given the particular importance of sympathy to Charlotte Smith's literary project, it is perhaps not surprising that her own brand of "fandom" seems to have manifested itself in the publication of seemingly endless sequences of poems by other poets both celebrating Smith's work and lamenting the sad circumstances that produced it. Many readers seem to have identified personally with Smith's experiences, and her poetry provided them, in turn, with a language capable of expressing their own feelings of loss and suffering. For women in particular, "Smith stood for many of them as a brilliant—but also terrible—illustration of the woman who selflessly devotes herself to the interests of her family, even at the cost of comfort, happiness and public approbation."[1]

As early as 1786 we see readers like the anonymous author of "Sonnet to Mrs. Smith" (see Appendix E1) lamenting the "REAL woe" that lies at the heart of Smith's sonnets and celebrating the "sympathetic love" that the poems evoke in their readers:

> For sure than thine more sweet no strains can flow,
> Than thine no tenderer plaints the heart can move,
> More rouse the soul to sympathetic love;
> And yet—sad source! They spring from REAL woe.

Even poems that are ostensibly critical of Smith, such as Ticklepitcher's "Ode to Charlotte Smith" (see Appendix E4) testify to the public visibility of the writer and to a widespread interest in her literary and private life. Ticklepitcher's opening gambit is designed to intrigue the reader by alluding to gossip ("dirt") written about and by the author:

> CHARLOTTE, my dear! I'm really hurt,
> To see you throw about your dirt,
> And give yourself such dreadful labour,
> To soil and vilify your neighbour.

---

1   Stephen Behrendt, "Charlotte Smith, Women Poets and the Culture of Celebrity," Labbe, *Charlotte Smith in British Romanticism* 197.

Smith's popularity was clearly a sore point for literary rivals like Anna Seward, whose own poetry never reached the same level of public visibility as that of her contemporary. "I forget if I ever spoke to you about Mrs C. Smith's everlasting lamentables, which she calls sonnets," she writes cuttingly in a letter to a friend, "made up of hackneyed scraps of dismality, with which her memory furnished from our various poets. Never were poetical whipt syllabubs, in black glasses, so eagerly swallowed by the odd taste of the public."[1] Seward presents Smith's popularity here as a fad, as being as ephemeral as a "syllabub," an airy dessert made of whipped cream and alcohol. But if Smith's poetry was a fad, it was a long-lived one—"whipt syllabubs, in black glasses" seem not to have gone out of style for some fifteen years at least. During this time her poetry was hugely influential on a new generation of Romantics.[2]

Alongside new and carefully annotated editions of Smith's major poems, this Broadview Edition includes additional materials for readers who are interested in understanding more about Smith, her popularity with her audience, and the literary and social contexts within which she wrote. In Appendix A we reproduce precursory and contemporary texts that help to situate Smith's poetry in relation to a broader literary and cultural conversation. Appendix B reproduces some of the key writings from the period on the sonnet, and on Smith's place within a specifically English sonnet tradition. Smith discusses her poetry in her own words in Appendix C, which includes sections from the author's letters, while contemporary reviewers and critics offer their opinion of Smith's poetry in Appendix D. In order to give readers a sense of the popularity of the writer's work, Appendix E offers a small selection of the significant number of poems written about Smith that appeared in the newspapers and magazines of the period. Finally, Appendix F aims to give scholars in particular a sense of the evolution and transformation of Smith's best-known work, *Elegiac Sonnets*, through a list of the tables of contents for the various volumes of the work.

The central position that Smith's poetry has come to hold in accounts of the literature of the Romantic era is suggested by its

---

1 Anna Seward to Theophilus Swift, 9 July 1789, *Letters of Anna Seward Written between the years 1784 and 1807. In Six Volumes* (Edinburgh: George Ramsay and Company, 1811), 2:287.

2 For a detailed examination of Smith's influence see Knowles, *Sensibility and Female Poetic Tradition: 1780–1860*, and Feldman and Robinson's "Introduction" to *A Century of Sonnets*.

key role not only in major new assessments of women's writing such as those by Paula Backscheider, Stephen Behrendt, Susan Staves, Harriet Guest, and many others but also in more general critical assessments of the writing of the period.[1] We hope that this edition allows readers to read Smith's poetry in as close a form as possible to the way in which it was originally published. We also hope that readers will, through the appendices, gain a sense of the writer herself and a better understanding of the powerful reaction that she evoked from the late-eighteenth- and early-nineteenth-century reading public. Stephen Behrendt reminds us that Smith's poetry and the response that it generated in its readers are testaments to "the extent to which the Romantic writing community was an interactive and dialogic one."[2] It is not until the arrival of Byron (1788–1824) on the scene in the second decade of the nineteenth century that we again see a poet inspire the same heady mixture of admiration, respect, hostility, and imitation as Charlotte Smith, and it is not until Byron that we again see such a popular fascination with the circumstances of an author's private life. Charlotte Smith's major works remind us that one of the worldliest poets of the early Romantic period wrote not from the vantage point of the hustle and bustle of London, nor from the serene grandeur of the Lake District, but from the downs and cliffs of West Sussex, from where Britain faces out toward Europe.

---

1   Paula Backscheider, *Eighteenth-Century Women Poets and Their Poetry: Inventing Agency, Inventing Genre* (Baltimore: Johns Hopkins UP, 2005); Susan Staves, *A Literary History of Women's Writing in Britain, 1660–1789* (Cambridge: Cambridge UP, 2006); Behrendt, *British Women Poets*; Guest, *Unbounded Attachment*. For an example of Smith's central role in work on Romantic poetry more generally, see Wolfson, *Romantic Interactions*.
2   Behrendt, "Charlotte Smith" 194.

Charlotte Smith: A Brief Chronology

1749	Born in London on 4 May, the eldest child of Nicholas and Anna Towers Turner. Charlotte later baptized at Stoke Park, near Guildford in Sussex, where the family lives.
1752	Charlotte's mother dies.
1764	Charlotte's father remarries.
1765	Charlotte (aged 15) marries Benjamin Smith on 23 February. They move to Cheapside in London later that year to live with his parents.
1766	First son born. His name and birth date are unknown.
1767	Benjamin's father, Richard Smith, marries Charlotte's aunt, Lucy Towers. Benjamin and Charlotte's son Benjamin Berney is born, and the first son dies.
1768	Third child, William Towers, born.
1769	Fourth child, Charlotte Mary, born.
1770	Fifth child, Braithwaite, christened.
1771	Smiths move to Tottenham, just outside London. Sixth child, Nicholas Hankey, born.
1773	Seventh child, Charles Dyer, christened.
1774	Eighth child, Anna Augusta, christened. Smiths move to Lys Farm, Hampshire.
1776	Ninth child, Lucy Eleanor, christened. On 13 October, Charlotte's father-in-law, Richard Smith, dies, leaving a large estate and a contested will.
1777	Eldest child, Benjamin Berney, dies of consumption (aged 11). Tenth child, Lionel, born.
1782	Eleventh child, Harriet Amelia, born.
1783	Benjamin is imprisoned for debt in December and does not leave prison until July 1784. Typically for the time, Charlotte spends part of this time in jail with him, where she writes a number of the poems later published in *Elegiac Sonnets*.
1784	The first edition of *Elegiac Sonnets and Other Essays* is published. Charlotte and the children spend the winter of

1784–85 near Dieppe, where Benjamin has settled
as he is again in debt.

1785   Twelfth child, George Augustus Frederick, is born in
France in February.
The Smiths return to England in October and settle
in Woolbeding, Sussex.
William Cowper's *The Task* is published.

1786   Charlotte publishes an English translation of *Manon
Lescaut* by Abbé Prévost.
Braithwaite dies (aged 16).

1787   *The Romance of Real Life.*
Charlotte formally separates from Benjamin and
moves to a cottage near Wyhe (now called Wyke),
near Guildford in Surrey.

1788   *Emmeline, the Orphan of the Castle.*

1789   *Ethelinde, or the Recluse of the Lake.*
The fifth edition of *Elegiac Sonnets*, the first with il-
lustrations, is published by subscription.
Having spent time in London, Charlotte moves to
Brighton with her children who remain at home. She
lives predominantly in Brighton for the next few
years.
French Revolution begins.

1790   Edmund Burke publishes *Reflections on the Revolution
in France.*
Mary Wollstonecraft publishes *A Vindication of the
Rights of Men.*

1791   *Celestina, a novel.*
Thomas Paine publishes *Rights of Man.*

1792   *Desmond, a novel.*
Mary Wollstonecraft publishes *A Vindication of the
Rights of Woman.*

1793   *The Old Manor House.*
The Emigrants.
Daughter Augusta marries Alexandre Marc-
Constant de Foville, a French émigré. Son Charles
is wounded at the siege of Dunkirk, and his leg is
amputated.
Charlotte and family leave Brighton. She moves fre-
quently for the rest of her life.
King Louis XVI of France executed (21 January).
War declared between France and England.

1794   *The Banished Man.*

	The Wanderings of Warwick.
	Habeas corpus suspended in Britain.
1795	*Rural Walks: in dialogues. Intended for the use of young persons.*
	Montalbert, a novel.
	Anna Augusta dies on 23 April.
1796	*Rambles Farther: A Continuation of Rural Walks.*
	Marchmont, a novel.
	Mary Robinson publishes *Sappho and Phaon.*
1797	Two-volume subscription edition of *Elegiac Sonnets* is published.
1798	*Minor Morals, interspersed with sketches of natural history, historical anecdotes, and original stories.*
	The Young Philosopher.
	William Wordsworth and Samuel Taylor Coleridge publish *Lyrical Ballads, with a few other poems.*
1799	Smith's play *What Is She?* premieres.
1800–02	*The Letters of a Solitary Wanderer: containing narratives of various description.*
1801	Charles dies of yellow fever in Barbados (aged 28).
1804	*Conversations Introducing Poetry: chiefly on subjects of natural history. For the use of children and young persons.*
1806	*The History of England, from the earliest records, to the Peace of Amiens, in a series of letters to a young lady at school.*
	Benjamin dies in debtors' prison on 26 February.
	George dies of yellow fever in Surinam on 16 September (aged 22).
	Charlotte dies on 28 October at Tilford, in Surrey. She is buried at Stoke Church, near Guildford.
1807	*Beachy Head: with other Poems.*
	A Natural History of Birds, intended chiefly for young persons.
1813	Richard Smith's estate finally settled.

A Note on the Texts

The present texts of Charlotte Smith's poems are based on the following copy-texts: the two-volume ninth edition of *Elegiac Sonnets, and Other Poems* (London: Cadell and Davies, 1800), which was the first edition to include all 92 sonnets and the complete set of additional poems; the first and only edition of *The Emigrants, A Poem, in Two Books* (London: Cadell, 1793); and *Beachy Head, Fables, and Other Poems* (London: J. Johnson, 1807), published posthumously. Sonnets 1–59, "Elegy," and "Thirty-Eight" are from *Elegiac Sonnets, and Other Poems* (1800), Volume One; while Sonnets 60–92, "The Dead Beggar," and "The Female Exile" are from *Elegiac Sonnets, and Other Poems* (1800), Volume Two. Our central aim has been to present Smith's three major poetic works— *Elegiac Sonnets, The Emigrants,* and *Beachy Head*—in their entirety and to give a sense of her wider body of poetic work through the presentation of a select group of additional poems at the end.

Over the many editions of *Elegiac Sonnets* there were many small changes made, in particular to punctuation. However, as per Broadview Press practice, and in order to create as readable a text as possible, we have not collected these variants here. A list of variants can be found in Stuart Curran's edition of *The Poems of Charlotte Smith* (Oxford: Oxford UP, 1993) and in Jacqueline Labbe's edition of Smith's poetry in *The Works of Charlotte Smith*, vol. 14 (London: Pickering and Chatto, 2007).

In all cases, Smith's endnotes have been changed to footnotes, and we have clearly demarcated them from our own editorial notes by identifying them as [Smith's note]. This has also involved editorial decisions about where to insert superscript footnote numbers within Smith's text. In some cases, largely in *Beachy Head*, Smith footnotes her endnotes. We have identified these notes within notes using {braces}. In line with usual editorial practices, quotation marks have been regularized throughout this edition, capitalizations have been kept, and obvious typesetting errors have been silently corrected. Small capitals, however, commonly used in eighteenth-century newspaper poetry and in poem titles, have been standardized to normal capitals. Following Judith Phillips Stanton, we have kept Smith's original spelling from her letters.

ELEGIAC SONNETS (1784–1800)

TO WILLIAM HAYLEY, ESQ.[1]

SIR,

WHILE I ask your protection for these Essays, I cannot deny having myself some esteem for them. Yet permit me to say, that did I not trust to your candour and sensibility, and hope they will plead for the errors your judgement must discover, I should never have availed myself of the liberty I have obtained—that of dedicating these simple effusions to the greatest modern Master of that charming talent, in which I can never be more than a distant copyist.

I am, SIR, Your most obedient and obliged servant,
CHARLOTTE SMITH.

---

1 Smith dedicated the first edition of *ES* to William Hayley (1745–1820), who was her neighbour and whom she valued as a careful reader and corrector of her works. He was a poet, novelist, and patron of other writers, including William Blake (1757–1827).

PREFACE TO THE FIRST AND SECOND EDITIONS
(both published 1784)

THE little Poems which are here called Sonnets, have I believe no very just claim to that title; but they consist of fourteen lines, and appear to me no improper vehicle for a single Sentiment. I am told, and read it as the opinion of very good judges, that the legitimate Sonnet is ill calculated for our language.[1] The specimen Mr. Hayley has given,[2] though they form a strong exception, prove no more than that the difficulties of the attempt vanish before uncommon powers.

Some very melancholy moments have been beguiled, by expressing in verse the sensations those moments brought. Some of my friends, with partial indiscretion, have multiplied the copies they procured of several of these attempts, till they found their way into the prints of the day in a mutilated state; which concurring with other circumstances, determined me to put them into their present form. I can hope for readers only among the few, who to sensibility of heart, join simplicity of taste.

PREFACE TO THE THIRD AND FOURTH EDITIONS
(both published in 1786)

THE reception given by the public, as well as my particular friends, to the two first Editions of these Poems, has induced me to add to the present such other Sonnets as I have written since, or have recovered from my acquaintance, to whom I have given them without thinking well enough of them at the time to preserve any copies myself. A few of those last written, I have attempted on the Italian model; with which success I know not, but I am persuaded that to the generality of readers those which are less regular will be more pleasing.

As a few notes were necessary, I have added them at the end.[3] I have there quoted such lines as I have borrowed; and even

---

1 By "legitimate sonnet," Smith means the Italian, or Petrarchan form of the sonnet. The English (or Shakespearean) sonnet, and Smith's variations on this form, offers more scope for rhymes in the English language. See Introduction, p. 18, as well as Mary Robinson's discussion in Appendix B2.

2 Smith is probably referring to William Hayley's *Essay on Epic Poetry* (1782), in which Hayley translates into English a number of Italian sonnets.

3 In this edition we have changed these notes to footnotes.

where I am conscious the ideas were not my own, I have restored them to their original possessors.

PREFACE TO THE FIFTH EDITION (1789)

IN printing a list of so many noble, literary, and respectable names, it would become me, perhaps, to make my acknowledgements to those friends, to whose exertions in my favor, rather than to any merit of my own, I owe the brilliant assemblage.[1] With difficulty I repress what I feel on this subject; but in the conviction that such acknowledgements would be painful to them, I forbear publicly to speak of those particular obligations, the sense of which will ever be deeply impressed on my heart.

PREFACE TO THE SIXTH EDITION (1792)

WHEN a sixth Edition of these little Poems was lately called for, it was proposed to me to add such Sonnets, or other pieces, as I might have written since the publication of the fifth—Of these, however, I had only a few; and on shewing them to a friend,[2] of whose judgement I had an high opinion, he remarked that some of them, particularly "The Sleeping Woodman," and "The Return of the Nightingale," resembled in their subjects, and still more in the plaintive tone in which they are written, the greater part of those in the former Editions—and that, perhaps, some of a more lively cast might be better liked by the Public—"'Toujours perdrix,'" said my friend—"'Toujours perdrix' you know, 'ne vaut rien.'[3]—I am far from supposing that *your* compositions can be

---

1 The fifth edition of the sonnets, published in 1789, was printed by subscription. There is a long list of subscribers (817 in all) appended to the volume, and the success of this edition reflects Smith's status in the literary sphere of the time. For Smith's discussion of subscription see Appendix C1a, pp. 243–44. The 1789 edition of *ES* was also the first edition to include illustrations along with the poetry. The letter on *ES* (Appendix C1a) shows how involved Smith was in the illustration process of her work.

2 Stuart Curran notes that "according to Smith's sister, Catherine Anne Dorset [c. 1753–c. 1820], this friend is probably Bryan Edwards, himself a poet." *The Poems of Charlotte Smith* (Oxford: Oxford UP, 1993), 5.

3 In her "Notes to the Fables" published in *Beachy Head, Fables, and Other Poems* (1807), Smith explains the origin of this saying in an apology made by Henry IV of France (r. 1589–1610): "Toujours perdrix, toujours Chapon bouilli ne vaut rien" [If one always has boiled partridge or capon, then it is nothing special] (180).

neglected or disapproved, on whatever subject: but perhaps 'tou-jours Rossignols, toujours des chanson triste,'[1] may not be so well received as if you attempted, what you would certainly execute as successfully, a more cheerful style of composition." "Alas!" Replied I, "Are grapes gathered from thorns, or figs from this-tles?"[2] Or can the *effect* cease, while *cause* remains? *You know* that when in the Beech Woods of Hampshire, I first struck the chords of the melancholy lyre, its notes were never intended for the public ear! It was unaffected sorrows drew them forth: I wrote mournfully because I was unhappy—And I have unfortunately no reason yet, though nine years have elapsed, to *change my tone.* The time is indeed arrived, when I have been promised by "*the Honourable Men*" who, *nine years ago*, undertook to see that my family obtained the provision their grandfather designed for them,[3]—that "all should be well, all should be settled." But still I am condemned to feel the "*hope delayed that maketh the heart sick.*"[4] Still to receive—not a repetition of promises indeed—*but of scorn and insult*, when I apply to those gentlemen, who, though they acknowledge that all the impediments to a division of the estate they have undertaken to manage, are done away—will neither tell me *when* they will proceed to divide it, or *whether they will ever do so at all.* You know the circumstances under which I have now so long been labouring; and you have done me the honour to say that few Women could so long have contended with them. With these, however, as they are some of them of a domes-tic and painful nature, I will not trouble the Public *now*; but while they exist in all their force, that indulgent Public must accept all I am able to achieve—"Toujours des Chansons tristes!"

Thus ended the short dialogue between my friend and me, and I repeat it as an apology for that apparent despondence, which, when it is observed for a long series of years, may look like affectation. *I should be sorry*, if on some future occasion, I should feel myself compelled to detail its causes more at length; for, notwithstanding I am thus frequently appearing as an Authoress,

---

1 "Always nightingales, always sad songs." In classical mythology, the nightingale is associated with melancholy song.

2 Matthew 7:16.

3 Charlotte Smith's father-in-law, Richard Smith, died in 1776, leaving an estate of £36,000. However, the settlement of this estate would be held up in the courts until after Smith's death. See Introduction, p. 24.

4 "Hope deferred maketh the heart sick: but when the desire cometh, it is a tree of life" (Proverbs 13:12).

and have derived from thence many of the greatest advantages of my life, (since it has procured me friends whose attachment is most invaluable), I am well aware that for a woman—"The Post of Honor is a Private Station."[1]

London, May 14, 1792.

---

1 In Joseph Addison's play *Cato: A Tragedy* (London, 1713), the Roman statesman Cato advises his son to "Content thyself to be obscurely good. / When vice prevails, and impious men bear sway, / The post of honour is a private station" (4.4.142–44).

Elegiac Sonnets

Volume One

SONNET I

THE partial° Muse has from my earliest hours   *favourable*
    Smiled on the rugged path I'm doom'd to tread,
And still with sportive° hand has snatch'd wild flowers,   *playful*
    To weave fantastic garlands for my head:
5 But far, far happier is the lot of those
    Who never learn'd her dear delusive art;
Which, while it decks the head with many a rose,
    Reserves the thorn, to fester in the heart.
For still she bids soft Pity's melting eye
10   Stream o'er the ills she knows not to remove,
Points every pang, and deepens every sigh
    Of mourning Friendship, or unhappy Love.
Ah! then, how dear the Muse's favours cost,
    If those paint sorrow best—who feel it most![1]

SONNET II

Written at the Close of Spring

THE garland's fade that Spring so lately wove,
    Each simple flower which she had nurs'd in dew,
Anemonies,[2] that spangled every grove,
    The primrose wan, and hare-bell mildly blue.
5 No more shall violets linger in the dell,
    Or purple orchis variegate the plain,
Till Spring again shall call forth every bell,
    And dress with humid hands her wreaths again—
Ah! poor Humanity! so frail, so fair,
10   Are the fond visions of thy early day,
Till tyrant Passion, and corrosive Care,
    Bid all thy fairy colours fade away!
Another May new buds and flowers shall bring;
Ah! why has happiness—no second Spring?

---

1 [Smith's note:] "The well sung woes shall soothe my pensive ghost; / He best can paint them, who shall feel them most." [Alexander] Pope's *Eloisa to Abelard* [1717], 366th line.

2 [Smith's note:] Anemony Nemeroso. The Wood anemone.

SONNET III

To A Nightingale[1]

POOR melancholy bird—that all night long
    Tell'st to the Moon thy tale of tender woe;
    From what sad cause can such sweet sorrow flow,
And whence this mournful melody of song?

5 Thy poet's musing fancy would translate
    What mean the sounds that swell thy little breast,
    When still at dewy eve thou leavest thy nest,
Thus to the listening Night to sing thy fate?

Pale Sorrow's victims wert thou once among,
10   Tho' now released in woodlands wild to rove?
    Say—hast thou felt from friends some cruel wrong,
Or died'st thou—martyr of disastrous love?
Ah! songstress sad! that such my lot might be,
To sigh, and sing at liberty—like thee!

SONNET IV

To the Moon

QUEEN of the silver bow![2]—by thy pale beam,
    Alone and pensive, I delight to stray
And watch thy shadow trembling in the stream,
    Or mark the floating clouds that cross thy way.
5 And while I gaze, thy mild and placid light
    Sheds a soft calm upon my troubled breast;
And oft I think—fair planet of the night,
    That in thy orb the wretched may have rest:
The sufferers of the earth perhaps may go,
10   Released by death—to thy benignant sphere;

---

1 [Smith's note:] The idea from the 43rd Sonnet of Petrarch. Secondo
   parte. "Quel rosigniuol, che si soave piagne." ["That nightingale that so
   sweetly weeps," Sonnet 311. See *Petrarch's Lyric Poems*, trans. and ed.
   Robert M. Durling (Cambridge, MA: Harvard UP, 1976), 490–91. All
   translations of Petrarch are taken from this edition.]
2 A reference to Diana, the Roman goddess of the moon, who was also
   the goddess of the hunt.

Arbaild del. Milton sculpt.

Publish'd Jan:1.1789.by T.Cadell, Strand.

Queen of the Silver Bow, &c

ELEGIAC SONNETS   59

And the sad children of Despair and Woe
    Forget, in thee, their cup of sorrow here.
Oh! that I soon may reach thy world serene,
Poor wearied pilgrim—in this toiling scene!

SONNET V

To the South Downs

AH! hills belov'd!—where once a happy child,
    Your beechen shades, "your turf, your flowers among,"[1]
I wove your blue-bells into garlands wild,
    And woke your echoes with my artless song.
5 Ah! hills belov'd!—your turf, your flow'rs remain;
    But can they peace to this sad breast restore;
For one poor moment sooth the sense of pain,
    And teach a breaking heart to throb no more?
And you, Aruna![2]—in the vale below,
10   As to the sea your limpid waves you bear,
Can you one kind Lethean[3] cup bestow,
    To drink a long oblivion to my care?
Ah, no!—when all, e'en Hope's last ray is gone,
There's no oblivion—but in death alone!

SONNET VI

To Hope

O HOPE! thou soother sweet of human woes!
    How shall I lure thee to my haunts forlorn?
For me wilt thou renew the wither'd rose,
    And clear my painful path of pointed thorn?
5 Ah, come, sweet nymph! in smiles and softness drest,
    Like the young Hours that lead the tender Year;

---

1 [Smith's note:] "Whose turf, whose shades, whose flowers among."
    Gray. [Thomas Gray (1716–71), "Ode on a Distant Prospect of Eton
    College" (1747), line 8.]
2 [Smith's note:] The river Arun. [A river that runs through West Sussex,
    where Smith grew up.]
3 In Greek mythology, the river Lethe was one of the five rivers of Hades.
    Drinking from the river erased the memories of earthly life. Only once a
    soul had drunk from the river could it be reincarnated.

Enchantress! come, and charm my cares to rest:—
    Alas! the flatterer flies, and will not hear!
A prey to fear, anxiety, and pain,
10   Must I a sad existence still deplore?
    Lo!—the flowers fade, but all the thorns remain,
       "For me the vernal garland blooms no more."[1]
Come, then, "pale Misery's love!"[2] be thou my cure,
And I will bless thee, who, tho' slow, art sure.

SONNET VII

On the Departure of the Nightingale

SWEET poet of the woods!—a long adieu!
    Farewel, soft minstrel of the early year!
Ah! 'twill be long ere thou shalt sing anew,
    And pour thy music on "the Night's dull ear."[3]
5 Whether on Spring thy wandering flights await,[4]
    Or whether silent in our groves you dwell,
The pensive Muse shall own thee for her mate,[5]
    And still protect the song she loves so well.
With cautious step the love-lorn youth shall glide
10   Thro' the lone brake° that shades thy mossy nest;   *thicket*
And shepherd girls from eyes profane shall hide
    The gentle bird, who sings of pity best:
For still thy voice shall soft affections move,
And still be dear to Sorrow, and to Love!

---

1 [Smith's note:] Pope's "Imitation of the 1st Ode of the 4th Book of
    Horace." ["Horace his ode to Venus" (London: 1737), I.32.]
2 [Smith's note:] Shakespeare's *King John* ["Misery's love, / O come to
    me!" 3.4.35–63].
3 [Smith's note:] Shakespeare. ["Steed threatens steed, in high and boast-
    ful neighs / Piercing the night's dull ear." *Henry V*, Prologue, 10–11.]
4 [Smith's note:] Alludes to the supposed migration of the Nightingale.
5 [Smith's note:] Whether the Muse or Love call thee his mate, / Both
    them I serve, and of their train am I." Milton's "First Sonnet." [John
    Milton (1608–74), "O Nightingale" (1645), lines 13–14. For Milton's
    full sonnet, see Appendix B1, p. 238.]

SONNET VIII

To Spring

AGAIN the wood, and long-withdrawing vale,
    In many a tint of tender green are drest,
Where the young leaves, unfolding, scarce conceal
    Beneath their early shade, the half-form'd nest
5 Of finch or woodlark; and the primrose pale,
    And lavish cowslip, wildly scatter'd round,
Give their sweet spirits to the sighing gale.
    Ah! season of delight!—could aught be found
    To sooth awhile the tortur'd bosom's pain,
10 Of Sorrow's rankling shaft to cure the wound,
    And bring life's first delusions once again,
'Twere surely met in thee!—thy prospect fair,
Thy sounds of harmony, thy balmy air,
Have power to cure all sadness—but despair.[1]

SONNET IX

BLEST is yon shepherd, on the turf reclined,
    Who on the varied clouds which float above
Lies idly gazing—while his vacant mind
    Pours out some tale antique of rural love!
5 Ah! *he* has never felt the pangs that move
    Th' indignant spirit, when with selfish pride,
Friends, on whose faith the trusting heart rely'd,
    Unkindly shun th' imploring eye of woe!
The ills they ought to sooth, with taunts deride,
10   And laugh at tears themselves have forced to flow.[2]
Nor *his* rude bosom those fine feelings melt,
    Children of Sentiment and Knowledge born,
Thro' whom each shaft with cruel force is felt,
Empoison'd by deceit—or barb'd with scorn.

---

1   [Smith's note:] "To the heart inspires / Vernal delight and joy, able to drive / All sadness but despair." [Milton, *Paradise Lost* (1667), 4.152–54.]

2   [Smith's note:] Sonnet IX, line 10. "And hard unkindness' alter'd eye / That mocks the tear it forc'd to flow." Gray. ["Ode on a Distant Prospect of Eton College," lines 76–77.]

SONNET X

To Mrs. G.

AH! why will Mem'ry with officious care
    The long-lost visions of my days renew?
Why paint the vernal landscape green and fair,
    When Life's gay dawn was opening to my view?
5 Ah! wherefore bring those moments of delight,
    When with my Anna, on the southern shore,
I thought the future, as the present, bright?
    Ye dear delusions!—ye return no more!
Alas! how diff'rent does the truth appear,
10   From the warm picture youth's rash hand pourtrays
How fades the scene, as we approach it near,
    And pain and sorrow strike—how many ways!
Yet of that tender heart, ah! still retain
A share for me—and I will not complain.

SONNET XI

To Sleep

COME, balmy Sleep! tired Nature's soft resort!
    On these sad temples all thy poppies shed;
And bid gay dreams, from Morpheus'[1] airy court,
    Float in light vision round my aching head![2]
5 Secure of all thy blessings, partial Power!
    On his hard bed the peasant throws him down;
And the poor sea-boy, in the rudest hour,
    Enjoys thee more than he who wears a crown.[3]
Clasp'd in her faithful shepherd's guardian arms,
10   Well may the village-girl sweet slumbers prove;
And they, O gentle Sleep! still taste thy charms,
    Who wake to labour, liberty, and love.

---

1 Greek and Roman god of dreams.
2 [Smith's note:] Sonnet XI, line 4. "Float in light vision round the poet's head." Mason. [William Mason (1724–97), "Elegy V. On the Death of a Lady" (1760), line 12.]
3 [Smith's note:] Sonnet XI, lines 7–8. "Wilt thou, upon the high and giddy mast / Seal up the ship boy's eyes, and rock his brains / in cradle of the rude impetuous surge?" Shakespeare's *Henry IV*. [*Henry IV Part 2*, 3.1.18–20; "imperious surge" in original.]

But still thy opiate aid dost thou deny
To calm the anxious breast; to close the streaming eye.

SONNET XII

Written on the sea shore.—October, 1784

ON some rude fragment of the rocky shore,
   Where on the fractured cliff the billows break,
   Musing, my solitary seat I take,
And listen to the deep and solemn roar.

5 O'er the dark waves the winds tempestuous howl;
   The screaming sea-bird quits the troubled sea:
   But the wild gloomy scene has charms for me,
And suits the mournful temper of my soul.[1]

Already shipwreck'd by the storms of Fate,
10   Like the poor mariner, methinks, I stand,
   Cast on a rock; who sees the distant land
From whence no succour comes—or comes too late.
Faint and more faint are heard his feeble cries,
'Till in the rising tide the exhausted sufferer dies.

SONNET XIII

From Petrarch[2]

OH! place me where the burning noon[3]
   Forbids the wither'd flower to blow;
   Or place me in the frigid zone,

---

1 [Smith's note:] Young. [Edward Young (1683–1765), *The Revenge* (1721),
    "Rage on, ye winds, burst clouds, and waters roar! / You bear a just resem-
    blance of my fortune, / And suit the gloomy habit of my soul" 1.1.5–7.]
2 Francesco Petrarcha (Petrarch) (1304–74) was an Italian scholar and
    poet. The sonnets from Petrarch's *Il Canzioniere* ("songbook"), particu-
    larly those to his married love, Laura, were to become an important
    model for lyric poetry in the centuries that followed. Petrarch's influence
    on the Romantic-era sonnet revival is evident in Smith, and in the
    poetry of contemporaries such as Mary Robinson (1757–1800) and
    William Lisle Bowles (1762–1850).
3 [Smith's note:] Sonnet XIII, "Pommi ove'l Sol, occide i fiori e l'erba."
    ["Place me where the sun kills the flowers and the grass." Sonnet 145,

Petrarch's Lyric Poems, 290–91.] Petrarch, *Sonnetto 112. Parte Primo.*
[Smith's "Sonnet XIII" draws on the themes of Petrarch's "Sonnet 145"
but is quite different in content.]

On mountains of eternal snow:
5 Let me pursue the steps of Fame,
    Or Poverty's more tranquil road;
    Let youth's warm tide my veins inflame,
      Or sixty winters chill my blood:
Tho' my fond soul to heaven were flown,
10   Or tho' on earth 'tis doom'd to pine,
Prisoner or free—obscure or known,
    My heart, O Laura! still is thine.
Whate'er my destiny may be,
That faithful heart still burns for thee!

SONNET XIV

From Petrarch

LOOSE to the wind her golden tresses stream'd,[1]
    Forming bright waves, with amorous Zephyr's[2] sighs;
    And tho' averted now, her charming eyes
Then with warm love, and melting pity beam'd.
5 Was I deceived?—Ah! surely, nymph divine!
    That fine suffusion on thy cheek was love;
    What wonder then those beauteous tints should move,
Should fire this heart, this tender heart of mine!
Thy soft melodious voice, thy air, thy shape,
10   Were of a goddess—not a mortal maid;
    Yet tho' thy charms, thy heavenly charms should fade,
My heart, my tender heart could not escape;
    Nor cure for me in time or change be found:
    The shaft extracted does not cure the wound!

SONNET XV

From Petrarch

WHERE the green leaves exclude the summer beam,[3]
    And softly bend as balmy breezes blow,
    And where, with liquid lapse, the lucid stream

---

1 [Smith's note:] "Erano i capei d'oro all aura [l'aura] sparsi." *Sonnetto 69.*
   Parte Primo. ["Her golden hair was loosed to the breeze," Sonnet 90,
   Petrarch's Lyric Poems, 192–93.]
2 The west wind, after Zephyrus, the Greek god of the west wind.
3 [Smith's note:] "Se lamentar augelli o verdi fronde." *Sonnetto 21. Parte*

Across the fretted° rock is heard to flow,   *ridged*
5 Pensive I lay: when she whom earth conceals,
        As if still living to my eyes appears,
    And pitying Heaven her angel form reveals,
        To say—"Unhappy Petrarch! dry your tears:
    Ah! why, sad lover! thus before your time,
10   In grief and sadness should your life decay,
    And like a blighted flower, your manly prime
        In vain and hopeless sorrow fade away?
    Ah! yield not thus to culpable despair,
    But raise thine eyes to heaven—and think I wait thee there."

SONNET XVI

From Petrarch

YE vales and woods! fair scenes of happier hours;[1]
        Ye feather'd people! tenants of the grove;
    And you, bright stream! befring'd with shrubs and flowers;
        Behold my grief, ye witnesses of love!

5 For ye beheld my infant passion rise,
        And saw thro' years unchang'd my faithful flame;
    Now cold, in dust, the beauteous object lies,
        And you, ye conscious scenes, are still the same!

    While busy Memory still delights to dwell
10   On all the charms these bitter tears deplore,
    And with a trembling hand describes too well
        The angel form I shall behold no more!
    To heaven she's fled! and nought to me remains
    But the pale ashes which her urn contains.

Secondo. ["If I hear birds lamenting, or green leaves," Sonnet 279, *Petrarch's Lyric Poems*, 458–59.]

1 [Smith's note:] "Valle che de lamenti miei se piena." *Sonnetto 33. Parte Secondo.* ["O valley full of my laments," Sonnet 301, *Petrarch's Lyric Poems*, 480–81.]

SONNET XVII

From the Thirteenth Cantata of Metastasio[1]

ON thy grey bark, in witness of my flame,[2]
   I carve Miranda's cipher—Beauteous tree!
Graced with the lovely letters of her name,
   Henceforth be sacred, to my love and me!
5 Tho' the tall elm, the oak, and darker pine,
   With broader arms may noon's fierce ardours break,
To shelter me, and her I love, be thine;
   And thine to see her smile and hear her speak.
No bird, ill-omen'd, round thy graceful head
10   Shall clamour harsh, or wave his heavy wing,
But fern and flowers arise beneath thy shade,
   Where the wild bees their lullabies shall sing.
And in thy boughs the murmuring ring-dove rest;
And there the nightingale shall build her nest.

SONNET XVIII

To the Earl of Egremont[3]

WYNDHAM! 'tis not thy blood, tho' pure it runs,
   Thro' a long line of glorious ancestry,
Percys and Seymours,[4] Britain's boasted sons,
   Who trust the honors of their race to thee:

---

1 Pietro Trapessi (1698–1782), known as "Metastasio," was an Italian poet and librettist.
2 [Smith's note:] "Scrivo in te l'amato nome / Di colei, per cui, mi moro" [from Metastasio's cantata *Il Nome*: "I write on you the beloved name / Of her for whom I die"]. This is not meant as a translation; the original is much longer, and full of images, which could not be introduced in a Sonnet.—And some of them, though very beautiful in Italian, would not appear to advantage in English dress.
3 Sir George O'Brien Wyndham, third Earl of Egremont (1751–1837). Egremont became a trustee of Smith's father-in-law Richard Smith's will in 1797. He had previously paid off debts to the estate that had been holding up final settlement, and Smith was hopeful that he would be more sympathetic to her cause than previous trustees. However, by 1802 Egremont and his steward, William Tyler, were withholding the interest payments Smith had previously received from the trust (see *CL* xxvii–xxix).
4 Labbe notes that "Percy was the family name of the earls of Northumberland, and Seymour was the family name of the dukes of Somerset.

5   'Tis not thy splendid domes, where Science loves
        To touch the canvas, and the bust to raise;
    Thy rich domains, fair fields, and spreading groves,
        'Tis not all these the Muse delights to praise:

    In birth, and wealth, and honors, great thou art!
10   But nobler in thy independent mind;
    And in that liberal hand and feeling heart
        Given thee by Heaven—a blessing to mankind!
    Unworthy oft may titled fortune be;
    A soul like thine—is true Nobility!

SONNET XIX

To Mr. Hayley,
On receiving some elegant lines from him

    FOR me the Muse a simple band design'd
        Of "idle" flowers that bloom the woods among,
    Which, with the cypress and the willow[1] join'd,
        A garland form'd as artless as my song.
5   And little dared I hope its transient hours
        So long would last; composed of buds so brief;
    'Till Hayley's hand among the vagrant flowers
        Threw from his verdant crown a deathless leaf.
    For high in Fame's bright fane° has Judgment placed   *temple*
10   The laurel wreath Serena's[2] poet won,
    Which, woven with myrtles by the hands of Taste,
        The Muse decreed for this her favourite son.
    And those immortal leaves his temples shade,
    Whose fair, eternal verdure—shall not fade!

Both families had been in and out of royal favour since the sixteenth
century" (*Works of Charlotte Smith*, vol. 14, ed. Jacqueline Labbe
[London: Pickering and Chatto, 2007], 220).
1   Both the cypress and the willow are associated with mourning and
    weeping.
2   The laurel wreath was awarded to great poets. Serena is the heroine of
    Hayley's poem *The Triumphs of Temper* (1781).

SONNET XX

To the Countess of A——[1]

Written on the anniversary of her marriage

ON this blest day may no dark cloud, or shower,
    With envious shade the Sun's bright influence hide!
But all his rays illume the favour'd hour,
    That saw thee, Mary!—Henry's lovely bride!

5 With years revolving may it still arise,
    Blest with each good approving Heaven can send!
And still, with ray serene, shall those blue eyes
    Enchant the husband, and attach the friend!

For you fair Friendship's amaranth[2] shall blow,
10   And Love's own thornless roses bind your brow;
And when—long hence—to happier worlds you go,
    Your beauteous race shall be what you are now!
And future Nevills[3] thro' long ages shine,
With hearts as good, and forms as fair as thine!

SONNET XXI

Supposed to be written by Werter[4]

GO, cruel tyrant of the human breast!
    To other hearts thy burning arrows bear;
Go where fond Hope, and fair Illusion rest;

---

1 Mary, Lady Abergavenny (1760–96) was Charlotte Smith's niece, the daughter of her brother-in-law, John Robinson.
2 A mythical flower with petals that never fade.
3 Mary married Henry Nevill, Earl of Abergavenny (1755–1843), on 3 October 1781.
4 Werter is the hero of Johann Wolfgang von Goethe's partly autobiographical novel *Die Leiden des jungen Werthers* (1774), translated into English as *The Sorrows of Werter: A German Story* (London: J. Dodsley, 1779). In this epistolary novel, Werter meets and falls in love with a young woman named Lotte (Charlotte). She, however, is already engaged to marry a man named Albert. Werter becomes good friends with both Lotte and Albert but is tortured by his unrequited love. Famously, at the end of the novel young Werter kills himself.

Ah! why should Love inhabit with Despair?
5 Like the poor maniac[1] I linger here,
    Still haunt the scene where all my treasure lies;
  Still seek for flowers where only thorns appear,
    "And drink delicious poison from her eyes!"[2]
  Tow'rds the deep gulf that opens on my sight
10   I hurry forward, Passion's helpless slave!
  And scorning Reason's mild and sober light,
    Pursue the path that leads me to the grave!
  So round the flame the giddy insect flies,
  And courts the fatal fire, by which it dies!

SONNET XXII

By the same. To Solitude

O SOLITUDE! to thy sequester'd vale[3]
    I come to hide my sorrow and my tears,
  And to thy echoes tell the mournful tale
    Which scarce I trust to pitying Friendship's ears!
5 Amidst thy wild-woods, and untrodden glades,
    No sounds but those of melancholy move;
  And the low winds that die among thy shades,
    Seem like soft Pity's sighs for hopeless love!
  And sure some story of despair and pain,
10   In yon deep copse thy murm'ring doves relate;
  And, hark, methinks in that long plaintive strain,
    Thine own sweet songstress weeps my wayward fate!
  Ah, Nymph! that fate assist me to endure,
  And bear awhile—what Death alone can cure!

---

1 [Smith's note:] See the Story of the Lunatic. "Is this the destiny of man?
   Is he only happy before he possesses his reason, or after he has lost it?—
   Full of hope, you go to gather flowers in Winter, and are grieved not to
   find any—and do not know why they cannot be found." *Sorrows of
   Werter. Volume Second* [2.94].
2 [Smith's note:] "And drink delicious poison from thine eye." [Alexan-
   der] Pope. ["Eloisa to Abelard," line 122.]
3 [Smith's note:] "I climb steep rocks, I break my way through copses,
   among thorns and briars which tear me to pieces, and I feel a little
   relief." *Sorrows of Werter. Volume First* [1.153–54. For Anne Bannerman's
   sonnet based on the same scene, see Appendix A8].

SONNET XXIII

By the Same. To the North Star[1]

TO thy bright beams[2] I turn my swimming eyes,
   Fair, fav'rite planet! which in happier days
Saw my young hopes, ah, faithless hopes!—arise,
   And on my passion shed propitious rays!
5 Now nightly wandering 'mid the tempests drear
   That howl the woods and rocky steeps among,
I love to see thy sudden light appear
   Thro' the swift clouds—driven by the wind along;
Or in the turbid water, rude and dark,
10   O'er whose wild stream the gust of Winter raves,
Thy trembling light with pleasure still I mark,
   Gleam in faint radiance on the foaming waves!
So o'er my soul short rays of reason fly,
Then fade:—and leave me to despair and die!

SONNET XXIV

By the same

MAKE there my tomb, beneath the lime-tree's shade,[3]
   Where grass and flowers in wild luxuriance wave;
Let no memorial mark where I am laid,
   Or point to common eyes the lover's grave!
5 But oft at twilight morn, or closing day,
   The faithful friend with falt'ring step shall glide,
Tributes of fond regret by stealth to pay,
   And sigh o'er the unhappy suicide!
And sometimes, when the sun with parting rays
10   Gilds the long grass that hides my silent bed,
The tears shall tremble in my CHARLOTTE's eyes;

---

1 The North Star is a fixed point for navigation, particularly useful when sailing.

2 [Smith's note:] "The greater Bear, favourite of all the constellations; for when I left you of an evening it us'd to shine opposite your window." *Sorrows of Werter. Volume Second* [2.164].

3 [Smith's note:] "At the corner of the church yard which looks towards the fields, there are two lime trees—it is there I wish to rest." *Sorrows of Werter. Volume Second* [2.165].

Dear, precious drops!—they shall embalm the dead!
Yes!—CHARLOTTE o'er the mournful spot shall weep,
Where her poor WERTER—and his sorrows sleep!

SONNET XXV

By the same. Just before his death

WHY should I wish to hold in this low sphere[1]
    "A frail and feverish being?" Wherefore try
Poorly from day to day to linger here,
    Against the powerful hand of Destiny?
5 By those who know the force of hopeless care
    On the worn heart—I sure shall be forgiven,
If to elude dark guilt, and dire despair,
    I go uncall'd—to mercy and to heaven!
O thou! to save whose peace I now depart,
10   Will thy soft mind thy poor lost friend deplore,
When worms shall feed on this devoted heart,
    Where even thy image shall be found no more?[2]
Yet may thy pity mingle not with pain,
For then thy hapless lover—dies in vain!

SONNET XXVI

To the River Arun

ON thy wild banks, by frequent torrents worn,
    No glittering fanes,° or marble domes appear,   *temples*
Yet shall the mournful Muse thy course adorn,
    And still to her thy rustic waves be dear.
5 For with the infant Otway, lingering here,[3]
    Of early woes she bade her votary dream,

---

1 [Smith's note:] "May my death remove every obstacle to your happi-
ness.—Be at peace, I intreat you be at peace." *Sorrows of Werter. Volume
Second* [2. 162 ("May ... happiness,"); 168 ("Be at peace")].

2 [Smith's note:] From a line in Rousseau's *Eloisa*. [Swiss philosopher and
writer Jean-Jacques Rousseau's (1712–78) novel *Julie, ou la novelle
Héloïse* (1761) was widely read and admired as a key text in the litera-
ture of sensibility.]

3 [Smith's note:] Otway was born at Trotten, a village in Sussex. Of
Woolbeding, another village on the banks of the Arun, (which runs
through them both), his father was rector. Here it was   (*continued*)

While thy low murmurs sooth'd his pensive ear,
  And still the poet—consecrates the stream.
Beneath the oak and birch that fringe thy side,
10   The first-born violets of the year shall spring;
And in thy hazles, bending o'er the tide,
  The earliest nightingale delight to sing:
While kindred spirits, pitying, shall relate
Thy Otway's sorrows, and lament his fate!

SONNET XXVII

SIGHING I see yon little troop at play,
  By Sorrow yet untouch'd, unhurt by Care;
While free and sportive they enjoy to-day,
  "Content and careless of to-morrow's fare!"[1]
5 O happy age! when Hope's unclouded ray
  Lights their green path, and prompts their simple mirth;
Ere yet they feel the thorns that lurking lay,
  To wound the wretched pilgrims of the earth;
Making them rue the hour that gave them birth,
10   And threw them on a world so full of pain,
Where prosperous folly treads on patient worth,
  And, to deaf Pride, Misfortune pleads in vain!
Ah!—for their future fate how many fears
Oppress my heart—and fill mine eyes with tears!

SONNET XXVIII

To Friendship

O THOU! whose name too often is profaned;
  Whose charms celestial few have hearts to feel!
Unknown to Folly—and by Pride disdain'd!
  —To thy soft solace may my sorrows steal!
5 Like the fair moon, thy mild and genuine ray
  Thro' Life's long evening shall unclouded last;

---

therefore that he probably passed many of his early years. The Arun is
here an inconsiderable stream, winding in a channel deeply worn,
among meadow, heath, and wood. [Thomas Otway (1652–85) was a
popular playwright and author who ended his years in poverty.]
1 [Smith's note:] Thomson. [James Thomson (1700–48), *Autumn*, in *The
Seasons* (1726–30), line 191.]

Plate 3.   Sonnet 26.

Stothard del.   Thornthwaite sculp.

Published Jan.ʸ 1.1789.by T.Cadell Strand.

For with the infant Otway lingering here.

While Pleasure's frail attachments fleet away,
  As fades the rainbow from the northern blast!
'Tis thine, O Nymph! with "balmy hands to bind"[1]
10   The wounds inflicted in Misfortune's storm,
  And blunt severe Affliction's sharpest dart!
    —'Tis thy pure spirit warms my Anna's mind,
  Beams thro' the pensive softness of her form,
  And holds its altar—on her spotless heart!

SONNET XXIX

To Miss C— On being desired to attempt writing a comedy[2]

WOULD'ST thou then have *me* tempt the comic scene
  Of gay Thalia?° used so long to tread   *the muse of comedy*
  The gloomy paths of Sorrow's cypress shade;
And the lorn° lay with sighs and tears to stain?   *forlorn*
5 Alas! how much unfit her sprightly vein,
  Arduous to try!—and seek the sunny mead,
  And bowers of roses, where she loves to lead
The sportive subjects of her golden reign!
Enough for me, if still to sooth my days,
10   Her fair and pensive sister[3] condescend
  With tearful smile to bless my simple lays°   *lyrics or songs*
    Enough, if her soft notes she sometimes lend,
  To gain for me of feeling hearts the praise,
  And chiefly thine, my ever partial friend!

SONNET XXX

To the River Arun

BE the proud Thames of trade the busy mart!
  Arun! to thee will other praise belong;

---

1 [Smith's note:] Collins. ["With balmy hands his wounds to bind,"
  William Collins (1721–59), "Ode to Pity" (1746), line 2.]
2 Somewhat ironically, an anonymous comedy *What Is She?* (1798) is now
  attributed to Smith. See Diego Saglia, "'This Village Wonder': Charlotte
  Smith's *What Is She?* and the Ideological Comedy of Curiosity," *Char-
  lotte Smith in British Romanticism*, ed. Jacqueline Labbe (London: Picker-
  ing and Chatto, 2008), 145–58.
3 Thalia's sister Erato, the muse of lyric poetry.

Dear to the lover's, and the mourner's heart,
   And ever sacred to the sons of song!

5 Thy banks romantic, hopeless Love shall seek,
     Where o'er the rocks the mantling bindwith[1] flaunts;
  And Sorrow's drooping form and faded cheek
     Choose on thy willow'd shore her lonely haunts!

  Banks! which inspired thy Otway's plaintive strain!
10   Wilds!—whose lorn echoes learn'd the deeper tone
  Of Collins' powerful shell![2] yet once again
     Another poet—Hayley is thine own!
  Thy classic stream anew shall hear a lay,
  Bright as its waves, and various as its way!

SONNET XXXI

Written on Farm Wood, South Downs, in May 1784

SPRING'S dewy hand on this fair summit weaves
   The downy grass with tufts of Alpine flowers:[3]
And shades the beechen slopes with tender leaves,
   And leads the shepherd to his upland bowers,
5 Strewn with wild thyme; while slow-descending showers

---

1 [Smith's note:] The plant Clematis, Bindwith, Virgin's Bower, or Traveller's Joy, which towards the end of June begins to cover the hedges and sides of rocky hollows, with its beautiful foliage, and flowers of a yellowish white of an agreeable fragrance; these are succeeded by seed pods, that bear some resemblance to feathers or hair, whence it is sometimes called Old Man's Beard.

2 [Smith's note:] [William] Collins, as well as Otway, was a native of this country, and probably at some period of his life an inhabitant of this neighbourhood, since in his beautiful Ode on the death of Colonel Ross, he says: "The Muse shall still, with social aid, / Her gentlest promise keep, / E'en humble Harting's cottag'd vale / Shall learn the sad repeated tale, / And bid her shepherds weep" ["Ode, to a Lady on the Death of Colonel Ross" (1746), lines 56–60 ("aid" reads "grief" in the original)]. And in the "Ode to Pity": "Wild Arun too has heard thy strains, / And Echo, midst my native plains, / Been sooth'd with Pity's lute" [lines 16–18].

3 [Smith's note:] An infinite variety of plants are found on these hills, particularly about this spot: many sorts of Orchis and Cistus of singular beauty, with several others.

Feed the green ear,° and nurse the future sheaves!   *grain*
—Ah! blest the hind°—whom no sad thought   *farm assistant*
    bereaves
Of the gay season's pleasures!—All his hours
To wholesome labour given, or thoughtless mirth;
10   No pangs of sorrow past, or coming dread,
Bend his unconscious spirit down to earth,
    Or chase calm slumbers from his careless head!
Ah! what to me can those dear days restore,
When scenes could charm that now I taste no more!

SONNET XXXII

To Melancholy. Written on the banks of the Arun, October, 1785

WHEN latest Autumn spreads her evening veil,
    And the grey mists from these dim waves arise,
    I love to listen to the hollow sighs,
Thro' the half-leafless wood that breathes the gale:
5 For at such hours the shadowy phantom pale,
    Oft seems to fleet before the poet's eyes;
    Strange sounds are heard, and mournful melodies,
As of night-wanderers, who their woes bewail!
Here, by his native stream, at such an hour,
10   Pity's own Otway[1] I methinks could meet,
        And hear his deep sighs swell the sadden'd wind!
Oh Melancholy!—such thy magic power,
    That to the soul these dreams are often sweet,
        And sooth the pensive visionary mind!

SONNET XXXIII

To the Naiad of the Arun

GO, rural Naiad![2] wind thy stream along
    Thro' woods and wilds: then seek the ocean caves
Where sea-nymphs meet their coral rocks among,
    To boast the various honors of their waves!
5 'Tis but a little, o'er thy shallow tide,
    That toiling trade her burden'd vessel leads;

---

1 Thomas Otway. See Sonnet XXVI.
2 A water nymph said to inhabit a river, spring, or waterfall.

But laurels grow luxuriant on thy side,
    And letters live along thy classic meads.
Lo! where 'mid British bards thy natives[1] shine!
10   And now another poet helps to raise
Thy glory high—the poet of the MINE![2]
    Whose brilliant talents are his smallest praise:
And who, to all that genius can impart,
Adds the cool head, and the unblemish'd heart!

SONNET XXXIV

To a Friend

CHARM'D by thy suffrage° shall I yet aspire   *prayers*
    (All inauspicious as my fate appears,
    By troubles darken'd, that increase with years,)
To guide the crayon, or to touch the lyre?
5   Ah me!—the sister Muses still require
    A spirit free from all intrusive fears,
    Nor will they deign to wipe away the tears
Of vain regret, that dim their sacred fire.
But when thy envied sanction crowns my lays,
10   A ray of pleasure lights my languid mind,
For well I know the value of thy praise;
    And to how few the flattering meed° confin'd,   *reward*
    That thou,—their highly favour'd brows to bind,
Wilt weave green myrtle and unfading bays!

SONNET XXXV

To Fortitude

NYMPH of the rock! whose dauntless spirit braves
    The beating storm, and bitter winds that howl
Round thy cold breast; and hear'st the bursting waves
    And the deep thunder with unshaken soul;
5   Oh come!—and show how vain the cares that press
    On my weak bosom—and how little worth

---

1   [Smith's note:] Otway, Collins, Hayley.
2   John Sargent (1750–1831) was a politician and the author of *The Mine*
    (1785), the story of a man who was condemned to the quicksilver mines
    of Idria, Slovenia, as a punishment for duelling.

Is the false fleeting meteor, Happiness,
    That still misleads the wanderers of the earth!
Strengthen'd by thee, this heart shall cease to melt
10   O'er ills that poor Humanity must bear;
Nor friends estranged, or ties dissolv'd be felt
    To leave regret, and fruitless anguish there:
And when at length it heaves its latest sigh,
Thou and mild Hope shall teach me how to die!

SONNET XXXVI

SHOULD the lone Wanderer, fainting on his way,
    Rest for a moment of the sultry hours,
And tho' his path thro' thorns and roughness lay,
    Pluck the wild rose, or woodbine's gadding[1] flowers,
5 Weaving gay wreaths beneath some sheltering tree,
    The sense of sorrow he awhile may lose;
So have I sought thy flowers, fair Poesy!
    So charm'd my way with Friendship and the Muse.
But darker now grows life's unhappy day,
10   Dark with new clouds of evil yet to come,
Her pencil sickening Fancy throws away,
    And weary Hope reclines upon the tomb;
And points my wishes to that tranquil shore,
Where the pale spectre Care pursues no more.

SONNET XXXVII

Sent to the Honourable Mrs. O'Neill,[2] with painted flowers

THE poet's fancy takes from Flora's realm
    Her buds and leaves to dress fictitious powers,
With the green olive shades Minerva's° helm,   *goddess of wisdom*
    And give to Beauty's Queen the Queen of flowers.[3]
5 But what gay blossoms of luxuriant Spring,
    With rose, mimosa, amaranth entwin'd,
Shall fabled Sylphs° and fairy people bring,   *spirit of the air*

---

1 Wandering idly.
2 Henrietta Boyle O'Neill (1758–93) was a poet and a friend of Smith's.
    O'Neill was a significant source of literary and personal support, and
    Smith was devastated when her friend died in 1793.
3 "Beauty's Queen" is Venus, and she is given roses, "the Queen of flowers."

Corbould del.   Neagle sculp.

Publish'd as the Act directs by T. Cadell Strand Jan.ʳ 1 1789.

Her pencil sickening fancy throws away
And weary hope reclines upon the tomb.

As a just emblem of the lovely mind?
    In vain the mimic pencil tries to blend
10   The glowing dyes that dress the flowery race,
        Scented and colour'd by a hand divine!
    Ah! not less vainly would the Muse pretend
      On her weak lyre, to sing the native grace
      And native goodness of a soul like thine!

SONNET XXXVIII

From the novel of Emmeline[1]

WHEN welcome slumber sets my spirit free,
    Forth to fictitious happiness it flies,
    And where Elysian° bowers of bliss arise,   *heavenly*
I seem, my Emmeline—to meet with thee!
5 Ah! Fancy then, dissolving human ties,
    Gives me the wishes of my soul to see;
Tears of fond pity fill thy soften'd eyes:
    In heavenly harmony—our hearts agree.
Alas! these joys are mine in dreams alone,
10 When cruel Reason abdicates her throne!
    Her harsh return condemns me to complain
Thro' life unpitied, unrelieved, unknown!
    And as the dear delusions leave my brain,
    She bids the truth recur—with aggravated pain!

SONNET XXXIX

To Night. From the same

I LOVE thee, mournful, sober-suited Night!
    When the faint moon, yet lingering in her wane,
And veil'd in clouds, with pale uncertain light
    Hangs o'er the waters of the restless main.
5 In deep depression sunk, the enfeebled mind
    Will to the deaf cold elements complain,
    And tell the embosom'd grief, however vain,
To sullen surges and the viewless wind.

---

1   This sonnet and the next one were first printed in Smith's novel *Emmeline, the Orphan of the Castle* (1788). They are supposed to have been written by Godolphin, the man who is to become Emmeline's husband.

Tho' no repose on thy dark breast I find,
10   I still enjoy thee—cheerless as thou art;
     For in thy quiet gloom the exhausted heart
Is calm, tho' wretched; hopeless, yet resign'd.
While to the winds and waves its sorrows given,
May reach—tho' lost on earth—the ear of Heaven!

SONNET XL

From the Same[1]

FAR on the sands, the low, retiring tide,
     In distant murmurs hardly seems to flow;
And o'er the world of waters, blue and wide,
     The sighing summer-wind forgets to blow.
5 As sinks the day-star° in the rosy West,   *the sun*
     The silent wave, with rich reflection glows:
Alas! can tranquil nature give *me* rest,
     Or scenes of beauty sooth me to repose?
Can the soft lustre of the sleeping main,°   *the ocean*
10   Yon radiant heaven, or all creation's charms,
     "Erase the written troubles of the brain,"[2]
     Which Memory tortures, and which Guilt alarms?
Or bid a bosom transient quiet prove,
That bleeds with vain remorse and unextinguish'd love!

SONNET XLI

To Tranquillity

IN this tumultuous sphere, for thee unfit,
     How seldom art thou found—Tranquillity!
     Unless 'tis when with mild and downcast eye
By the low cradles thou delight'st to sit
5 Of sleeping infants—watching the soft breath,
     And bidding the sweet slumberers easy lie;
Or sometimes hanging o'er the bed of death,

---

1 This poem is supposed to have been written by Emmeline's friend, Lady
    Adelina Trelawny.
2 "Pluck out from the memory a rooted sorrow, / Raze out the written
    troubles of the brain." Shakespeare, *Macbeth* 5.3.41–42.

Where the poor languid sufferer—hopes to die.
　　O beauteous sister of the halcyon[1] peace!
10　　I sure shall find thee in that heavenly scene
　　　　Where Care and Anguish shall their power resign;
　　Where hope alike, and vain regret shall cease,
　　　　And Memory—lost in happiness serene,
　　　　Repeat no more—that misery has been mine!

SONNET XLII

Composed during a walk on the Downs, in November, 1787

THE dark and pillowy cloud, the sallow trees,
　　Seem o'er the ruins of the year to mourn;
And, cold and hollow, the inconstant breeze
　　Sobs thro' the falling leaves and wither'd fern.
5　　O'er the tall brow of yonder chalky bourn,°   *outcrop*
The evening shades their gather'd darkness fling,
　　While, by the lingering light, I scarce discern
The shrieking night-jar[2] sail on heavy wing.
　　Ah! yet a little—and propitious Spring
10 Crown'd with fresh flowers shall wake the woodland strain;
　　But no gay change revolving seasons bring
To call forth pleasure from the soul of pain!
Bid Syren Hope resume her long-lost part,
And chase the vulture Care—that feeds upon the heart!

SONNET XLIII

THE unhappy exile, whom his fates confine
　　To the bleak coast of some unfriendly isle,
　　Cold, barren, desart, where no harvests smile,
But thirst and hunger on the rocks repine;
5 When, from some promontory's fearful brow,
　　Sun after sun he hopeless sees decline

1　A mythical time of peace and calm.
2　[Smith's note:] The night-jar or night hawk, a dark bird not so big as a
　　rook, which is frequently seen of an evening on the downs. It has a short
　　heavy flight, then rests on the ground, and again, uttering a mournful
　　cry, flits before the traveller, to whom its appearance is supposed by the
　　peasants to portend misfortune. As I have never seen it dead, I know not
　　to what species it belongs.

In the broad shipless sea—perhaps may know
    Such heartless pain, such blank despair as mine!
And, if a flattering cloud appears to show
10   The fancied semblance of a distant sail,
    Then melts away—anew his spirits fail,
While the lost hope but aggravates his woe!
Ah! so for me delusive Fancy toils,
Then, from contrasted truth—my feeble soul recoils.

SONNET XLIV

Written in the Church Yard at Middleton in Sussex

PRESS'D by the Moon, mute arbitress of tides,
    While the loud equinox its power combines,
    The sea no more its swelling surge confines,
But o'er the shrinking land sublimely rides.
5 The wild blast, rising from the Western cave,
    Drives the huge billows from their heaving bed;
    Tears from their grassy tombs the village dead,[1]
And breaks the silent sabbath of the grave!
With shells and sea-weed mingled, on the shore
10   Lo! their bones whiten in the frequent wave;
    But vain to them the winds and waters rave;
They hear the warring elements no more:
While I am doom'd—by life's long storm opprest,
To gaze with envy on their gloomy rest.

---

1 [Smith's note:] Middleton is a village on the margin of the sea in
Sussex, containing only two or three houses. There were formerly several
acres of ground between its small church and the sea; which now, by its
continual encroachments, approaches within a few feet of this half
ruined and humble edifice. The wall, which once surrounded the church
yard, is entirely swept away, many of the graves broken up, and the
remains of bodies interred washed into the sea: whence human bones
are found among the sand and shingles on the shore. [A companion
poem, "Elegy," was first published in the same 1789 edition; see pp.
193–96. "Elegy" is explicitly set in the same location and Smith makes
the graveyard the site of "the proud aggressor's tomb," where "Avarice
finds a quiet grave!" (lines 67 and 12).]

SONNET XLV

On leaving a Part of Sussex

FAREWEL, Aruna! on whose varied shore
    My early vows were paid to Nature's shrine,
    When thoughtless joy, and infant hope were mine,
And whose lorn stream has heard me since deplore
5   Too many sorrows! Sighing I resign
Thy solitary beauties—and no more
    Or on thy rocks, or in thy woods recline,
Or on the heath, by moonlight lingering, pore
    On air-drawn phantoms—While in Fancy's ear
10 As in the evening wind thy murmurs swell,
    The Enthusiast of the Lyre, who wander'd here,[1]
Seems yet to strike his visionary shell,°   *lyre*
    Of power to call forth Pity's tenderest tear,
Or wake wild Phrenzy—from her hideous cell!

SONNET XLVI

Written At Penshurst,[2] in Autumn 1788

YE towers sublime! deserted now and drear!
    Ye woods! deep sighing to the hollow blast,
The musing wanderer loves to linger near,
    While History points to all your glories past:
5 And startling from their haunts the timid deer,
    To trace the walks obscured by matted fern,
    Which Waller's[3] soothing lyre were wont to hear,
    But where now clamours the discordant hern!°[4]   *heron*
The spoiling hand of Time may overturn
10   These lofty battlements, and quite deface

---

1 [Smith's note:] Collins. [See note to Sonnet XXX, p. 77.]
2 Penshurst Place, in Kent, is the ancestral home of the Sidney family. It
    had begun to deteriorate at the time that Smith wrote this poem, and it
    was not restored and refurbished until 1818.
3 Edmund Waller (1606–87) wrote two poems "To Penshurst."
4 [Smith's note:] In the park at Penshurst is an heronry. The house is at
    present uninhabited, and the windows of the galleries and other rooms,
    in which there are many invaluable pictures, are never opened but when
    strangers visit it.

The fading canvass whence we love to learn
　　Sydney's[1] keen look, and Sacharissa's[2] grace;
But fame and beauty still defy decay,
　　Saved by the historic page—the poet's tender lay!

SONNET XLVII

To Fancy

THEE, Queen of Shadows!—shall I still invoke,
　　Still love the scenes thy sportive pencil drew,
When on mine eyes the early radiance broke
　　Which shew'd the beauteous rather than the true!
5　Alas! long since those glowing tints are dead,
　　And now 'tis thine in darkest hues to dress
The spot where pale Experience hangs her head
　　O'er the sad grave of murder'd Happiness!
Thro' thy false medium, then, no longer view'd,
10　　May fancied pain and fancied pleasure fly,
　　And I, as from me all thy dreams depart,
Be to my wayward destiny subdued:
　　Nor seek perfection with a poet's eye,
　　Nor suffer anguish with a poet's heart!

SONNET XLVIII

*To Mrs. *****

NO more my wearied soul attempts to stray
　　From sad reality and vain regret,
Nor courts enchanting Fiction to allay
　　Sorrows that Sense refuses to forget:
5　For of Calamity so long the prey,
　　Imagination now has lost her powers,
Nor will her fairy loom again essay
　　To dress Affliction in a robe of flowers.

1　[Smith's note:] Algernon Sidney. [Sidney, or Sydney (1623–83), was a republican political theorist, and a parliamentary leader during the English commonwealth (1650–60). Upon the restoration of the monarchy he was tried and executed for plotting against the king. After his death he became a celebrated martyr to liberty.]
2　Sacharissa was the name given to Lady Dorothea Sidney (1617–84), to whom Waller wrote amorous verse.

But if no more the bowers of Fancy bloom,
10   Let one superior scene attract my view,
Where Heaven's pure rays the sacred spot illume,
    Let *thy* loved hand with palm and amaranth[1] strew
The mournful path approaching to the tomb,
While Faith's consoling voice endears the friendly gloom.

SONNET XLIX

From the novel of *Celestina*

Supposed to have been written in a church-yard,
over the grave of a young woman of nineteen[2]

O THOU! who sleep'st where hazle-bands entwine
    The vernal grass, with paler violets drest;
I would, sweet maid! thy humble bed were mine,
    And mine thy calm and enviable rest.
5 For never more by human ills opprest
    Shall thy soft spirit fruitlessly repine:
    Thou canst not now thy fondest hopes resign
Even in the hour that should have made thee blest.
Light lies the turf upon thy virgin breast;
10   And lingering here, to Love and Sorrow true,
The youth who once thy simple heart possest
    Shall mingle tears with April's early dew;
While still for him shall faithful Memory save
Thy form and virtues from the silent grave.

SONNET L

From the novel of *Celestina*[3]

FAREWEL, ye lawns!—by fond remembrance blest,
    As witnesses of gay unclouded hours;

---

1 The palm represents triumph, and amaranth immortality. Amaranth is a
mythical flower that never fades and is associated with immortality in
myth and poetry. Cf. *Paradise Lost* 3.353–61.

2 This sonnet is supposed to have been written by the eponymous heroine
of *Celestina* (1791).

3 This sonnet, also supposed to have been written by Celestina, extols the
virtues of Alvestone, the country seat of the hero of the novel, Willoughby.
This poem has clear similarities to Sonnet V, "To the South Downs."

Where, to maternal Friendship's bosom prest,
    My happy childhood past among your bowers.
5 Ye wood-walks wild!—where leaves and fairy flowers
    By Spring's luxuriant hand are strewn anew;
Rocks!—whence with shadowy grace rude Nature lours°   *frowns*
    O'er glens and haunted streams!—a long adieu!
And you!—O promised Happiness!—whose voice
10   Deluded Fancy heard in every grove,
Bidding this tender, trusting heart, rejoice
    In the bright prospect of unfailing love:
Tho' lost to me—still may thy smile serene
Bless the dear lord of this regretted scene.

SONNET LI

From the novel of *Celestina*

Supposed to have been written in the Hebrides[1]

ON this lone island, whose unfruitful breast
    Feeds but the Summer-shepherd's little flock
    With scanty herbage from the half-clothed rock,
Where osprays,[2] cormorants, and sea-mews° rest;   *the common gull*
5   Even in a scene so desolate and rude
I could with *thee* for months and years be blest;
And of thy tenderness and love possest,
    Find all *my* world in this wild solitude!
When summer suns these northern seas illume,
10   With thee admire the light's reflected charms,
And when drear Winter spreads his cheerless gloom,
    Still find Elysium in thy shelt'ring arms:
For thou to me canst sovereign bliss impart,
Thy mind my empire—and my throne thy heart.

---

1 As the title suggests, this poem and the two poems that follow, are sup-
    posed to have been written by Celestina as she tours the Hebrides, off
    the west coast of Scotland.
2 [Smith's note:] The sea-eagle.

SONNET LII

The Pilgrim

FAULTERING and sad the unhappy Pilgrim roves,
    Who, on the eve of bleak December's night,
Divided far from all he fondly loves,
    Journeys alone, along the giddy height
5 Of these steep cliffs; and as the sun's last ray
    Fades in the west, sees, from the rocky verge,
Dark tempest scowling o'er the shortened day,
    And hears, with ear appall'd, the impetuous surge
Beneath him thunder!—So, with heart oppress'd,
10   Alone, reluctant, desolate, and slow,[1]
By Friendship's cheering radiance *now* unblest,
    Along Life's rudest path I seem to go;
Nor see where yet the anxious heart may rest,
That, trembling at the past—recoils from future woe.

SONNET LIII

THE shivering native, who by Tenglio's[2] side,
    Beholds with fond regret the parting light
Sink far away, beneath the darkening tide,
    And leave him to long months of dreary night,
5 Yet knows, that springing from the eastern wave
    The sun's glad beams shall re-illume his way,
And from the snows secured—within his cave
    He waits in patient hope—returning day.
Not so the sufferer feels, who, o'er the waste
10   Of joyless life, is destin'd to deplore
Fond love forgotten, tender friendship past,
    Which, once extinguish'd, can revive no more!
O'er the blank void he looks with hopeless pain;
For him those beams of heaven shall never shine again.

---

1   This line echoes in cadence the iconic opening lines of Oliver Gold-
    smith's (1730–74) *The Traveller, or A Prospect of Society* (1764): "Remote,
    unfriended, melancholy, slow."

2   According to Scottish poet James Thomson's *The Seasons* (1726–30), the
    Tenglio is a river in Lapland: "Where pure Niemi's fairy mountains rise, /
    And fringed with roses Tenglio rolls his stream" ("Winter," lines 875–76).
    Smith's sonnet is clearly inspired by this passage from Thomson's poem.

SONNET LIV

The sleeping woodman. Written in April 1790

YE copses wild, where April bids arise
    The vernal grasses, and the early flowers;
My soul depress'd—from human converse flies
    To the lone shelter of your pathless bowers.

5 Lo!—where the Woodman, with his toil oppress'd,
    His careless head on bark and moss reclined,
    Lull'd by the song of birds, the murmuring wind,
Has sunk to calm tho' momentary rest.

Ah! would 'twere mine in Spring's green lap to find
10   Such transient respite from the ills I bear!
Would I could taste, like this unthinking hind,
    A sweet forgetfulness of human care,[1]
Till the last sleep these weary eyes shall close,
And Death receive me to his long repose.

SONNET LV

The return of the Nightingale. Written in May 1791

BORNE on the warm wing of the western gale,
    How tremulously low is heard to float
Thro' the green budding thorns that fringe the vale,
    The early Nightingale's prelusive° note.   *introductory*

5 'Tis Hope's instinctive power that thro' the grove
    Tells how benignant Heaven revives the earth;
'Tis the soft voice of young and timid Love
    That calls these melting sounds of sweetness forth.

With transport, once, sweet bird! I hail'd thy lay,
10   And bade thee welcome to our shades again,
To charm the wandering poet's pensive way
    And sooth the solitary lover's pain;
But now!—such evils in my lot combine,
As shut my languid sense—to Hope's dear voice and thine!

---

1   [Smith's note:] Pope. ["The First Book of Statius's Thebaid," line 481.]

SONNET LVI

The captive escaped in the wilds of America

Addressed to the Hon. Mrs. O'Neill[1]

IF, by his torturing, savage foes untraced,
    The breathless Captive gain some trackless glade,
Yet hears the war-whoop howl along the waste,
    And dreads the reptile-monsters of the shade;
5 The giant reeds that murmur round the flood,
    Seem to conceal some hideous form beneath;
And every hollow blast that shakes the wood,
    Speaks to his trembling heart of woe and death.
With horror fraught, and desolate dismay,
10   On such a wanderer falls the starless night;
But if, far streaming, a propitious ray
    Leads to some amicable fort his sight,
He hails the beam benign that guides his way,
    As I, my Harriet, bless thy friendship's cheering light.

SONNET LVII

To Dependence

DEPENDENCE! heavy, heavy are thy chains,
    And happier they who from the dangerous sea,
Or the dark mine, procure with ceaseless pains
    An hard-earn'd pittance—than who trust to thee!
5 More blest the hind, who from his bed of flock
    Starts—when the birds of morn their summons give,
And waken'd by the lark—"the shepherd's clock,"[2]
    Lives but to labour—labouring but to live.
More noble than the sycophant, whose art
10   Must heap with taudry flowers thy hated shrine;
I envy not the meed thou canst impart
    To crown *his* service—while, tho' Pride combine
With Fraud to crush me—my unfetter'd heart
    Still to the Mountain Nymph[3] may offer mine.

---

1 See Sonnet XXXVII.
2 [Smith's note:] Shakespeare. ["And merry larks are ploughman's clocks," *Love's Labour's Lost*, 5.2.901.]
3 [Smith's note:] The mountain goddess, Liberty.

SONNET LVIII

The glow-worm

WHEN on some balmy-breathing night of Spring
    The happy child, to whom the world is new,
    Pursues the evening moth, of mealy wing,
      Or from the heath-bell beats the sparkling dew;
5 He sees before his inexperienced eyes
    The brilliant Glow-worm, like a meteor, shine
On the turf-bank;—amazed, and pleased, he cries,
    "Star of the dewy grass!¹—I make thee mine!"—
Then, ere he sleep, collects "the moisten'd" flower,²
10   And bids soft leaves his glittering prize enfold,
    And dreams that Fairy-lamps illume his bower:
    Yet with the morning shudders to behold
His lucid treasure, rayless as the dust!
—So turn the world's bright joys to cold and blank disgust.

SONNET LIX

*Written Sept. 1791, during a remarkable thunderstorm,
in which the moon was perfectly clear, while the tempest gathered
in various directions near the Earth*

WHAT awful pageants crowd the evening sky!
    The low horizon gathering vapours shroud;
    Sudden, from many a deep-embattled cloud
Terrific thunders burst, and lightnings fly—
5 While in serenest azure, beaming high,
    Night's regent,° of her calm pavilion proud,   *the moon*
Gilds the dark shadows that beneath her lie,
    Unvex'd by all their conflicts fierce and loud.
    —So, in unsullied dignity elate,
10   A spirit conscious of superior worth,

---

1 [Smith's note:] "Star of the earth." Dr. Darwin. [Erasmus Darwin,
  Economy of Vegetation (part one of *The Botanic Garden*, 1791), 1.196. On
  Darwin, see Appendix A9.]

2 [Smith's note:] "The moisten'd blade—" [Dr.] Walcot's beautiful "Ode
  to the Glow-worm." [John Wolcot (1738–1819) was a popular poet who
  wrote under the name of Peter Pindar. *The Works of Peter Pindar, Esq. In
  Three Volumes* (London, 1794), 2.493–95.]

In placid elevation firmly great,
    Scorns the vain cares that give Contention birth;
And blest with peace above the shocks of Fate,
Smiles at the tumult of the troubled earth.

Elegiac Sonnets

Volume Two

P. Conde sculp.

Oh: Time has Changed me since you saw me last,
And heavy Hours with Time's deforming Hand,
Have written strange Defeatures in my Face.

Published May 15th. 1797. by Cadell and Davies Strand.

PREFACE TO VOLUME TWO of *Elegiac Sonnets* (1797)[1]

IT so rarely happens that a second attempt in any species of writing equals the first, in the public opinion, when the first has been remarkably successful; that I send this second volume of small Poems into the world with a considerable degree of diffidence and apprehension.

Whatever inferiority may be adjudged to it, I cannot plead want of *time* for its completion, if I should attempt any excuse at all; for I do not forget that more than three years have elapsed since I reluctantly yielded to the pressing instances of some of my friends;[2] and accepted their offers to promote a subscription to another volume of Poems—I say, accepted the offers of my friends, because (with a single exception) I have never made any application myself.

Having once before had recourse to the indulgence of the public, in publishing a book by subscription, and knowing that it had been so often done by persons with whom it is honourable to be ranked, it was not pride that long withheld my consent from this manner of publication; and, certainly, the pecuniary inconveniencies I have been exposed to for so many years, never pressed upon me *more* heavily than at the moment this proposal was urged by my friends;[3] if then I declined it, it was because I even at *that* period doubted, either from extreme depression of spirit, I should have the power of fulfilling (so as to satisfy myself) the engagement I must feel myself bound by, the moment I had accepted subscription.

Could any one of the misfortunes that so rapidly followed have been foreseen, nothing should have induced me to have consented to it—for what expectation could I entertain of resisting such

---

1   This preface appeared in the 1797 edition of Volume Two of *ES* but was suppressed upon the publication of the 1800 edition, possibly for being too inflammatory in tone.

2   [Smith's note:] Particularly those of Joseph Cooper Walker, Esq. of Dublin, by whose friendly and successful applications in Ireland I am particularly obliged. [The Reverend Joseph Cooper (1761–1810) was an Irish antiquarian and author. He was introduced to Smith through Hayley and arranged the sale of some of the writer's works to Irish booksellers. See *CL* 782.]

3   The problems with settling Richard Smith's estate were still dragging on, and Smith had no reason to hope, at this stage, that the estate would be settled soon.

calamities as the detention of their property has brought on my children? Of four sons, all seeking in other climates the competence denied them in this, two were (for that reason) driven from their prospects in the Church to the Army, where one of them was maimed during the first campaign he served in, and is now a lieutenant of invalids.[1] The lovliest, the most beloved of my daughters, the darling of all her family, was torn from us forever.[2] The rest deprived of every advantage to which they are entitled; and the means of proper education for my youngest son denied me! while the money that their inhuman trustees have suffered yearly to be wasted, and what they keep possession of on false and frivolous pretences, would, if paid to those it belongs to, have saved me and them from all these now irremediable misfortunes.

I am well aware that the present is not a time when the complaints of individuals against private wrong are likely to be listened to; nor is this an opportunity fit to make those complaints; but I know so much has been said, (so much more than so trifling a matter could be worth) of the *delay* of this publication, that it becomes in some measure a matter of self-defence to account for that delay. Those who have expressed such impatience for it, were apprehensive (indeed they owned they were) of the loss of the half guinea they had paid. I have more than once thought of returning their money, rather than have remained under any obligation to persons who could suspect me of a design to accumulate, by gathering subscriptions for a work I never meant to publish, a sum, which no contrivance, no success, was likely to make equal to one year of the income I ought to possess. Surely, any who have entertained and *expressed* such an opinion of me, must either never have understood, *or must have forgotten*, what I was, what I am, or what I ought to be.

To be suspected even by arrogant ignorance of such an intention to impose on public generosity, has not been the least among the mortifications I have within these last years been subjected to; I place them to the same long account of injuries, where this,

---

1 In 1793, Smith's son, Charles Dyer Smith (chr. 27 February 1773–d. after June 1801), who had reached the rank of ensign in the army, had his leg amputated as a result of injuries received in the Siege of Dunkirk. See also Mary Robinson's poem on this event, Appendix A6.

2 Anna Augusta Smith de Foville (1774–95) was Smith's eighth child, and her mother's favourite. She died in April 1795 at the Clifton Hot Wells, where she was receiving treatment (possibly for consumption). She was 21. Smith felt the loss of her daughter acutely, and her death is referred to in a number of poems from this volume.

however, is almost lost in the magnitude of others! Let not the censors of literary productions, or the fastidious in private life, again reprove me for bringing forward "with querulous egotism," the mention of myself, and the sorrows, of which the men, who have withheld my family property, have been the occasion. Had they never so unjustly possessed, and so shamelessly exercised the power of reducing me to pecuniary distress, I should never, perhaps, have had occasion to ask the consideration of the *reader*, or to deprecate the severity of the *critic*. Certainly I should never have been compelled to make excuses as a defaulter in point of *punctuality* to the *subscriber*. Nor should I to any of these have found it necessary to state the causes that have rendered me miserable as an *individual*, though *now* I am compelled to complain of those who have crushed the poor abilities of the *author*, and by the most unheard of acts of injustice (*for twice seven years*) have added the painful sensations of *indignation* to the inconveniencies and deprivations of indigence; and aggravating by future dread, the present suffering, have frequently doubled the toil necessary for to-morrow, by palsying the hand and distracting the head, that were struggling against the evils of to-day!

It is passed!—The injuries I have so long suffered under are not mitigated; the aggressors are not removed: but however soon they may be disarmed their power, any retribution in this world is impossible—they can neither give back to the maimed the possession of health, or restore the dead. The time they have occasioned me to pass in anxiety, in sorrow, in anguish, they cannot recall to me—To my children they can make no amends, but they would not if they could; nor have I the poor consolation of knowing that I leave in the callous hearts of these persons, *thorns* to

"goad and sting them,"[1]

for they have conquered or outlived all sensibility of shame; they are alive neither to honesty, honour, or humanity; and at this moment, far from feeling compunction for the ruin they have occasioned, the dreadful misfortunes they have been the authors of, one shrinks from the very attempt to make such redress as he might yet give, and wraps himself up in the callous insolence of his imagined consequence; while the other uses such professional

---

1   Shakespeare, *Hamlet* 1.5.88. "Leave her to Heaven, / and to those
Thorns that in her bosom lodge, / To goad and sting her."

subterfuges as are the disgrace of his possession, to baffle me yet a little longer in my attempts to procure that restitution, that justice, which they dare not deny I am entitled to; and to insult me by a continuation of tormenting chicaneries,[1] perpetuating to the utmost of their power the distresses they have occasioned, and which their perseverance in iniquity has already put it out of the power of Heaven itself to remedy!

Would to God I could dismiss these oppressors from my mind for ever, as I now do from the notice of any future readers, whom I may engage to any work of mine (though very probably I may now take my last leave of the public). And let me, while I account for the delay of this work, and for many defects that may perhaps be found in it, assign the causes for both, and lament that such have been the circumstances under which I have composed it, as may rather render it a wonder I have produced it at all, than that it has been so long in appearing, and yet appears defective. Surely I shall be forgiven once more for "querulous egotism,"[2] when the disadvantages I have laboured under are considered; complaint may be pardoned when the consequences of what I deplore, mingle themselves in all my feelings, embitter every hour of my life, and leave me no hope but in the oblivion of the grave.

Some degree of pride which

"Still travels on, nor leaves us till we die,"[3]

makes me somewhat solicitous to account for the visible difference in point of numbers between the subscribers to this and the former volume. If I were willing to admit that these Poems are inferior to those that preceded them, I know that such a supposition would not have withheld a single subscription—but I also know, that as party can raise prejudices against the colour of a ribband, or the cut of a cape, it generates still stranger antipathies, even in regard to things almost equally trifling. And

---

1 Deceptions or subterfuges.
2 This was a charge not infrequently levelled at Smith as a result of her poetry's focus on the sufferings of its author. However, Samuel Taylor Coleridge (1772–1834), in the Preface to his *Poems on Various Subjects* (1796), reminds us that Smith was not the only poet to be accused of "querulous egotism." "Compositions resembling those of the present volume," he writes, "are not infrequently condemned for their querulous egotism" (v).
3 "Hope travels thro, nor quits us when we die," Alexander Pope, *An Essay on Man* (1734), line 274.

there are, who can never forgive an author that has, in the story of a Novel, or the composition of a Sonnet, ventured to hint at any opinions different from those which these liberal-minded personages are determined to find the best.

I know, therefore, perfectly well, how I have sinned against some ci-devant,[1] I was going to say friends, but I check myself, and change the word for acquaintance,

"Since friendship should be made of stronger stuff,"[2]

acquaintance, who when my writing first obtained popularity, erected themselves into patrons and patronesses. To the favor they *then* conferred I am not insensible; and I hope they will accept it as proof of my perfectly understanding the extent of the obligation, that I have so silently acquiesced in not expecting it to be repeated, and have never suffered them to be put under the painful necessity of avowing their dereliction in 1797, of the writer whom they affected so warmly to patronize in 1787. Ten years do indeed operate most wonderful changes in this state of existence.

Perhaps in addition to the friend, or *soi-disant tel,*[3] whose notice and whose names have for some such causes as these, been withheld, I might add as *another cause,* that for many months past I have been so apprehensive of not having health enough to superintend the publication of even this small volume, that I had desired those few friends who had voluntarily engaged to collect subscriptions, not to persevere in their kind endeavours; and I had written to my elder sons, entreating them, should death overtake me before I could complete my engagements, to place, as soon afterwards as they could, in the hands of Messrs. Cadell and Davies,[4] a sum sufficient to reimburse them any expences they might have incurred, and to repay the subscriptions.

---

1 Former (French). In Revolutionary France the word was commonly used to refer to those who remained loyal to the values of pre-Revolutionary French society.
2 Appears to be a play on Mark Antony's funeral oration in Shakespeare's *Julius Caesar:* "Ambition should be made of sterner stuff" (3.2.92).
3 So-called friends (French).
4 London publishers Thomas Cadell (1742–1802) and William Davies (d. 1820) published a number of Smith's early works. Cadell's son, Thomas Cadell Jr., took over his father's publishing firm in 1793. The firm published all of the editions of *ES* that appeared in Smith's lifetime. For an example of Smith's correspondence with them, see Appendix C1a.

I am at length enabled to send it into the world—and have certainly omitted nothing that was in my power to make it not intirely unworthy the general favor, and of the particular kindness of *those* without whose support I believe it would have been impossible for me to have prepared the few verses I had by me, or to have composed others. That these are gloomy, none will surely have a right to complain; for I never engaged they should be gay. But I am unhappily exempt from the suspicion of *feigning* sorrow for an opportunity of shewing the pathos with which it can be described—a suspicion that has given rise to much ridicule, and many invidious remarks, among certain critics, and others, who carry into their closets the same aversion to any thing tragic, as influences, at the present period, their theatrical taste.

It is, indeed, a melancholy truth, that at this time there is so much tragedy in real life,[1] that those who having escaped private calamity, can withdraw their minds a moment from that which is general, very naturally prefer to melancholy books, or tragic representations, those lighter and gayer amusements, which exhilarate the senses, and throw a transient veil over the extensive and still threatening desolation, that overspreads this country, and in some degree, every quarter of the world.

CHARLOTTE SMITH

May 15th 1797.

---

1 Britain and France had been at war since February 1793, and by 1797 the effects of sustained warfare—from the arrival of French emigrants, to injured soldiers, to food shortages—were becoming increasingly visible. See Introduction, pp. 30–33.

SONNET LX

To an Amiable Girl[1]

MIRANDA! mark where shrinking from the gale,
    Its silken leaves yet moist with early dew,
That fair faint flower, the Lily of the Vale,
    Droops its meek head, and looks, methinks, like you!
5 Wrapp'd in a shadowy veil of tender green,
    Its snowy bells a soft perfume dispense,
And bending as reluctant to be seen,
    In simple loveliness it sooths the sense.
With bosom bared to meet the garish day,
10   The glaring Tulip, gaudy, undismay'd,
Offends the eye of taste; that turns away
    To seek the Lily in her fragrant shade.
With such unconscious beauty, pensive, mild,
Miranda charms—Nature's soft modest child.

SONNET LXI

Supposed to have been written in America[2]

ILL-omen'd bird! whose cries portentous float[3]
    O'er yon savannah with the mournful wind;
While, as the Indian hears your piercing note,
    Dark dread of future evil fills his mind;
5 Wherefore with early lamentation break
    The dear delusive visions of repose?
Why from so short felicity awake
    My wounded senses to substantial woes?

---

1 This sonnet was originally written for Smith's children's book *Rural Walks: in dialogues intended for the use of young persons* (1795).

2 This poem and the next one are supposed to have been written by Orlando Somerive, the hero of Smith's novel *The Old Manor House* (1793).

3 [Smith's note:] This sonnet, first inserted in the Novel called *The Old Manor House*, is founded on a superstition attributed (*vide* Bertram's Travels in America) to the Indians, who believe that the cry of this night-hawk (Caprimulgus Americanus) portends some evil, and when they are at war, assert that it is never heard near their tents or habitations but to announce the death of some brave warrior of their tribe, or some other calamity.

O'er my sick soul thus rous'd from transient rest,
10   Pale Superstition sheds her influence drear,
And to my shuddering fancy would suggest
      Thou com'st to speak of ev'ry woe I fear.
Ah! Reason little o'er the soul prevails,
When, from ideal ill, the enfeebled spirit fails!

SONNET LXII

*Written on passing by moon-light through a village,
while the ground was covered with snow*[1]

WHILE thus I wander, cheerless and unblest,
      And find in change of place but change of pain;
In tranquil sleep the village labourers rest,
      And taste that quiet I pursue in vain!
5 Hush'd is the hamlet now, and faintly gleam
      The dying embers, from the casement low
Of the thatch'd cottage; while the Moon's wan beam
      Lends a new lustre to the dazzling snow.
O'er the cold waste, amid the freezing night,
10   Scarce heeding whither, desolate I stray;
For me, pale Eye of Evening, thy soft light
      Leads to no happy home; *my* weary way
Ends but in sad vicissitudes of care:
I only fly from doubt—to meet despair!

SONNET LXIII

The Gossamer

O'ER faded heath-flowers spun, or thorny furze,[2]
      The filmy Gossamer is lightly spread;
Waving in every sighing air that stirs,
      As Fairy fingers had entwined the thread:
5 A thousand trembling orbs of lucid dew
      Spangle the texture of the fairy loom,

---

1 [Smith's note:] First published in the same work [*The Old Manor House*].
2 [Smith's note:] The web, charged with innumerable globules of bright
    dew, that is frequently on heaths and commons in autumnal mornings,
    can hardly have escaped the observation of any lover of nature—the
    slender web of the field spider is again alluded to in Sonnet lxxvii.

As if soft Sylphs, lamenting as they flew,
    Had wept departed Summer's transient bloom:
But the wind rises, and the turf receives
10   The glittering web:—So, evanescent, fade
Bright views that Youth with sanguine heart believes:
    So vanish schemes of bliss, by Fancy made;
Which, fragile as the fleeting dreams of morn,
Leave but the wither'd heath, and barren thorn!

SONNET LXIV

Written at Bristol in the summer of 1794[1]

HERE from the restless bed of lingering pain
    The languid sufferer seeks the tepid wave,
And feels returning health and hope again
    Disperse "the gathering shadows of the grave!"[2]
5 And here romantic rocks that boldly swell,
    Fringed with green woods, or stain'd with veins of ore,
Call'd native Genius forth, whose Heav'n-taught skill
    Charm'd the deep echos of the rifted shore.
But tepid waves, wild scenes, or summer air,
10   Restore they palsied Fancy, woe-deprest?
Check they the torpid influence of Despair,
    Or bid warm Health re-animate the breast;
Where Hope's soft visions have no longer part,
And whose sad inmate—is a broken heart?

SONNET LXV

To Dr. Parry of Bath, with some botanic drawings
which had been made some years[3]

IN happier hours, ere yet so keenly blew
    Adversity's cold blight, and bitter storms,

---

1 This poem first appeared in *The Banished Man* (1794), where it was
   titled "Sonnet written at Bristol Hotwell, in answer to a friend, who rec-
   ommended a residence there to the author." In the novel it is written by
   Mrs. Denzil, and addressed to her friend Mrs. Armitage.
2 William Hayley, "Epistle to a Friend on the Death of John Thornton"
   (London: J. Dodsley, 1780), 1.190.
3 [Smith's note:] To the excellent friend and Physician to whom these
   lines are addressed, I was obliged for the kindest attention, (*continued*)

Luxuriant Summer's evanescent forms,
And Spring's soft blooms with pencil light I drew:
5 But as the lovely family of flowers
    Shrink from the bleakness of the Northern blast,
    So fail from present care and sorrow past
The slight botanic pencil's mimic powers—
Nor will kind Fancy even by Memory's aid,
10   Her visionary garlands now entwine;
Yet while the wreaths of Hope and Pleasure fade,
    Still is one flower of deathless blossom mine,
That dares the lapse of Time, and Tempest rude,
The unfading Amaranth[1] of Gratitude.

SONNET LXVI

Written in a tempestuous night, on the coast of Sussex[2]

THE night-flood rakes upon the stony shore;
    Along the rugged cliffs and chalky caves
Mourns the hoarse Ocean, seeming to deplore
    All that are buried in his restless waves—
5 Mined by corrosive tides, the hollow rock
    Falls prone, and rushing from its turfy height,
Shakes the broad beach with long-resounding shock,
    Loud thundering on the ear of sullen Night;
Above the desolate and stormy deep,
10   Gleams the wan Moon, by floating mist opprest;
Yet here while youth, and health, and labour sleep,
    Alone I wander—Calm untroubled rest,
"Nature's soft nurse,"[3] deserts the sigh-swoln breast,
And shuns the eyes, that only wake to weep!

---

and for the recovery from one dangerous illness, of that beloved child
whom a few months afterwards his skill and most unremitted and disin-
terested exertions could not save! [Smith is talking here of the death of
her daughter Anna Augusta in 1795.]
1 See p. 70, note 2.
2 [Smith's note:] Written on the coast of Sussex during very tempestuous
  weather in December 1791, but first published in the Novel of Mont-
  albert [*Montalbert: A Novel* (1795)].
3 Shakespeare, *Henry IV Part 2*, 3.1.6. "Oh sleep, O gentle sleep, /
  Nature's soft nurse."

SONNET LXVII

On passing over a dreary tract of country,
and near the ruins of a deserted chapel, during a tempest[1]

SWIFT fleet the billowy clouds along the sky,
    Earth seems to shudder at the storm aghast;
While only beings as forlorn as I,
    Court the chill horrors of the howling blast.
5 Even round yon crumbling walls, in search of food,
    The ravenous Owl foregoes his evening flight,
And in his cave, within the deepest wood,
    The Fox eludes the tempest of the night.
But to *my* heart congenial is the gloom
10   Which hides me from a World I wish to shun;
That scene where Ruin saps the mouldering tomb,
    Suits with the sadness of a wretch undone.
Nor is the deepest shade, the keenest air,
Black as my fate, or cold as my despair.

SONNET LXVIII

Written at Exmouth, midsummer, 1795

FALL, dews of Heaven, upon my burning breast,
    Bathe with cool drops these ever-streaming eyes;
Ye gentle Winds, that fan the balmy West,
    With the soft rippling tide of morning rise,
5 And calm my bursting heart, as here I keep
    The vigil of the wretched!—Now away
Fade the pale stars, as wavering o'er the deep
    Soft rosy tints announce another day,
The day of Middle Summer!—Ah! in vain
10   To those who mourn like me, does radiant June
Lead on her fragrant hours; for hopeless pain
    Darkens with sullen clouds the Sun of Noon,
And veil'd in shadows Nature's face appears
To hearts o'erwhelm'd with grief, to eyes suffused with tears.

---

1 [Smith's note:] Printed in the same work [*Montalbert*].

SONNET LXIX

*Written at the same place, on seeing a Seaman return
who had been imprisoned at Rochfort*[1]

CLOUDS, gold and purple, o'er the westering ray
    Threw a bright veil, and catching lights between,
    Fell on the glancing sail, that we had seen
With soft, but adverse winds, throughout the day
5 Contending vainly: as the vessel nears,
    Encreasing numbers hail it from the shore;
Lo! on the deck a pallid form appears,
    Half wondering to behold himself once more
Approach his home—And now he can discern
10   His cottage thatch amid surrounding trees;
    Yet, trembling, dreads lest sorrow or disease
Await him there, embittering his return:
But all he loves are safe; with heart elate,
Tho' poor and plunder'd, he absolves his fate!

SONNET LXX

*On being cautioned against walking on an headland
overlooking the sea, because it was frequented by a lunatic*

IS there a solitary wretch who hies
    To the tall cliff, with starting pace or slow,
And, measuring, views with wild and hollow eyes
    Its distance from the waves that chide below;
5 Who, as the sea-born gale with frequent sighs
    Chills his cold bed upon the mountain turf,
With hoarse, half utter'd lamentation, lies
    Murmuring responses to the dashing surf?
In moody sadness, on the giddy brink,
10   I see him more with envy than with fear;
He has no *nice felicities* that shrink[2]
    From giant horrors; wildly wandering here,
He seems (uncursed with reason) not to know
The depth or the duration of his woe.

---

1 Rochefort, north of Bordeaux, was the location of a French naval prison
   during the Napoleonic wars.
2 [Smith's note:] "'Tis delicate felicity that shrinks / When rocking winds
   are loud." Walpole. [Horace Walpole (1717–97), *The Mysterious Mother:
   A Tragedy* (1781), 2.3.5–6.]

R. Corbould del.   J. Heath R.A. sculp.

In moody Sadness on the giddy Brink
I view him more with Envy than with Fear.

Published May 25th 1797, by Cadell and Davies Strand.

SONNET LXXI

Written at Weymouth in winter

THE chill waves whiten in the sharp North-east;
    Cold, cold the night-blast comes, with sullen sound;
And black and gloomy, like my cheerless breast,
    Frowns the dark pier and lonely sea-view round.
5 Yet a few months—and on the peopled strand
    Pleasure shall all her varied forms display;
Nymphs lightly tread the bright reflecting sand,
    And proud sails whiten all the summer bay:
Then, for these winds that whistle keen and bleak,
10   Music's delightful melodies shall float
O'er the blue waters; but 'tis mine to seek
    Rather, some unfrequented shade, remote
From sights and sounds of gaiety—I mourn
All that gave *me* delight—Ah! never to return!

SONNET LXXII

To the morning star. Written near the sea

THEE! lucid arbiter 'twixt day and night,[1]
    The Seaman greets, as on the Ocean stream
    Reflected, thy precursive friendly beam
Points out the long-sought haven to his sight.

5 Watching for thee, the lover's ardent eyes
    Turn to the eastern hills; and as above
Thy brilliance trembles, hails the lights that rise
    To guide his footsteps to expecting love!

I mark thee too, as night's dark clouds retire,
10   And thy bright radiance glances on the sea;
But never more shall thy heraldic fire
    Speak of approaching morn with joy to me!
Quench'd in the gloom of death that heavenly ray
Once lent to light me on my thorny way!

---

1   [Smith's note:] Milton. ["The sun was sunk, and after him the star / Of
    Hesperus, whose office is to bring / Twilight upon the Earth, short
    arbiter / 'Twixt day and night." *Paradise Lost*, 9.48–51.]

SONNET LXXIII

To a querulous acquaintance

THOU! whom Prosperity has always led
    O'er level paths, with moss and flow'rets strewn;
For whom she still prepares a downy bed
    With roses scatter'd, and to thorns unknown,
5 Wilt thou yet murmur at a mis-placed leaf?[1]
    Think, ere thy irritable nerves repine,
    How many, born with feelings keen as thine,
Taste all the sad vicissitudes of grief;
    How many steep in tears their scanty bread;
10   Or, lost to reason, Sorrow's victims! rave:
How many know not where to lay their head;
    While some are driven by anguish to the grave!
Think; nor impatient at a feather's weight,
Mar the uncommon blessings of thy fate!

SONNET LXXIV

The winter night

"SLEEP, that knits up the ravell'd sleeve of care,"[2]
    Forsakes me, while the chill and sullen blast,
    As my sad soul recalls its sorrows past,
Seems like a summons, bidding me prepare
5 For the last sleep of death—Murmuring I hear
    The hollow wind around the ancient towers,[3]
While night and silence reign; and cold and drear
    The darkest gloom of Middle Winter lours;°   *lowers*
But wherefore fear existence such as mine,
10   To change for long and undisturb'd repose?
Ah! when this suffering being I resign,
    And o'er my miseries the tomb shall close,

---

1 [Smith's note:] From a story (I know not where told) of a fastidious being, who on a bed of rose leaves complained that his or her rest was destroyed because one of those leaves was doubled.

2 [Smith's note:] Shakespeare [*Macbeth*, 2.2.36].

3 [Smith's note:] These lines were written in a residence among ancient public buildings.

By her,[1] whose loss in anguish I deplore,
I shall be laid, and feel that loss no more!

SONNET LXXV

WHERE the wild woods and pathless forests frown,
    The darkling° Pilgrim seeks his unknown way,   *night-time*
Till on the grass he throws him weary down,
    To wait in broken sleep the dawn of day:
5 Thro' boughs just waving in the silent air,
    With pale capricious light the Summer Moon
Chequers his humid couch; while Fancy there,
    That loves to wanton in the Night's deep noon,
Calls from the mossy roots and fountain edge
10   Fair visionary Nymphs that haunt the shade,
Or Naiads[2] rising from the whispering sedge;
    And, 'mid the beauteous group, his dear loved maid
Seems beckoning him with smiles to join the train:
Then, starting from his dream, he feels his woes again!

SONNET LXXVI

To a young man entering the world

GO now, ingenious Youth!—The trying hour
    Is come: The World demands that thou shouldst go
To active life: There titles, wealth, and power
    May all be purchas'd—Yet I joy to know
5 Thou wilt not pay their price. The base controul
    Of petty despots in their pedant reign
    Already hast thou felt;[3]—and high disdain
Of Tyrants is imprinted on thy soul—
    Not, where mistaken Glory, in the field
10 Rears her red banner, be thou ever found;
    But, against proud Oppression raise the shield
Of Patriot daring—So shalt thou renown'd

---

1 Her daughter, Anna Augusta.
2 Female spirits of the trees and streams respectively.
3 [Smith's note:] This was not addressed to my son, who suffered with
   many others in an event which will long be remembered by those
   parents who had sons at a certain public school, in 1793, but to another
   young man, not *compelled* as he was, in consequence of that dismission,
   to abandon the fairest prospects of his future life. [At the age of 14,

For the best virtues *live*; or that denied
May'st die, as Hampden or as Sydney died![1]

SONNET LXXVII

To the insect of the gossamer

SMALL, viewless[2] Æronaut, that by the line[3]
    Of Gossamer suspended, in mid air
    Float'st on a sun beam—Living Atom, where
Ends thy breeze-guided voyage;—with what design
5   In Æther dost thou launch thy form minute,
    Mocking the eye?—Alas! before the veil
    Of denser clouds shall hide thee, the pursuit
Of the keen Swift may end thy fairy sail!—
    Thus on the golden thread that Fancy weaves
10 Buoyant, as Hope's illusive flattery breathes,
    The young and visionary Poet leaves
Life's dull realities, while sevenfold wreaths
    Of rainbow-light around his head revolve.
    Ah! soon at Sorrow's touch the radiant dreams dissolve!

Smith's son Lionel was dismissed from Winchester College as a result of
his participation in what came to be known as "the rebellion of 1793."
For more information on this event see *CL* 37, note 2.]

1 Both John Hampden (1594–1643) and Algernon Sydney, or Sidney,
were seen as heroes for their support of the liberties of the English
people. See note to Sonnet XLVI.

2 Unable to be seen by the eye.

3 [Smith's note:] The almost imperceptible threads floating in the air,
towards the end of Summer or Autumn, in a still evening, sometimes are
so numerous as to be felt on the face and hands. It is on these that a
minute species of spider convey themselves from place to place; some-
times rising with the wind to a great height in the air. Dr. Lister among
other naturalists, remarked these insects, "to fly they cannot strictly be
said, they being carried into the air by external force; but they can, in
case the wind suffer them, steer their course, perhaps mount and
descend at pleasure: and to the purpose of rowing themselves along in
the air, it is observable that they ever take their flight backwards, that is,
their head looking a contrary way like a sculler upon the Thames. It is
scarcely credible to what height they will mount; which is yet precisely
true, and a thing easily to be observed by one that shall fix his eye from
some time on any part of the heavens, the white web, at a vast distance,
very distinctly appearing from the azure sky—But this is in Autumn only,
and that in very fair and calm weather." From the Encyclop. Britan.

SONNET LXXVIII

Snowdrops

WAN Heralds of the Sun and Summer gale!
    That seem just fallen from infant Zephyr's wing;
Not now, as once, with heart revived I hail
    Your modest buds, that for the brow of Spring
5 Form the first simple garland—Now no more
    Escaping for a moment all my cares,
Shall I, with pensive, silent step, explore
    The woods yet leafless; where to chilling airs
Your green and pencil'd blossoms, trembling, wave.
10   Ah! ye soft, transient, children of the ground,
More fair was she[1] on whose untimely grave
    Flow my unceasing tears! Their varied round
The Seasons go; while I through all repine:
For fix'd regret, and hopeless grief are mine.

SONNET LXXIX

To the Goddess of Botany[2]

OF Folly weary, shrinking from the view
    Of Violence and Fraud, allow'd to take
    All peace from humble life; I would forsake

---

1   This is yet another reference to Smith's daughter Anna Augusta.

2   [Smith's note:] "Rightly to spell," as Milton wishes, in *Il Penseroso*
[1645], "of every herb that sips the dew" [lines 170–72], seems to be a
resource for the sick at heart—for those who from sorrow or disgust
may without affectation say "Society is nothing to one not sociable!" [a
slight misquotation from Shakespeare's *Cymbeline*, 3.2.12–13], and
whose wearied eyes and languid spirits find relief and repose amid the
shades of vegetable nature—*I cannot now turn to any other pursuit that
for a moment sooths my wounded mind.*

    "Je pris goût a cette récréation des yeux, qui dans l'infortune, repose,
distrait l'esprit, et suspend le sentiment des peines." [Rousseau, *Les rêveries
du promeneur solitaire* (1782): "I delighted in this ocular recreation which in
misfortune relaxes, amuses, distracts the mind, and suspends the troubled
feeling," *The Reveries of the Solitary Walker* (1782), trans. Charles E. Butter-
worth (Indianapolis/Cambridge: Hackett, 1992), Seventh Walk, 92.]

    Thus speaks the singular, the unhappy Rousseau; when in his "Prom-
enades" he enumerates the causes that drove him from the society of

Their haunts for ever, and, sweet Nymph! with you
5   Find shelter; where my tired, and tear-swoln eyes,
Among your silent shades of soothing hue,
       Your "bells and florets of unnumber'd dyes"[1]
       Might rest—And learn the bright varieties
That from your lovely hands are fed with dew;
10   And every veined leaf, that trembling sighs
In mead or woodland; or in wilds remote,
       Or lurk with mosses in the humid caves,
Mantle the cliffs, on dimpling rivers float,
       Or stream from coral rocks beneath the Ocean's waves.

---

men, and occasioned his pursuing with renewed avidity the study of
Botany. "I was," says he, "Forcé de m'abstenir de penser, de peur de
penser à mes malheurs malgré moi; forcé de contenir les restes d'une
imagination riante, mais languissante, que tant d'angoisses pourroient
effaroucher à la fin—" ["Forced to abstain from thinking for fear of
thinking about my misfortunes in spite of myself, forced to keep in
check the remainders of a cheerful but languishing imagination which so
much anguish could end up by frightening...." *Reveries of the Solitary
Walker*, Seventh Walk, 95.]

Without any pretensions to those talents which were in him so heavily
taxed with that excessive irritability, too often if not always the attendant
on genius, it has been my misfortune to have endured real calamities
that have disqualified me for finding any enjoyment in the pleasures and
pursuits which occupy the generality of the world. I have been engaged
in contending with persons whose cruelty has left so painful an impres-
sion on my mind, that I may well say

"Brillantes fleurs, émail des près, ombrages frais, bosquets,
verdure venez purifier mon imagination de tous ces hideux objets!"
["Brilliant flowers, diverse colours of the meadows, fresh shady
spots, brooks, thickets, greenery, come purify my imagination
sullied by all those hideous objects" *Reveries of the Solitary Walker*,
Seventh Walk, 97.]

Perhaps, if any situation is more pitiable than that which compels us to
wish to escape from the common business and forms of life, it is that
where the sentiment is forcibly felt, while it cannot be indulged; and
where the sufferer, chained down to the discharge of duties from
which the wearied spirit recoils, feels like the wretched Lear, when
Shakespeare makes him exclaim "Oh! I am bound upon a wheel of
fire, / Which my own tears do scald like melted lead" [*King Lear*,
3.7.47–48].

1   John Milton, *Lycidas* (1637), line 135.

SONNET LXXX

To the Invisible Moon[1]

DARK and conceal'd art thou, soft Evening's Queen,
　　And Melancholy's votaries that delight
To watch thee, gliding thro' the blue serene,
　　Now vainly seek thee on the brow of night—
5　Mild Sorrow, such as Hope has not forsook,
　　May love to muse beneath thy silent reign;
But *I* prefer from some steep rock to look
　　On the obscure and fluctuating main,
What time the martial star[2] with lurid glare,
10　　Portentous, gleams above the troubled deep;
Or the red comet shakes his blazing hair;
　　Or on the fire-ting'd waves the lightnings leap;
While thy fair beams illume another sky,
And shine for beings less accurst than I.

SONNET LXXXI[3]

HE may be envied, who with tranquil breast
　　Can wander in the wild and woodland scene,
When Summer's glowing hands have newly drest
　　The shadowy forests, and the copses green;
5　Who, unpursued by care, can pass his hours
　　Where briony and woodbine fringe the trees,[4]
　　On thymy banks reposing, while the bees
Murmur "their fairy tunes, in praise of flowers";[5]

1　[Smith's note:] I know not whether this is correctly expressed—I suspect
　　that it is not—What I mean, however, will surely be understood—I address
　　the moon when not visible at night in our hemisphere. "The Sun to me is
　　dark, / And silent as the Moon / When she deserts the night / Hid in her
　　secret interlunar cave." Milton, *Samson Agonistes* [1671, lines 86–89].
2　Mars, named after the Roman god of war.
3　[Smith's note:] First printed in a publication for the use of young
　　persons, called *Rambles Farther* [1796].
4　[Smith's note:] Briony, Bryonica dioica, foliis palmatis, &c. White
　　Briony, growing plentifully in woods and hedges, and twisting around
　　taller plants.
5　[Smith's note:] A line taken, *I believe*, from a Poem called "Vacuna,"
　　printed in Dodsley's collection. ["Vacuna," Dr D—, printed in *A Collec-
　　tion of Poems* (London: J. Dodsley, 1770).]

Or on the rock with ivy clad, and fern
10 That overhangs the ozier-whispering[1] bed
Of some clear current, bid his wishes turn
From this bad world; and by calm reason led,
Knows, in refined retirement, to possess
By friendship hallow'd—rural happiness!

SONNET LXXXII

To the Shade of Burns[2]

MUTE is thy wild harp, now, O Bard sublime!
Who, amid Scotia's mountain solitude,
Great Nature taught to "build the lofty rhyme,"[3]
And even beneath the daily pressure, rude,
5 Of labouring Poverty, thy generous blood,
Fired with the love of freedom—Not subdued
Wert thou by thy low fortune: But a time
Like this we live in, when the abject chime
Of echoing Parasite is best approved,
10 Was not for thee—Indignantly is fled
Thy noble Spirit; and no longer moved
By all the ills o'er which thine heart has bled,
Associate worthy of the illustrious dead,
Enjoys with them "the Liberty it loved."[4]

---

1 Willow-whispering.

2 [Smith's note:] Whoever has tasted the charm of the original genius so
evident in the composition of this genuine Poet, A Poet "of nature's own
creation," cannot surely fail to lament his unhappy life, (latterly passed,
as I have understood, in an employment to which such a mind as his
must have been averse,) nor his premature death. For one, herself made
the object of *subscription*, it is proper to add, that whoever *has* thus been
delighted with the wild notes of the Scottish bard, must have a melan-
choly pleasure in relieving by their benevolence, the unfortunate family
he has left? [The quintessential Scottish poet Robert Burns (1759–96)
had died recently and his family hoped to publish an edition of his col-
lected works with a biography by subscription to help support his many
children.]

3 Milton, *Lycidas*, line 11.

4 [Smith's note] Pope. ["Epitaph on Sir William Trumbull" (1717), line
12.]

SONNET LXXXIII

The sea view

THE upland Shepherd, as reclined he lies[1]
    On the soft turf that clothes the mountain brow,
Marks the bright Sea-line mingling with the skies;
    Or from his course celestial, sinking slow,
5   The Summer-Sun in purple radiance low,
Blaze on the western waters; the wide scene
    Magnificent, and tranquil, seems to spread
Even o'er the Rustic's breast a joy serene,
    When, like dark plague-spots by the Demons shed,
10 Charged deep with death, upon the waves, far seen,
    Move the war-freighted ships; and fierce and red,
    Flash their destructive fires—The mangled dead
And dying victims then pollute the flood.
Ah! thus man spoils Heaven's glorious works with blood.

SONNET LXXXIV

To the Muse

WILT thou forsake me who in life's bright May
    Lent warmer lustre to the radiant morn;
    And even o'er Summer scenes by tempests torn,
Shed with illusive light the dewy ray
5 Of pensive pleasure?—Wilt thou, while the day
    Of saddening Autumn closes, as I mourn
In languid, hopeless sorrow, far away
    Bend thy soft step, and never more return?—
Crush'd to the earth, by bitterest anguish prest,
10   From my faint eyes thy graceful form recedes;
    Thou canst not heal an heart like mine that bleeds;
But, when in quiet earth that heart shall rest,

---

1 [Smith's note:] Suggested by the recollection of having seen, some years
since, on a beautiful evening of Summer, an engagement between two
armed ships, from the high down called the Beacon Hill, near
Brighthelmstone. [Modern Brighton, on the south coast of England.
This is also the setting of *The Emigrants*.]

Haply may'st thou one sorrowing vigil keep,
Where Pity and Remembrance bend and weep![1]

SONNET LXXXV[2]

THE fairest flowers are gone! for tempests fell,
   And with wild wing swept some unblown away,
While on the upland lawn or rocky dell
   More faded in the day-star's° ardent ray;   *the sun*
5 And scarce the copse, or hedge-row shade beneath,
   Or by the runnel's° grassy course, appear   *a brook or stream*
   Some lingering blossoms of the earlier year,
Mingling bright florets, in the yellow wreath
That Autumn with his poppies and his corn
10   Binds on his tawny temples——So the schemes
Rais'd by fond Hope in youth's unclouded morn,
   While sanguine youth enjoys delusive dreams,
Experience withers; till scarce one remains
Flattering the languid heart, where only Reason reigns.

SONNET LXXXVI

Written near a Port on a dark Evening

HUGE vapours brood above the clifted shore,
   Night on the Ocean settles, dark and mute,
Save where is heard the repercussive roar
   Of drowsy billows, on the rugged foot
5 Of rocks remote; or still more distant tone
   Of seamen in the anchor'd bark that tell
The watch reliev'd; or one deep voice alone
   Singing the hour, and bidding "Strike the bell,"
All is black shadow, but the lucid line
10   Mark'd by the light surf on the level sand,
Or where afar the ship-lights faintly shine

---

1 [Smith's note:] "Where melancholy friendship bends and weeps." Gray.
   ["Epitaph on Sir William Williams" (1775), line 12.]
2 [Smith's note:] Sonnets LXXXV, LXXXVI, and LXXXVII. First
   printed in a novel *The Young Philosopher* [1798].

Like wandering fairy fires,[1] that oft on land
Mislead the Pilgim——Such the dubious ray
That wavering Reason lends, in life's long darkling way.

SONNET LXXXVII

Written in October

THE blasts of Autumn as they scatter round
    The faded foliage of another year,
And muttering many a sad and solemn sound,
    Drive the pale fragments o'er the stubble sere,[2]
5 Are well attuned to my dejected mood;
    (Ah! better far than airs that breathe of Spring!)
    While the high rooks, that hoarsely clamouring
Seek in black phalanx[3] the half-leafless wood,
    I rather hear, than that enraptured lay
10 Harmonious, and of Love and Pleasure born,
    Which from the golden furze, or flowering thorn
      Awakes the Shepherd in the ides of May;
Nature delights *me* most when most she mourns,
For never more to me the Spring of Hope returns!

SONNET LXXXVIII

Nepenthe[4]

OH! for imperial Polydamna's art,
    Which to bright Helen was in Egypt taught,
    To mix with magic power the oblivious draught
Of force to staunch the bleeding of the heart,
5 And to Care's wan and hollow cheek impart

---

1 "Ignis fatuus," a light that appears over marshy ground at night thought
    to be the result of a combustion of gases from decomposing organic
    matter. Also known as "will-o'-the-wisp."
2 Dry or withered.
3 A body of troops moving in formation.
4 [Smith's note:] Of what nature this Nepenthe was, has ever been a
    matter of doubt and dispute. See [Gilbert] Wakefield's note to Pope's
    Odyssey, Book IV, verse 302. [1796, 1.205–06. The note is actually origi-
    nally Pope's. In the *Odyssey* nepenthe was a drug given to Helen of Troy
    by Polydamna to quell rage and despair. Pope notes that it may be
    understood metaphorically as history, music, or philosophy.]

The smile of happy youth, uncurled with thought.
　　Potent indeed the charm that could appease
　　　Affection's ceaseless anguish, doom'd to weep
　　O'er the cold grave; or yield even transient ease
10　　By soothing busy Memory to sleep!
　　—Around me those who surely must have tried
　　　Some charm of equal power, I daily see,
　　But still to *me* Oblivion is denied,
　　　There's no Nepenthe, now, on earth for me.

SONNET LXXXIX

To the Sun[1]

WHETHER awaken'd from unquiet rest
　　I watch "the opening eyelids of the Morn,"[2]
When thou, O Sun! from Ocean's silver'd breast
　　Emerging, bidst another day be born—
5　Or whether in thy path of cloudless blue,
　　Thy noontide fires I mark with dazzled eyes;
Or to the West thy radiant course pursue,
　　Veil'd in the gorgeous broidery of the skies,
Celestial lamp! thy influence bright and warm
10　　That renovates the world with life and light
Shines not for me—for never more the form
　　I loved—so fondly loved, shall bless my sight;
And nought thy rays illumine, *now* can charm
　　My misery, or to day convert my night!

SONNET XC

To Oblivion

FORGETFULNESS! I would thy hand could close
　　These eyes that turn reluctant from the day;
　　So might this painful consciousness decay,
And, with my memory, end my cureless woes.
5　　Sister of Chaos and eternal Night!
　　Oblivion! take me to thy quiet reign,

1　[Smith's note:] "I woke, she fled, and day brought back my night."
　Milton [Sonnet 23 (1658?), line 14].
2　Milton, *Lycidas*, line 26.

Since robb'd of all that gave my soul delight,
I only ask exemption from the pain
    Of knowing "such things were"—and are no more;
10 Of dwelling on the hours for ever fled,
    And heartless, helpless, hopeless to deplore
"Pale misery living, joy and pleasure dead":[1]
While dragging thus unwish'd a length of days,
"Death seems prepared to strike, yet still delays."[2]

SONNET XCI

Reflections on some Drawings of Plants

I CAN in groups these mimic flowers compose,
    These bells and golden eyes, embathed in dew;
Catch the soft blush that warms the early Rose,
    Or the pale Iris cloud with veins of blue;
5 Copy the scallop'd leaves, and downy stems,
    And bid the pencil's varied shades arrest
Spring's humid buds, and Summer's musky gems:
    But, save the portrait on my bleeding breast,
I have no semblance of that form adored,
10   That form, expressive of a soul divine,
    So early blighted; and while life is mine,
With fond regret, and ceaseless grief deplored—
    That grief, my angel! with too faithful art
Enshrines thy image in thy Mother's heart.

SONNET XCII

Written at Bignor Park in Sussex, in August, 1799

LOW murmurs creep along the woody vale,
    The tremulous Aspens shudder in the breeze,
Slow o'er the downs the leaden vapours sail,
    While I, beneath these old paternal trees,

---

1   [Smith's note:] Sir Brook Boothby. [Sir Brooke Boothby (1744–1824),
    Sonnet XIII, line 6 in *Sorrows. Sacred to the Memory of Penelope* (1796),
    19.]
2   [Smith's note:] Thomas Warton. ["Ode I. To Sleep," line 16 in *Poems, a
    new edition* (1777), 27.]

5   Mark the dark shadows of the threaten'd storm,
       As gathering clouds o'erveil the morning sun;
    They pass!—But oh! ye visions bright and warm
       With which even here my sanguine youth begun,
    Ye are obscured for ever!—And too late
10   The poor Slave shakes the unworthy bonds away
       Which crush'd her!—Lo! the radiant star of day
    Lights up this lovely scene anew—My fate
       Nor hope nor joy illumines—Nor for me
       Return those rosy hours which here I used to see!

THE EMIGRANTS,
A POEM, IN TWO BOOKS (1793)

TO
WILLIAM COWPER, ESQ.[1]

DEAR SIR,

THERE is, I hope, some propriety in my addressing a Composition to you, which would never perhaps have existed, had I not, amid the heavy pressure of many sorrows, derived infinite consolation from your Poetry, and some degree of animation and of confidence from your esteem.

The following performance is far from aspiring to be considered as an imitation of your inimitable Poem, THE TASK; I am perfectly sensible, that it belongs not to a feeble and feminine hand to draw the Bow of Ulysses.[2]

The force, clearness, and sublimity of your admirable Poem; the felicity, almost peculiar to your genius, of giving to the most familiar objects dignity and effect, I could never hope to reach; yet, having read "The Task" almost incessantly from its first publication to the present time, I felt that kind of enchantment described by Milton, when he says,

> The Angel ended, and in Adam's ear
> So charming left his voice, that he awhile
> Thought him still speaking.—[3]

And from the force of this impression, I was gradually led to attempt, in Blank Verse, a delineation of those interesting objects which happened to excite my attention, and which even pressed upon an heart, that has learned, perhaps from its own sufferings, to feel with acute, though unavailing compassion, the calamity of others.

---

1 William Cowper (1731–1800) was the author of *The Task* (1785), a hugely popular six-book poem in blank verse. In August 1792, shortly before she began writing *The Emigrants*, Smith spent two weeks with Cowper at the home of their mutual acquaintance, William Hayley (1745–1820). Cowper was not himself completely approving of Smith's poem, writing to Hayley that it should have contained less "severity" toward the emigrants themselves and more "righteous invective" about those in France who had forced their exile. ("To William Hayley" [1 April 1793], *Letters and Prose Works of William Cowper*, ed. James King and Charles Ryskamp, vol. 1 [Oxford: Clarendon, 1984], 318–19.)

2 In the *Odyssey* Penelope proposed that she would marry the suitor who could bend Ulysses' bow, and so prove himself a match for her absent husband.

3 John Milton (1608–74), *Paradise Lost* (1667), 8.1–3.

A Dedication usually consists of praises and of apologies; *my* praise can add nothing to the unanimous and loud applause of your country. She regards you with pride, as one of the few, who, at the present period, rescue her from the imputation of having degenerated in Poetical talents; but in the form of Apology, I should have much to say, if I again dared to plead the pressure of evils, aggravated by their long continuance, as an excuse for the defects of this attempt.

Whatever may be the faults of its execution, let me vindicate myself from those, that may be imputed to the design.—In speaking of the Emigrant Clergy,[1] I beg to be understood as feeling the utmost respect for the integrity of their principles; and it is with pleasure I add my suffrage to that of those, who have had a similar opportunity of witnessing the conduct of the Emigrants of all descriptions during their exile in England;[2] which has been such as does honour to *their* nation, and ought to secure to them in ours the esteem of every liberal mind.

Your philanthropy, dear Sir, will induce you, I am persuaded, to join with me in hoping, that this painful exile may finally lead to the extirpation of that reciprocal hatred so unworthy of great and enlightened nations; that it may tend to humanize both countries, by convincing each, that good qualities exist in the other; and at length annihilate the prejudices that have so long existed to the injury of both.

Yet it is unfortunately but too true, that with the body of the English, this national aversion has acquired new force by the dreadful scenes which have been acted in France during the last summer[3]—even those who are the victims of the Revolution, have not escaped the odium, which the undistinguishing multitude annex to all the natives of a country where such horrors have been acted: nor is this the worst effect those events have had on the minds of the English; by confounding the original cause with

---

1   Catholic clergy were the most prominent and recognizable group amongst the emigrants. They had fled France after the abolition of state religion, the banning of monastic vows, and the nationalization of church property.

2   Hannah More (1745–1833) and Frances Burney (1752–1840) both published pamphlets specifically on the situation of the emigrant clergy. See Introduction, p. 33.

3   A reference to the September massacres of 1792, in which hundreds of French Royalists were killed and thousands more fled to Britain over the following months. See Introduction, pp. 31–32.

the wretched catastrophes that have followed its ill management; the attempts of public virtue, with the outrages that guilt and folly have committed in its disguise, the very name of Liberty has not only lost the charm it used to have in British ears, but many, who have written, or spoken, in its defence, have been stigmatized as promoters of Anarchy, and enemies to the prosperity of their country. Perhaps even the Author of "The Task," with all his goodness and tenderness of heart, is in the catalogue of those, who are reckoned to have been too warm in a cause, which it was once the glory of Englishmen to avow and defend—The exquisite Poem, indeed, in which you have honoured Liberty, by a tribute highly gratifying to her sincerest friends, was published some years before the demolition of regal despotism in France, which, in the fifth book, it seems to foretell[1]—All the truth and energy of the passage to which I allude, must have been strongly felt, when, in the Parliament of England, the greatest Orator of our time quoted the sublimest of our Poets—when the eloquence of Fox did justice to the genius of Cowper.[2]

I am, dear SIR,
With the most perfect esteem,
Your obliged and obedient servant,
CHARLOTTE SMITH

Brighthelmstone, May 10, 1793.

---

1 Book Five of *The Task* contains a long passage in praise of liberty and an imagining of the fall of the Bastille. See especially 5.363–448, part of which appears in Appendix A2.

2 In May 1792, the Whig leader, Charles James Fox (1749–1806), had quoted *The Task* Book 5 (lines 384–92, 396–99, and 432–42) in a speech on the need for religious toleration in which he also praised the Revolution in the by-then politically charged term of "liberty." Fox particularly emphasized Cowper's sentiment that "There's not an English heart that would not leap" on hearing of the Bastille's fall (*Speeches of the Right Honourable Charles James Fox, in the House of Commons* vol. 4 [London, 1815], 426–28). Smith's allusion establishes the complexity of her politics in *The Emigrants*, both calling for acceptance of those made homeless by the Revolution and continuing to support the Revolution in principle.

THE
EMIGRANTS

BOOK THE FIRST.

BOOK I.

SCENE, on the Cliffs to the Eastward of the Town of
Brighthelmstone¹ in Sussex.
TIME, a Morning in November, 1792.

SLOW in the Wintry Morn, the struggling light
Throws a faint gleam upon the troubled waves;
Their foaming tops, as they approach the shore
And the broad surf that never ceasing breaks
5 On the innumerous pebbles, catch the beams
Of the pale Sun, that with reluctance gives
To this cold northern Isle, its shorten'd day.
Alas! how few the morning wakes to joy!
How many murmur at oblivious night
10 For leaving them so soon; for bearing thus
Their fancied bliss (the only bliss they taste!),
On her black wings away!—Changing the dreams
That sooth'd their sorrows, for calamities
(And every day brings its own sad proportion)
15 For doubts, diseases, abject dread of Death,
And faithless friends, and fame and fortune lost;
Fancied or real wants; and wounded pride,
That views the day star,° but to curse his beams.   *the sun*
      Yet He, whose Spirit into being call'd
20 This wond'rous World of Waters; He who bids
The wild wind lift them till they dash the clouds,
And speaks to them in thunder; or whose breath,
Low murmuring o'er the gently heaving tides,
When the fair Moon, in summer night serene,
25 Irradiates with long trembling lines of light
Their undulating surface; that great Power,

---

1 Modern Brighton. This is also the location of many of the sonnets,
and of humanitarian poems such as "The Dead Beggar. An Elegy,"
pp. 199–200. Smith's timing and location of *The Emigrants* is precise,
situating Book I at the height of the emigrant crisis. See Introduction,
pp. 31–33.

Who, governing the Planets, also knows
If but a Sea-Mew falls,[1] whose nest is hid
In these incumbent cliffs; He surely means
30 To us, his reasoning Creatures, whom He bids
Acknowledge and revere his awful hand,
Nothing but good: Yet Man, misguided Man,
Mars the fair work that he was bid enjoy,
And makes himself the evil he deplores.
35 How often, when my weary soul recoils
From proud oppression, and from legal crimes[2]
(For such are in this Land, where the vain boast
Of equal Law is mockery, while the cost
Of seeking for redress is sure to plunge
40 Th' already injur'd to more certain ruin
And the wretch starves, before his Counsel pleads)
How often do I half abjure Society,
And sigh for some lone Cottage, deep embower'd
In the green woods, that these steep chalky Hills
45 Guard from the strong South West; where round their base
The Beach[3] wide flourishes, and the light Ash
With slender leaf half hides the thymy turf!—
There do I wish to hide me; well content
If on the short grass, strewn with fairy flowers,
50 I might repose thus shelter'd;[4] or when Eve
In Orient crimson lingers in the west,
Gain the high mound, and mark these waves remote
(Lucid tho' distant), blushing with the rays
Of the far-flaming Orb, that sinks beneath them;
55 For I have thought, that I should then behold
The beauteous works of God, unspoil'd by Man
And less affected then, by human woes
I witness'd not; might better learn to bear
Those that injustice, and duplicity
60 And faithlessness and folly, fix on me:
For never yet could I derive relief,

---

1 Cf. *Hamlet*: "There's a special providence in the fall of a sparrow"
  (5.2.157–58), which in turn echoes Matthew 10:29.
2 A reference to her legal troubles. See Introduction, p. 24.
3 As Curran suggests, the context suggests the beech tree (*Poems of Char-
  lotte Smith* [New York: Oxford UP, 1993], 139n).
4 Smith's language here echoes that of her sonnets. See, for example,
  Sonnets XXXVI, L, and LIX.

When my swol'n heart was bursting with its sorrows,
From the sad thought, that others like myself
Live but to swell affliction's countless tribes!
65 —Tranquil seclusion I have vainly sought;
Peace, who delights solitary shade,
No more will spread for me her downy wings,
But, like the fabled Danaïds[1]—or the wretch,
Who ceaseless, up the steep acclivity,
70 Was doom'd to heave the still rebounding rock,[2]
Onward I labour; as the baffled wave,
Which yon rough beach repulses, that returns
With the next breath of wind, to fail again.—
Ah! Mourner—cease these wailings: cease and learn,
75 That not the Cot[3] sequester'd, where the briar
And wood-bine wild, embrace the mossy thatch,
(Scarce seen amid the forest gloom obscure!)
Or more substantial farm, well fenced and warm,
Where the full barn, and cattle fodder'd round
80 Speak rustic plenty; nor the statelier dome
By dark firs shaded, or the aspiring pine,
Close by the village Church (with care conceal'd
By verdant foliage, lest the poor man's grave
Should mar the smiling prospect of his Lord),
85 Where offices well rang'd, or dove-cote stock'd,[4]
Declare manorial residence; not these
Or any of the buildings, new and trim
With windows circling towards the restless Sea,
Which ranged in rows, now terminate my walk,[5]
90 Can shut out for an hour the spectre Care,
That from the dawn of reason, follows still
Unhappy Mortals, 'till the friendly grave

---

1 In Greek mythology the Danaids, the daughters of Danaus, were condemned to forever drawing water in a sieve for the crime of killing their husbands.

2 A reference to Sisyphus and his eternal task in Greek mythology of pushing a rock to the top of a hill, only to watch it roll back down again.

3 A small house or cottage.

4 Well-stocked outbuildings, such as kitchen, dairy, and stables (Curran, *Poems of Charlotte Smith* 138n).

5 Smith refers here to the building of new houses as symbolic of the new wealth of Brighton associated with the residence there of the Prince of Wales (Curran, *Poems of Charlotte Smith* 138n).

(Our sole secure asylum) "ends the chace."[1]
    Behold, in witness of this mournful truth,
95 A group approach me, whose dejected looks,
    Sad Heralds of distress! proclaim them Men
    Banish'd for ever and for conscience sake
    From their distracted Country,[2] whence the name
    Of Freedom misapplied, and much abus'd
100 By lawless Anarchy, has driven them far
    To wander; with the prejudice they learn'd
    From Bigotry (the Tut'ress of the blind),
    Thro' the wide World unshelter'd; their sole hope,
    That German spoilers,[3] thro' that pleasant land
105 May carry wide the desolating scourge
    Of War and Vengeance; yet unhappy Men,
    Whate'er your errors, I lament your fate:
    And, as disconsolate and sad ye hang
    Upon the barrier of the rock, and seem
110 To murmur your despondence, waiting long
    Some fortunate reverse that never comes;
    Methinks in each expressive face, I see
    Discriminated anguish; there droops one,
    Who in a moping cloister long consum'd
115 This life inactive,[4] to obtain a better,
    And thought that meagre abstinence, to wake
    From his hard pallet with the midnight bell,
    To live on eleemosynary bread,[5]

---

1 [Smith's note:] I have a confused notion that this expression, with nearly
   the same application, is to be found in Young: but I cannot refer to it.
   [Most likely Edward Young's play *The Brothers* (Drury Lane, 1753):
   "Nor ends the fruitless chace but in the grave" (*The Dramatic works of
   Dr. Edward Young* [London: 1783], 177). The phrase is also picked up by
   Smith's contemporary Anne Hunter (1742–1821), in her poem "Tomor-
   row" ("Nor ends the chase but in the grave"). Hunter's poems were
   widely circulated in manuscript beginning in the 1780s (*The Life and
   Poems of Anne Hunter: Haydn's Tuneful Voice*, ed. Caroline Grigson [Liver-
   pool: Liverpool UP, 2009])].
2 Laws had been passed banishing emigrants from returning to French
   soil. See Introduction, p. 32.
3 A reference to the Austro-Prussian forces that invaded Revolutionary
   France. They were pushed back at the Battle of Valmy in September
   1792.
4 Here Smith singles out a monk.
5 Bread distributed to the poor by way of alms or charity.

And to renounce God's works, would please that God.
120 And now the poor pale wretch receives, amaz'd,
     The pity, strangers give to his distress,
     Because these Strangers are, by his dark creed,
     Condemn'd as Heretics°—and with sick heart   *i.e., Protestants*
     Regrets his pious prison, and his beads.[1] —
125 Another,[2] of more haughty port, declines
     The aid he needs not; while in mute despair
     His high indignant thoughts go back to France,
     Dwelling on all he lost—the Gothic dome,
     That vied with splendid palaces;[3] the beds
130 Of silk and down, the silver chalices,
     Vestments with gold enwrought for blazing altars;
     Where, amid clouds of incense, he held forth
     To kneeling crowds the imaginary bones
     Of Saints suppos'd, in pearl and gold enchas'd,
135 And still with more than living Monarchs' pomp
     Surrounded; was believ'd by mumbling bigots
     To hold the keys of Heaven, and to admit
     Whom he thought good to share it—Now alas!
     He, to whose daring soul and high ambition
140 The World seem'd circumscrib'd; who, wont to dream,
     Of Fleuri, Richelieu, Alberoni,[4] men
     Who trod on Empire, and whose politics

---

1 [Smith's note:] Lest the same attempts at misrepresentation should now
   be made, as have been made on former occasions, it is necessary to
   repeat, that nothing is farther from my thoughts, than to reflect invidi-
   ously on the Emigrant Clergy, whose steadiness of principle excites ven-
   eration, as much as their sufferings compassion. Adversity has now
   taught them the charity and humility they perhaps wanted, when they
   made it a part of their faith, that salvation could be obtained in no other
   religion than their own.
2 She draws attention, now, to a Cardinal.
3 [Smith's note:] Let it not be considered as an insult to men in fallen
   fortune, if these luxuries (undoubtedly inconsistent with their profes-
   sion) be here enumerated—France is not the only country, where the
   splendour and indulgences of the higher, and the poverty and depres-
   sion of the inferior Clergy, have alike proved injurious to the cause of
   Religion.
4 Cardinal André Hercule de Fleury (1653–1743), Armand Jean du
   Plessis, Duc de Richelieu (1585–1643), and Cardinal Giulio Alberoni
   (1664–1752) were all cardinals who held powerful political positions
   (Curran, *Poems of Charlotte Smith* 140n).

Were not beyond the grasp of his vast mind,
Is, in a Land once hostile, still prophan'd
145 By disbelief, and rites un-orthodox,
The object of compassion—At his side,
Lighter of heart than these, but heavier far
Than he was wont, another victim comes,
An Abbé[1]—who with less contracted brow
150 Still smiles and flatters, and still talks of Hope;
Which, sanguine as he is, he does not feel,
And so he cheats the sad and weighty pressure
Of evils present;——Still, as Men misled
By early prejudice (so hard to break),
155 I mourn your sorrows; for I too have known
Involuntary exile;[2] and while yet
England had charms for me, have felt how sad
It is to look across the dim cold sea,
That melancholy rolls its refluent tides
160 Between us and the dear regretted land
We call our own—as now ye pensive wait
On this bleak morning, gazing on the waves
That seem to leave your shore; from whence the wind
Is loaded to your ears, with the deep groans
165 Of martyr'd Saints and suffering Royalty,
While to your eyes the avenging power of Heaven
Appears in aweful anger to prepare
The storm of vengeance, fraught with plagues and death.
Even he of milder heart, who was indeed
170 The simple shepherd in a rustic scene,
And, 'mid the vine-clad hills of Languedoc,[3]
Taught to the bare-foot peasant, whose hard hands
Produc'd[4] the nectar he could seldom taste,

---

1 An abbot in France. In French the term was often used for young or
lower-ranking clergymen.
2 A reference to time Smith spent in Normandy between late 1784 and
early 1785 to escape her husband's debts. Her twelfth child was born
there. See Introduction, pp. 23–24.
3 The former province in the central part of southern France.
4 [Smith's note:] See the finely descriptive Verses written at Montauban in
France in 1750, by Dr. Joseph Warton. Printed in Dodsley's Miscella-
nies, Vol. IV. page 203. [Warton's (1722–1800) poem is addressed to
LIBERTY and Smith invokes his opening image of the state of peasants
in Southern France: "Tarn, how delightful wind thy willow'd waves, /
But ah! they fructify a land of slaves! / In vain, thy bare-foot, sun-burnt

Submission to the Lord for whom he toil'd;
175 He, or his brethren, who to Neustria's sons[1]
Enforc'd religious patience, when, at times,
On their indignant hearts Power's iron hand
Too strongly struck; eliciting some sparks
Of the bold spirit of their native North;
180 Even these Parochial Priests, these humbled men,
Whose lowly undistinguish'd cottages
Witness'd a life of purest piety,
While the meek tenants were, perhaps, unknown
Each to the haughty Lord of his domain,
185 Who mark'd them not; the Noble scorning still
The poor and pious Priest, as with slow pace
He glided thro' the dim arch'd avenue
Which to the Castle led; hoping to cheer
The last sad hour of some laborious life
190 That hasten'd to its close—even such a Man
Becomes an exile; staying not to try
By temperate zeal to check his madd'ning flock,
Who, at the novel sound of Liberty
(Ah! most intoxicating sound to slaves!),
195 Start into licence—Lo! dejected now,
The wandering Pastor mourns, with bleeding heart,
His erring people, weeps and prays for them,
And trembles for the account that he must give
To Heaven for souls entrusted to his care.—
200 Where the cliff, hollow'd by the wintry storm,
Affords a seat with matted sea-weed strewn,
A softer form reclines; around her run,
On the rough shingles, or the chalky bourn,°   *a small stream*
Her gay unconscious children, soon amus'd;
205 Who pick the fretted stone, or glossy shell,
Or crimson plant marine: or they contrive
The fairy vessel, with its ribband sail
And gilded paper pennant: in the pool,
Left by the salt wave on the yielding sands,
210 They launch the mimic navy—Happy age!

---

peasants hide / With luscious grapes yon' hill's romantic side; / No cups
nectareous shall their toils repay, / The priest's, the soldier's, and the
fermier's prey" (in Robert Dodsley [1703–64], *A Collection of Poems in
Six volumes*, vol. 4. [1775], lines 1–6).]
1 Inhabitants of Normandy in the north.

Unmindful of the miseries of Man!—
Alas! too long a victim to distress,
Their Mother, lost in melancholy thought,[1]
Lull'd for a moment by the murmurs low
215 Of sullen billows, wearied by the task
Of having here, with swol'n and aching eyes
· Fix'd on the grey horizon, since the dawn
Solicitously watch'd the weekly sail
From her dear native land, now yields awhile
220 To kind forgetfulness, while Fancy brings,
In waking dreams, that native land again!
Versailles[2] appears—its painted galleries,
And rooms of regal splendour, rich with gold,
Where, by long mirrors multiply'd, the crowd
225 Paid willing homage—and, united there,
Beauty gave charms to empire—Ah! too soon
From the gay visionary pageant rous'd,
See the sad mourner start!—and, drooping, look
With tearful eyes and heaving bosom round
230 On drear reality—where dark'ning waves,
Urg'd by the rising wind, unheeded foam
Near her cold rugged seat:—To call her thence
A fellow-sufferer comes: dejection deep
Checks, but conceals not quite, the martial air,
235 And that high consciousness of noble blood,
Which he has learn'd from infancy to think
Exalts him o'er the race of common men:
Nurs'd in the velvet lap of luxury,
And fed by adulation—could *he* learn,
240 That worth alone is true Nobility?
And that *the peasant* who, "amid the sons
"Of Reason, Valour, Liberty, and Virtue,
"Displays distinguish'd merit, is a Noble
"Of Nature's own creation!"[3]—If even here,

---

1 This passage was rewritten as "The Female Exile," which appeared
with an accompanying illustration in *ES* Volume Two (1797). See pp.
200–02.
2 The Palace of Versailles, which had been the location of the French
Royal Court from the mid-seventeenth century.
3 [Smith's note:] These lines are Thomson's, and are among those senti-
ments which are now called (when used by living writers), not common-
place declamation, but sentiments of dangerous tendency. [From James
Thomson's (1834–82) adaptation of *Coriolanus* 3.3, staged in 1749. In

245   If in this land of highly vaunted Freedom,
       Even Britons controvert the unwelcome truth,
       Can it be relish'd by the sons of France?
       Men, who derive their boasted ancestry
       From the fierce leaders of religious wars,
250   The first in Chivalry's emblazon'd page;
       Who reckon Gueslin, Bayard, or De Foix,[1]
       Among their brave Progenitors? *Their* eyes,
       Accustom'd to regard the splendid trophies
       Of Heraldry[2] (that with fantastic hand
255   Mingles, like images in feverish dreams,
       "Gorgons and Hydras, and Chimeras dire,"[3]
       With painted puns, and visionary shapes;),
       See not the simple dignity of Virtue,
       But hold all base, whom honours such as these
260   Exalt not from the crowd[4]—As one, who long
       Has dwelt amid the artificial scenes
       Of populous City, deems that splendid shows,
       The Theatre, and pageant pomp of Courts,
       Are only worth regard; forgets all taste
265   For Nature's genuine beauty; in the lapse

1792, performances of the play were barred from Covent Garden for fear of their effect on the British public (Susan Wolfson, *Romantic Interactions: Social Being and the Turns of Literary Action* [Baltimore: Johns Hopkins UP, 2010], 37).]

1   Bertrand De Guesclin (c. 1320–80) was a French commander in the Hundred Years' War. Pierre Terrail, seigneur de Bayard (1473–1524) and Gaston de Foix, duc de Nemours (1489–1512) were military commanders associated with chivalry.

2   Coats of arms held by noble families.

3   Milton, *Paradise Lost* 2.628. The trio of classical monsters are associated in Milton with Satan's Legions of fallen angels in Hell.

4   [Smith's note:] It has been said, and with great appearance of truth, that the contempt in which the Nobility of France held the common people, was remembered, and with all that vindictive asperity which long endurance of oppression naturally excites, when, by a wonderful concurrence of circumstances, the people acquired the power of retaliation. Yet let me here add, what seems to be in some degree inconsistent with the former charge, that the French are good masters to their servants, and that in their treatment of their Negro slaves, they are allowed to be more mild and merciful than other Europeans. [Curran notes that the only "other Europeans" with extensive slave-holdings were the British, so that Smith's innuendo here should not be lost (*Poems of Charlotte Smith* 144n).]

Of gushing waters hears no soothing sound,
Nor listens with delight to sighing winds,
That, on their fragrant pinions,° waft the notes   *wings*
Of birds rejoicing in the trangled[1] copse;
270   Nor gazes pleas'd on Ocean's silver breast,
While lightly o'er it sails the summer clouds
Reflected in the wave, that, hardly heard,
Flows on the yellow sands: so to *his* mind,
That long has liv'd where Despotism hides
275   His features harsh, beneath the diadem°   *crown*
Of worldly grandeur, abject Slavery seems,
If by that power impos'd, slavery no more:
For luxury wreathes with silk the iron bonds,
And hides the ugly rivets with her flowers,
280   Till the degenerate triflers, while they love
The glitter of the chains, forget their weight.
But more the Men,[2] whose ill acquir'd wealth
Was wrung from plunder'd myriads, by the means
Too often legaliz'd by power abus'd,
285   Feel all the horrors of the fatal change,
When their ephemeral greatness, marr'd at once
(As a vain toy that Fortune's childish hand

---

1   Curran suggests this is most likely a misprint for tangled (*Poems of Charlotte Smith* 145n).

2   [Smith's note:] The Financiers and Fermiers Generaux are here intended. In the present moment of clamour against all those who have spoken or written in favour of the first Revolution of France, the declaimers seem to have forgotten, that under the reign of a mild and easy tempered Monarch, in the most voluptuous Court in the world, the abuses by which men of this description were enriched, had arisen to such height, that their prodigality exhausted the immense resources of France: and, unable to supply the exigencies of Government, the Ministry were compelled to call Le Tiers Etat; a meeting that gave birth to the Revolution, which has since been so ruinously conducted. [*Fermiers Généraux* refers to the tax collection agencies that prior to the Revolution had become outsourced customs and excise operations, amassing great wealth as a result of unpopular taxation schemes. The First Estate (the clergy) and the Second Estate (the nobility) were largely exempt from these taxes, causing resentment amongst members of the Third Estate (*Le Tiers État*), which consisted of everyone else. In May 1789 a meeting of representatives of the Estates-General was called to discuss the country's financial problems, leading to the succession of the Third Estate, and the formation of the National Assembly, an assembly not of the estates but of "the people."]

Equally joy'd to fashion or to crush),
Leaves them expos'd to universal scorn
290 For having nothing else; not even the claim
To honour, which respect for Heroes past
Allows to ancient titles; Men, like these,
Sink even beneath the level, whence base arts
Alone had rais'd them;—unlamented sink,
295 And know that they deserve the woes they feel.
        Poor wand'ring wretches! whosoe'er ye are,
That hopeless, houseless, friendless, travel wide[1]
O'er these bleak russet downs; where, dimly seen,
The solitary Shepherd shiv'ring tends
300 His dun discolour'd flock (Shepherd, unlike
Him, whom in song the Poet's fancy crowns
With garlands, and his crook with vi'lets binds);
Poor vagrant wretches! outcasts of the world!
Whom no abode receives, no parish owns;
305 Roving, like Nature's commoners, the land
That boasts such general plenty: if the sight
Of wide-extended misery softens yours
Awhile, suspend your murmurs!—here behold
The strange vicissitudes of fate—while thus
310 The exil'd Nobles, from their country driven,
Whose richest luxuries were theirs, must feel
More poignant anguish, than the lowest poor,
Who, born to indigence, have learn'd to brave
Rigid Adversity's depressing breath!—
315 Ah! rather Fortune's worthless favourites!
Who feed on England's vitals—Pensioners
Of base corruption, who, in quick ascent
To opulence unmerited, become
Giddy with pride, and as ye rise, forgetting
320 The dust ye lately left, with scorn look down
On those beneath ye (tho' your *equals* once
In fortune, and *in worth superior still*,
They view the eminence, on which ye stand,
With wonder, not with envy; for they know

---

1 King Lear's lament is echoed here and reverberates through the lines
   that follow. Cf. "Poor naked wretches, wheresoe'er you are, ... How shall
   your houseless heads and unfed sides, / Your looped and windowed
   raggedness, defend you / From seasons such as these?" (*King Lear*
   3.4.29–33).

325 The means, by which ye reach'd it, have been such
    As, in all honest eyes, degrade ye far
    Beneath the poor dependent, whose sad heart
    Reluctant pleads for what your pride denies);
    Ye venal, worthless hirelings of a Court!
330 Ye pamper'd Parasites! whom Britons pay
    For forging fetters for them; rather here
    Study a lesson that concerns ye much;
    And, trembling, learn, that if oppress'd too long,
    The raging multitude, to madness stung,
335 Will turn on their oppressors; and, no more
    By sounding titles and parading forms
    Bound like tame victims, will redress themselves!
    Then swept away by the resistless torrent,
    Not only all your pomp may disappear,
340 But, in the tempest lost, fair Order sink
    Her decent head, and lawless Anarchy
    O'erturn celestial Freedom's radiant throne;—
    As now in Gallia;° where Confusion, born   *France*
    Of party rage and selfish love of rule,
345 Sully the noblest cause that ever warm'd
    The heart of Patriot Virtue[1]—There arise
    The infernal passions; Vengeance, seeking blood,
    And Avarice; and Envy's harpy fangs
    Pollute the immortal shrine of Liberty,
350 Dismay her votaries, and disgrace her name.
    Respect is due to principle; and they,
    Who suffer for their conscience, have a claim,
    Whate'er that principle may be, to praise.
    These ill-starr'd Exiles then, who, bound by ties,
355 To them the bonds of honour; who resign'd
    Their country to preserve them, and now seek
    In England an asylum—well deserve
    To find that (every prejudice forgot,
    Which pride and ignorance teaches), we for them
360 Feel as our brethren; and that English hearts,
    Of just compassion ever own the sway,
    As truly as our element, the deep,
    Obeys the mild dominion of the Moon—

---

1 [Smith's note:] This sentiment will probably *renew* against me the indig-
  nation of those, who have an interest in asserting that no such virtue any
  where exists.

This they *have* found; and may they find it still!
365 Thus may'st thou, Britain, triumph!—May thy foes,
By Reason's gen'rous potency subdued,
Learn, that the God thou worshippest, delights
In acts of pure humanity!—May thine
Be still such bloodless laurels! nobler far
370 Than those acquir'd at Cressy or Poictiers,[1]
Or of more recent growth, those well bestow'd
On him who stood on Calpe's[2] blazing height
Amid the thunder of a warring world,
Illustrious rather from the crowds he sav'd
375 From flood and fire, than from the ranks who fell
Beneath his valour!—Actions such as these,
Like incense rising to the Throne of Heaven,
Far better justify the pride, that swells
In British bosoms, than the deafening roar
380 Of Victory from a thousand brazen throats,
That tell with what success wide-wasting War
Has by our brave Compatriots thinned the world.

ALIGNED CENTER: END OF BOOK I.

---

1 The Battle of Crécy (1346) and the Battle of Poitiers (1356) were two decisive English victories in the Hundred Years' War.
2 Calpe is the Latin name for the Rock of Gibraltar; the reference is to George Augustus Eliot (1717–90), who commanded the Gibraltar garrison during the Siege of Gibraltar (1779–83).

THE
EMIGRANTS

BOOK THE SECOND.

Quippe ubi fas versum atque nefas: tot bella per orbem
Tam multæ scelerum facies; non ullus aratro
Dignus honos: squalent abductis arva colonis,
Et curva[e] rigidum falces conflantur in ensem
Hinc movet Euphrates, illinc Germania bellum
Vicinæ ruptis inter se legibus urbes
Arma ferunt: sævit toto Mars impius orbe.

GEOR. lib. i.[1]

BOOK II.

SCENE, on an Eminence on one of those Downs, which afford to the South
a View of the Sea; to the North of the Weald of Sussex.
TIME, an Afternoon in April, 1793.[2]

LONG wintry months are past; the Moon that now
Lights her pale crescent even at noon, has made
Four times her revolution; since with step,
Mournful and slow, along the wave-worn cliff,
5 Pensive I took my solitary way,[3]

---

1 For right and wrong change places; everywhere
So many wars, so many shapes of crime
Confront us; no due honour attends the plough,
The fields, bereft of tillers, are all unkempt,
And in the force the curving pruning-hook
Is many a straight hard sword. Euphrates here,
There Germany is in arms, and neighbour cities
Break covenants and fight; throughout the world
Impious War is raging.

Virgil, *The Georgics*, trans. and notes by L.P. Wilkinson
(London: Penguin, 1982), I.505–11.

2 Here, the precise dating places the poem after the execution of Louis
XVI on 21 January 1793; after the passing of the Aliens Act in Britain,
also in January, which curtailed the movements of foreigners on British
soil; and, after the declaration of war between France and England. See
Introduction, p. 32.
3 Cf. the closing lines of *Paradise Lost*: "with wandering steps and slow, /
Through *Eden* took their solitarie way" (12.648–49).

Lost in despondence, while contemplating
Not my own wayward destiny alone,
(Hard as it is, and difficult to bear!)
But in beholding the unhappy lot
10   Of the lorn Exiles; who, amid the storms
Of wild disastrous Anarchy, are thrown,
Like shipwreck'd sufferers, on England's coast,
To see, perhaps, no more their native land,
Where Desolation riots: They, like me,
15   From fairer hopes and happier prospects driven,
Shrink from the future, and regret the past.
But on this Upland scene, while April comes,
With fragrant airs, to fan my throbbing breast,
Fain would I snatch an interval from Care,
20   That weighs my wearied spirit down to earth;
Courting, once more, the influence of Hope
(For "Hope" still waits upon the flowery prime[1])
As here I mark Spring's humid hand unfold
The early leaves that fear capricious winds,
25   While, even on shelter'd banks, the timid flowers
Give, half reluctantly, their warmer hues
To mingle with the primroses' pale stars.
No shade the leafless copses[2] yet afford,
Nor hide the mossy labours of the Thrush,
30   That, startled, darts across the narrow path;
But quickly re-assur'd, resumes his talk,
Or adds his louder notes to those that rise
From yonder tufted brake; where the white buds
Of the first thorn are mingled with the leaves
35   Of that which blossoms on the brow of May.
        Ah! 'twill not be:——So many years have pass'd,
Since, on my native hills, I learn'd to gaze
On these delightful landscapes; and those years
Have taught me so much sorrow, that my soul
40   Feels not the joy reviving Nature brings;
But, in dark retrospect, dejected dwells

---

1   [Smith's note:] Shakspeare. [Actually comes from Edmund Waller's
     (1606–87) "To my young Lady Lucy Sidney," *Poems* (1645), line 13
     (Curran, *Poems of Charlotte Smith* 150n). Anna Laetitia Barbauld
     (1743–1825) also uses Waller's line as an epigraph to her popular "Ode
     to Spring," reprinted in her *Poems* (1792)].
2   Stands of small trees or bushes.

On human follies, and on human woes.——
What is the promise of the infant year,
The lively verdure, or the bursting blooms,
45 To those, who shrink 'from horrors such as War
Spreads o'er the affrighted world? With swimming eye,[1]
Back on the past they throw their mournful looks,
And see the Temple, which they fondly hop'd
Reason would raise to Liberty, destroy'd
50 By ruffian hands; while, on the ruin'd mass,
Flush'd with hot blood, the Fiend of Discord sits
In savage triumph; mocking every plea
Of policy and justice, as she shews
The headless corse° of one, whose only crime   *corpse*
55 Was being born a Monarch°—Mercy turns,   *Louis XVI*
From spectacle so dire, her swol'n eyes;
And Liberty, with calm, unruffled brow
Magnanimous, as conscious of her strength
In Reason's panoply,° scorns to distain   *full array*
60 Her righteous cause with carnage, and resigns
To Fraud and Anarchy the infuriate crowd.——
      What is the promise of the infant year
To those, who (while the poor but peaceful hind
Pens, unmolested, the encreasing flock
65 Of his rich master in this sea-fenc'd isle°)   *i.e., Britain*
Survey, in neighbouring countries, scenes that make
The sick heart shudder; and the Man, who thinks,
Blush for his species? *There* the trumpet's voice°   *call to arms*
Drowns the soft warbling of the woodland choir;
70 And violets, lurking in their turfy beds
Beneath the flow'ring thorn, are stain'd with blood.
There fall, at once, the spoiler and the spoil'd;
While War, wide-ravaging, annihilates
The hope of cultivation; gives to Fiends,
75 The meagre, ghastly Fiends of Want and Woe,
The blasted land—There, taunting in the van
Of vengeance-breathing armies, Insult stalks;
And, in the ranks, "Famine, and Sword, and Fire,
Crouch for employment."[2]—Lo! the suffering world,
80 Torn by the fearful conflict, shrinks, amaz'd,

---

1 The phrase "swimming eye" echoes Barbauld's "An Address to the
  Deity," line 74, also reprinted in her *Poems* (1792).
2 [Smith's note:] Shakspeare [*Henry V*, Prologue, lines 7–8].

From Freedom's name, usurp'd and misapplied,
And, cow'ring to the purple Tyrant's rod,
Deems *that* the lesser ill—Deluded Men!
Ere ye prophane her ever-glorious name,
85 Or catalogue the thousands that have bled
Resisting her; or those, who greatly died
Martyrs to *Liberty*—revert awhile
To the black scroll, that tells of regal crimes
Committed to destroy her; rather count
90 The hecatombs[1] of victims, who have fallen
Beneath a single despot; or who gave
Their wasted lives for some disputed claim
Between anointed robbers: Monsters both![2]
"Oh! Polish'd perturbation—golden care!"[3]
95 So strangely coveted by feeble Man
To lift him o'er his fellows;—Toy, for which
Such showers of blood have drench'd th' affrighted earth—
Unfortunate *his*° lot, whose luckless head   *Louis XVI*
Thy jewel'd circlet, lin'd with thorns, has bound;
100 And who, by custom's laws, obtains from thee
Hereditary right to rule, uncheck'd,
Submissive myriads: for untemper'd power,
Like steel ill form'd, injures the hand
It promis'd to protect—Unhappy France!
105 If e'er thy lilies,[4] trampled now in dust,
And blood-bespotted, shall again revive
In silver splendour, may the wreath be wov'n
By voluntary hands; and Freemen, such
As England's self might boast, unite to place
110 The guarded diadem on *his* fair brow,
Where Loyalty may join with Liberty
To fix it firmly.[5]—In the rugged school
Of stern Adversity so early train'd,

---

1 The public sacrifice of a great number.
2 [Smith's note:] Such was the cause of quarrel between the Houses of
   York and Lancaster [the dynastic wars for the throne known as the Wars
   of the Roses (1455–85)]; and of too many others, with which the page
   of History reproaches the reason of man.
3 [Smith's note:] Shakspeare [*Henry IV, Part II*, 4.3.153. In other words,
   the crown is a source of unease].
4 The fleur-de-lis symbol, associated with the French throne.
5 A reference to England's constitutional monarchy.

His future life, perchance, may emulate
115 That of the brave Bernois,[1] so justly call'd
The darling of his people; who rever'd
The Warrior less, than they ador'd the Man!
But ne'er may Party Rage, perverse and blind,
And base Venality, prevail to raise
120 To public trust, a wretch,[2] whose private vice
Makes even the wildest profligate recoil;
And who, with hireling ruffians leagu'd, has burst
The laws of Nature and Humanity!
Wading, beneath the Patriot's specious mask,
125 And in Equality's illusive name,
To empire thro' a stream of kindred blood—
Innocent prisoner![3]—most unhappy heir
Of fatal greatness, who art suffering now
For all the crimes and follies of thy race;
130 Better for thee, if o'er thy baby brow
The regal mischief never had been held:
Then, in an humble sphere, perhaps content,
Thou hadst been free and joyous on the heights
Of Pyrennean mountains, shagg'd with woods
135 Of chestnut, pine, and oak: as on these hills
Is yonder little thoughtless shepherd lad,
Who, on the slope abrupt of downy turf
Reclin'd in playful indolence, sends off
The chalky ball, quick bounding far below;
140 While, half forgetful of his simple task,
Hardly his length'ning shadow, or the bells'
Slow tinkling of his flock, that supping tend
To the brown fallows in the vale beneath,

---

1 [Smith's note:] Henry the Fourth of France. It may be said of this
monarch, that had all the French sovereigns resembled him, despotism
would have lost its horrors; yet he had considerable failings, and his
greatest virtues may be chiefly imputed to his education in the School of
Adversity. [As Curran notes, Henry IV (r. 1589–1610), who was the
first Bourbon king, stands as a natural foil for Smith to Louis XVI,
whom she presumed would be the last Bourbon king (*Poems of Charlotte
Smith* 153n).]
2 As Curran notes, probably the Jacobin Jean-Paul Marat (1743–93)
(*Poems of Charlotte Smith* 153n).
3 Louis-Charles (1785–95), son of Louis XVI, who was imprisoned with
his family. On his father's execution he had become the nominal king of
France.

Where nightly it is folded, from his sport
145 Recal the happy idler.[1]—While I gaze
On his gay vacant countenance, my thoughts
Compare with his obscure, laborious lot,
Thine, most unfortunate, imperial Boy!
Who round thy sullen prison daily hear'st
150 The savage howl of Murder, as it seeks
Thy unoffending life: while sad within
Thy wretched Mother,[2] petrified with grief,
Views thee with stony eyes, and cannot weep!—
Ah! much I mourn thy sorrows, hapless Queen!
155 And deem thy expiation made to Heaven
For every fault, to which Prosperity
Betray'd thee, when it plac'd thee on a throne
Where boundless power was thine, and thou wert rais'd
High (as it seem'd) above the envious reach
160 Of destiny! Whate'er thy errors were,
Be they no more remember'd; tho' the rage
Of Party swell'd them to such crimes, as bade
Compassion stifle every sigh that rose
For thy disastrous lot—More than enough
165 Thou hast endur'd; and every English heart,
Ev'n those, that highest beat in Freedom's cause,
Disclaim as base, and of that cause unworthy,
The Vengeance, or the Fear, that makes thee still
A miserable prisoner!—Ah! who knows,
170 From sad experience, more than I, to feel
For thy desponding spirit, as it sinks
Beneath procrastinated fears for those
More dear to thee than life! But eminence
Of misery is thine, as once of joy;
175 And, as we view the strange vicissitude,
We ask anew, where happiness is found?———
Alas! in rural life, where youthful dreams
See the Arcadia[3] that Romance describes,

---

1 Cf. 1.299–303 above.
2 Marie Antoinette, queen of France (1755–93). From August 1792 the royal family was imprisoned in Paris. Marie Antoinette would herself be executed in October 1793. The fate of Marie Antoinette had become a dominant image in British debates about the Revolution.
3 A mythical rural paradise.

Not even Content resides!—In yon low hut
180 Of clay and thatch, where rises the grey smoke
Of smold'ring turf, cut from the adjoining moor,
The labourer, its inhabitant, who toils
From the first dawn of twilight, till the Sun
Sinks in the rosy waters of the West,
185 Finds that with poverty it cannot dwell;
For bread, and scanty bread, is all he earns
For him and for his household—Should Disease,
Born of chill wintry rains, arrest his arm,
Then, thro' his patch'd and straw-stuff'd casement, peeps
190 The squalid figure of extremest Want;
And from the Parish the reluctant dole,[1]
Dealt by th' unfeeling farmer, hardly saves
The ling'ring spark of life from cold extinction:
Then the bright Sun of Spring, that smiling bids
195 All other animals rejoice, beholds,
Crept from his pallet, the emaciate wretch
Attempt, with feeble effort, to resume
Some heavy task, above his wasted strength,
Turning his wistful looks (how much in vain!)
200 To the deserted mansion, where no more
The owner (gone to gayer scenes) resides,[2]
Who made even luxury, Virtue; while he gave
The scatter'd crumbs to honest Poverty.—
But, tho' the landscape be too oft deform'd
205 By figures such as these, yet Peace is here,
And o'er our vallies, cloath'd with springing corn,
No hostile hoof shall trample, nor fierce flames
Wither the wood's young verdure, ere it form
Gradual the laughing May's luxuriant shade;
210 For, by the rude sea guarded, we are safe,
And feel not evils such as with deep sighs
The Emigrants deplore, as, they recal
The Summer past, when Nature seem'd to lose
Her course in wild distemperature, and aid,
215 With seasons all revers'd, destructive War.
     Shuddering, I view the pictures they have drawn

---

1 Under the Old Poor Law it was the responsibility of each parish to
  provide for those who were sick or unable to find work from funds pro-
  vided by local property rates.
2 Absentee landlords were a frequent target of criticism.

Of desolated countries,[1] where the ground,
Stripp'd of its unripe produce, was thick strewn
With various Death—the war-horse falling there
220 By famine, and his rider by the sword.
The moping clouds sail'd heavy charg'd with rain,
And bursting o'er the mountains misty brow,
Deluged, as with an inland sea, the vales;[2]
Where, thro' the sullen evening's lurid gloom,
225 Rising, like columns of volcanic fire,
The flames of burning villages illum'd
The waste of water; and the wind, that howl'd
Along its troubled surface, brought the groans
Of plunder'd peasants, and the frantic shrieks
230 Of mothers for their children; while the brave,
To pity still alive, listen'd aghast
To these dire echoes, hopeless to prevent
The evils they beheld, or check the rage,
Which ever, as the people of one land
235 Meet in contention, fires the human heart
With savage thirst of kindred blood, and makes
Man lose his nature; rendering him more fierce
Than the gaunt monsters of the howling waste.
Oft have I heard the melancholy tale,
240 Which, all their native gaiety forgot,
These Exiles tell—How Hope impell'd them on,
Reckless of tempest, hunger, or the sword,
Till order'd to retreat, they knew not why,
From all their flattering prospects, they became
245 The prey of dark suspicion and regret:[3]

---

1 Smith sheltered a group of emigrants in her home in 1792, one of
whom her daughter Anna Augusta later married. See Appendix C1b for
a letter by Smith from this period.

2 [Smith's note:] From the heavy and incessant rains during the last cam-
paign, the armies were often compelled to march for many miles
through marshes overflowed; suffering the extremities of cold and
fatigue. The peasants frequently misled them; and, after having passed
these inundations at the hazard of their lives, they were sometimes
under the necessity of crossing them a second and a third time; their
evening quarters after such a day of exertion were often in a wood
without shelter; and their repast, instead of bread, unripe corn, without
any other preparation than being mashed into a sort of paste.

3 [Smith's note:] It is remarkable, that notwithstanding the excessive
hardships to which the army of the Emigrants was exposed, very few

Then, in despondence, sunk the unnerv'd arm
Of gallant Loyalty—At every turn
Shame and disgrace appear'd, and seem'd to mock
Their scatter'd squadrons; which the warlike youth,
250 Unable to endure, often implor'd,
As the last act of friendship, from the hand
Of some brave comrade, to receive the blow
That freed the indignant spirit from its pain.
To a wild mountain, whose bare summit hides
255 Its broken eminence in clouds; whose steeps
Are dark with woods; where the receding rocks
Are worn by torrents of dissolving snow,
A wretched Woman, pale and breathless, flies!
And, gazing round her, listens to the sound
260 Of hostile footsteps——No! it dies away:
Nor noise remains, but of the cataract,
Or surly breeze of night, that mutters low
Among the thickets, where she trembling seeks
A temporary shelter—clasping close
265 To her hard-heaving heart, her sleeping child,
All she could rescue of the innocent groupe
That yesterday surrounded her—Escap'd
Almost by miracle! Fear, frantic Fear,
Wing'd her weak feet: yet, half repentant now
270 Her headlong haste, she wishes she had staid
To die with those affrighted Fancy paints
The lawless soldier's victims—Hark! Again
The driving tempest bears the cry of Death,
And, with deep sudden thunder, the dread sound
275 Of cannon vibrates on the tremulous earth;
While, bursting in the air, the murderous bomb
Glares o'er her mansion. Where the splinters fall,
Like scatter'd comets, its destructive path
Is mark'd by wreaths of flame!—Then, overwhelm'd
280 Beneath accumulated horror, sinks
The desolate mourner; yet, in Death itself,
True to maternal tenderness, she tries

---

in it suffered from disease till they began to retreat; then it was that
despondence consigned to the most miserable death many brave men
who deserved a better fate; and then despair impelled some to suicide,
while others fell by mutual wounds, unable to survive disappointment
and humiliation.

To save the unconscious infant from the storm
In which she perishes; and to protect
285 This last dear object of her ruin'd hopes
From prowling monsters, that from other hills,
More inaccessible, and wilder wastes,
Lur'd by the scent of slaughter, follow fierce
Contending hosts, and to polluted fields
290 Add dire increase of horrors—But alas!
The Mother and the Infant perish both!—
     The feudal Chief, whose Gothic battlements
Frown on the plain beneath, returning home
From distant lands, alone and in disguise,
295 Gains at the fall of night his Castle walls,
But, at the vacant gate, no Porter sits
To wait his Lord's admittance!—In the courts
All is drear silence!—Guessing but too well
The fatal truth, he shudders as he goes
300 Thro' the mute hall; where, by the blunted light
That the dim moon thro' painted casements lends,
He sees that devastation has been there:
Then, while each hideous image to his mind
Rises terrific, o'er a bleeding corse
305 Stumbling he falls; another interrupts
His staggering feet—all, all who us'd to rush
With joy to meet him—all his family
Lie murder'd in his way!—And the day dawns
On a wild raving Maniac, whom a fate
310 So sudden and calamitous has robb'd
Of reason; and who round his vacant walls
Screams unregarded, and reproaches Heaven!—
Such are thy dreadful trophies, savage War!
And evils such as these, or yet more dire,
315 Which the pain'd mind recoils from, all are thine—
The purple Pestilence,° that to the grave   *the plague*
Sends whom the sword has spar'd, is thine; and thine
The Widow's anguish and the Orphan's tears!—
Woes such as these does Man inflict on Man;
320 And by the closet murderers, whom we style
Wise Politicians; are the schemes prepar'd,
Which, to keep Europe's wavering balance even,
Depopulate her kingdoms, and consign
To tears and anguish half a bleeding world!—
325   Oh! could the time return, when thoughts like these

Spoil'd not that gay delight, which vernal Suns,
Illuminating hills, and woods, and fields,
Gave to my infant spirits—Memory come!
And from distracting cares, that now deprive
330 Such scenes of all their beauty, kindly bear
My fancy to those hours of simple joy,
When, on the banks of Arun,[1] which I see
Make its irriguous° course thro' yonder meads,   *serving to irrigate*
I play'd; unconscious then of future ill!
335 There (where, from hollows fring'd with yellow broom,
The birch with silver rind, and fairy leaf,
Aslant the low stream trembles) I have stood,
And meditated how to venture best
Into the shallow current, to procure
340 The willow herb of glowing purple spikes,
Or flags,[2] whose sword-like leaves conceal'd the tide,
Startling the timid reed-bird from her nest,
As with aquatic flowers I wove the wreath,
Such as, collected by the shepherd girls,
345 Deck in the villages the turfy shrine,
And mark the arrival of propitious May.—
How little dream'd I then the time would come,
When the bright Sun of that delicious month
Should, from disturb'd and artificial sleep,
350 Awaken me to never-ending toil,
To terror and to tears!—Attempting still,
With feeble hands and cold desponding heart,
To save my children from the o'erwhelming wrongs,
That have for ten long years been heap'd on me![3]—
355 The fearful spectres of chicane[4] and fraud
Have, Proteus like, still chang'd their hideous forms[5]
(As the Law lent its plausible disguise),
Pursuing my faint steps; and I have seen
Friendship's sweet bonds (which were so early form'd,)

---

1 Smith also refers to the River Arun in Sonnets V, XXVI, XXXII,
  XXXIII, and XLV.
2 A common name for wild irises.
3 Again, a reference to the litigation around her children's inheritance.
4 Trickery or deception, in particular in litigation.
5 In Greek mythology Proteus is the sea-god who can assume different
  shapes at will.

360   And once I fondly thought of amaranth[1]
      Inwove with silver seven times tried) give way,
      And fail; as these green fan-like leaves of fern
      Will wither at the touch of Autumn's frost.
      Yet there *are those*, whose patient pity still
365   Hears my long murmurs; who, unwearied, try
      With lenient hands to bind up every wound
      My wearied spirit feels, and bid me go
      "Right onward"[2]—a calm votary of the Nymph,
      Who, from her adamantine rock,[3] points out
370   To conscious rectitude the rugged path,
      That leads at length to Peace!—Ah! yes, my friends
      Peace will at last be mine; for in the Grave
      Is Peace—and pass a few short years, perchance
      A few short months, and all the various pain
375   I now endure shall be forgotten there,
      And no memorial shall remain of me,
      Save in your bosoms; while even *your* regret
      Shall lose its poignancy, as ye reflect
      What complicated woes that grave conceals!
380   But, if the little praise, that may await
      The Mother's efforts, should provoke the spleen
      Of Priest or Levite;[4] and they then arraign
      The dust that cannot hear them; be it yours
      To vindicate my humble fame; to say,
385   That, not in selfish sufferings absorb'd,
      "I gave to misery all I had, my tears."[5]
      And if, where regulated sanctity

---

1   See p. 70, note 2.

2   [Smith's note:] MILTON, Sonnet 22d. ["To Mr. Cyriac Skinner, Upon his Blindness," line 9 (manuscript circulation until 1694). Smith may have meant to mobilize the political reverberations of Milton's sonnet, which continues: "Right onward. What supports me, dost thou ask? / The Conscience, Friend, to have lost them over ply'd / In Liberties Defence, my noble task; / Of which all *Europe* rings from side to side" (lines 9–12).]

3   Literally, a rock of surpassing hardness; figuratively, unwavering or unyielding.

4   That is, those who judge by a strict code (Curran, *Poems of Charlotte Smith* 162n).

5   [Smith's note:] GRAY. [Thomas Gray (1716–71), "He gave to Mis'ry (all he had) a Tear," which appears on the poet's epitaph at the end of "An Elegy Written in a Country Churchyard" (1751)].

Pours her long orisons° to Heaven, my voice   *prayers*
Was seldom heard, that yet *my prayer* was made
390 To him who hears even silence; not in domes
Of human architecture, fill'd with crowds,
But on these hills, where boundless, yet distinct,
Even as a map, beneath are spread the fields
His bounty cloaths; divided here by woods,
395 And there by commons rude,[1] or winding brooks,
While I might breathe the air perfum'd with flowers,
Or the fresh odours of the mountain turf;
And gaze on clouds above me, as they sail'd
Majestic: or remark the reddening north,
400 When bickering arrows of electric fire[2]
Flash on the evening sky—I made my prayer
In unison with murmuring waves that now
Swell with dark tempests, now are mild and blue,
As the bright arch above; for all to me
405 Declare omniscient goodness; nor need I
Declamatory essays to incite
My wonder or my praise, when every leaf
That Spring unfolds, and every simple bud,
More forcibly impresses on my heart
410 His power and wisdom—Ah! while I adore
That goodness, which design'd to all that lives
Some taste of happiness, my soul is pain'd
By the variety of woes that Man
For Man creates—his blessings often turn'd
415 To plagues and curses: Saint-like Piety,
Misled by Superstition, has destroy'd
More than Ambition; and the sacred flame
Of Liberty becomes a raging fire,
When Licence and Confusion bid it blaze.
420 From thy high throne, above yon radiant stars,
O Power Omnipotent! with mercy view
This suffering globe, and cause thy creatures cease,
With savage fangs, to tear her bleeding breast:
Refrain that rage for power, that bids a Man,
425 Himself a worm, desire unbounded rule
O'er beings like himself: Teach the hard hearts
Of rulers, that the poorest hind, who dies

---

1 Undeveloped land held in common by the community.
2 The aurora borealis, or northern lights.

For their unrighteous quarrels, in thy sight
Is equal to the imperious Lord, that leads
430 His disciplin'd destroyers to the field.——
May lovely Freedom, in her genuine charms,
Aided by stern but equal Justice, drive
From the ensanguin'd earth the hell-born fiends
Of Pride, Oppression, Avarice, and Revenge,
435 That ruin what thy mercy made so fair!
Then shall these ill-starr'd wanderers, whose sad fate
These desultory lines lament, regain
Their native country; private vengeance then
To public virtue yield; and the fierce feuds,
440 That long have torn their desolated land,
May (even as storms, that agitate the air,
Drive noxious vapours from the blighted earth)
Serve, all tremendous as they are, to fix
The reign of Reason, Liberty, and Peace!

BEACHY HEAD (1807)

ADVERTISEMENT.

—

AS the following Poems were delivered to the Publisher as early as the month of May last, it may not be thought improper to state the circumstances that have hitherto delayed their appearance.

The fulfilling this duty to the public has since devolved to other hands; for alas! the admired author is now unconscious of their praise or censure, having fallen a victim to a long and painful illness, on the 28th of October last.

The delay which since that period has taken place, has been occasioned partly by the hope of finding a preface to the present publication, which there was some reason to suppose herself had written, and partly from an intention of annexing a short account of her life; but it having been since decided to publish biographical memoirs, and a selection of her correspondence, on a more enlarged plan, and under the immediate authority of her own nearest relatives,[1] it was thought unnecessary; and the motives for deferring the publication are altogether removed.

The public, who have received the several editions of Mrs. Smith's former Poems with unbounded approbation, will, without doubt, admit the claims of the present work to an equal share of their favour; and her friends and admirers cannot fail of being highly gratified in observing, that although most of the Poems included in this volume were composed during the few and short intervals of care which her infirmities permitted her to enjoy; yet they bear the most unquestionable evidence of the same undiminished genius, spirit, and imagination, which so imminently distinguished her former productions.

The Poem entitled BEACHY HEAD is not completed according to the original design. That the increasing debility of its author has been the cause of its being left in an imperfect state, will it is hoped be a sufficient apology.

There are two Poems in this collection, viz. FLORA, and STUDIES BY THE SEA, which have already been published in Mrs. Smith's "Conversations for the Use of Children and Young

---

1 Smith's sister, Catherine Ann Dorset (c. 1753–c. 1817), wrote a biography of Smith that was intended to accompany a volume that never made it into print. Sir Walter Scott (1771–1832) finally published the piece, simply titled "Charlotte Smith," in *The Miscellaneous Prose Works of Sir Walter Scott, Bart. Biographical Memoirs.* Vol. 4 (Boston: Wells and Lilly, 1829), 5–41.

Persons";[1] but as many of her friends considered them as misplaced in that work, and not likely to fall under the general observation of those who were qualified to appreciate their superior elegance and exquisite fancy, and had expressed a desire of seeing them transplanted into a more congenial soil, the Publisher, with his usual liberality, has permitted them to re-appear in the present volume.

January 31, 1807.

---

1   Charlotte Smith, *Conversations Introducing Poetry: Chiefly on Subjects of Natural History for the Use of Children and Young Persons* (London: J. Johnson, 1804).

BEACHY HEAD

ON thy stupendous summit, rock sublime!
That o'er the channel rear'd, half way at sea
The mariner at early morning hails,[1]
I would recline; while Fancy should go forth,
5 And represent the strange and awful hour
Of vast concussion; when the Omnipotent
Stretch'd forth his arm,[2] and rent the solid hills,
Bidding the impetuous main flood rush between
The rifted shores, and from the continent
10 Eternally divided this green isle.
Imperial lord of the high southern coast!
From thy projecting head-land I would mark
Far in the east the shades of night disperse,
Melting and thinned, as from the dark blue wave
15 Emerging, brilliant rays of arrowy light
Dart from the horizon; when the glorious sun
Just lifts above it his resplendent orb.
Advances now, with feathery silver touched,
The rippling tide of flood; glisten the sands,
20 While, inmates of the chalky clefts that scar
Thy sides precipitous, with shrill harsh cry,
Their white wings glancing in the level beam,
The terns, and gulls, and tarrocks,[3] seek their food,
And thy rough hollows echo to the voice
25 Of the gray choughs,[4] and ever restless daws,
With clamour, not unlike the chiding hounds,
While the lone shepherd, and his baying dog,
Drive to thy turfy crest his bleating flock.

---

1 [Smith's note:] In crossing the Channel from the coast of France,
Beachy-Head is the first land made.
2 [Smith's note:] Alluding to an idea that this Island was once joined to
the continent of Europe, and torn from it by some convulsion of
Nature. I confess I never could trace the resemblance between the two
countries. Yet the cliffs about Dieppe, resemble the chalk cliffs on the
Southern coast. But Normandy has no likeness whatever to the part of
England opposite to it.
3 [Smith's note:] Terns.—Sterna hirundo, or Sea Swallow. Gulls.—Larus
canus. Tarrocks.—Larus tridactylus.
4 [Smith's note:] Gray Choughs.—Corvus Graculus, Cornish Choughs,
or, as these birds are called by the Sussex people, Saddle-backed Crows,
build in great numbers on this coast.

The high meridian° of the day is past,   *noon*
30 And Ocean now, reflecting the calm Heaven,
Is of cerulean° hue; and murmurs low   *deep blue*
The tide of ebb, upon the level sands.
The sloop,¹ her angular canvas shifting still,
Catches the light and variable airs
35 That but a little crisp the summer sea,
Dimpling its tranquil surface.

                                        Afar off,
And just emerging from the arch immense
Where seem to part the elements, a fleet
Of fishing vessels stretch their lesser sails;
40 While more remote, and like a dubious spot
Just hanging in the horizon, laden deep,
The ship of commerce richly freighted, makes
Her slower progress, on her distant voyage,
Bound to the orient climates, where the sun
45 Matures the spice within its odorous shell,²
And, rivalling the gray worm's filmy toil,
Bursts from its pod the vegetable down;³
Which in long turban'd wreaths, from torrid heat
Defends the brows of Asia's countless casts.⁴
50 There the Earth hides within her glowing breast
The beamy adamant,⁵ and the round pearl
Enchased in rugged covering; which the slave,
With perilous and breathless toil, tears off
From the rough sea-rock, deep beneath the waves.
55 These are the toys of Nature; and her sport
Of little estimate in Reason's eye:
And they who reason, with abhorrence see
Man, for such gaudes and baubles, violate
The sacred freedom of his fellow man—

---

1 One-masted sailing boat.
2 Probably a reference to nutmeg. Nutmeg is the seed of a tree (*Myristica fragrans*) whose shell yields another spice (mace).
3 [Smith's note:] Cotton. (Gossypium herbaceum).
4 A reference to the caste system in India.
5 [Smith's note:] Diamonds, the hardest and most valuable of precious stones. For the extraordinary exertions of the Indians in diving for the pearl oysters, see the account of the Pearl Fisheries in Percival's View of Ceylon. [Robert Percival (1765–1826), *An Account of the Island of Ceylon* (1803). Ceylon is modern-day Sri Lanka.]

60 Erroneous estimate! As Heaven's pure air,
    Fresh as it blows on this aërial height,
    Or sound of seas upon the stony strand,
    Or inland, the gay harmony of birds,
    And winds that wander in the leafy woods;
65 Are to the unadulterate taste more worth
    Than the elaborate harmony, brought out
    From fretted stop, or modulated airs
    Of vocal science.—So the brightest gems,
    Glancing resplendent on the regal crown,
70 Or trembling in the high born beauty's ear,
    Are poor and paltry, to the lovely light
    Of the fair star, that as the day declines,
    Attendant on her queen, the crescent moon,
    Bathes her bright tresses in the eastern wave.
75 For now the sun is verging to the sea,
    And as he westward sinks, the floating clouds
    Suspended, move upon the evening gale,
    And gathering round his orb, as if to shade
    The insufferable brightness, they resign
80 Their gauzy whiteness; and more warm'd, assume
    All hues of purple. There, transparent gold
    Mingles with ruby tints, and sapphire gleams,
    And colours, such as Nature through her works
    Shews only in the ethereal canopy.
85 Thither aspiring Fancy fondly soars,
    Wandering sublime thro' visionary vales,
    Where bright pavilions rise, and trophies, fann'd
    By airs celestial; and adorn'd with wreaths
    Of flowers that bloom amid elysian° bowers.   *heavenly*
90 Now bright, and brighter still the colours glow,
    Till half the lustrous orb within the flood
    Seems to retire: the flood reflecting still
    Its splendor, and in mimic glory drest;
    Till the last ray shot upward, fires the clouds
95 With blazing crimson; then in paler light,
    Long lines of tenderer radiance, lingering yield
    To partial darkness; and on the opposing side
    The early moon distinctly rising, throws
    Her pearly brilliance on the trembling tide.
100 The fishermen, who at set seasons pass
    Many a league off at sea their toiling night,
    Now hail their comrades, from their daily task

Returning; and make ready for their own,
With the night tide commencing:—The night tide
105 Bears a dark vessel on, whose hull and sails
Mark her a coaster from the north. Her keel
Now ploughs the sand; and sidelong now she leans,
While with loud clamours her athletic crew
Unload her; and resounds the busy hum
110 Along the wave-worn rocks. Yet more remote,
Where the rough cliff hangs beetling° o'er its base,   *projecting*
All breathes repose; the water's rippling sound
Scarce heard; but now and then the sea-snipe's cry[1]
Just tells that something living is abroad;
115 And sometimes crossing on the moonbright line,
Glimmers the skiff, faintly discern'd awhile,
Then lost in shadow.

                    Contemplation here,
High on her throne of rock, aloof may sit,
And bid recording Memory unfold
120 Her scroll voluminous—bid her retrace
The period, when from Neustria's[2] hostile shore
The Norman launch'd his galleys, and the bay
O'er which that mass of ruin[3] frowns even now
In vain and sullen menace, then received
125 The new invaders; a proud martial race,
Of Scandinavia[4] the undaunted sons,

---

1 [Smith's note:] In crossing the channel this bird is heard at night, utter-
ing a short cry, and flitting along near the surface of the waves. The
sailors call it the Sea Snipe; but I can find no species of sea bird of which
this is the vulgar name. A bird so called inhabits the Lake of Geneva.
2 Normandy's. Smith indicates this line as the start point of the long note
that follows. In this passage, ending at line 142, she writes of the
Norman conquests up to the victory of William the Conqueror (c.
1028–87) in 1066 at the Battle of Hastings, after which he became the
first Norman king of England.
3 [Smith's note:] Pevensey Castle. [A medieval castle in East Sussex,
England.]
4 [Smith's note:] The Scandinavians, {Scandinavia.—Modern Norway,
Sweden, Denmark, Lapland, &c.} and other inhabitants of the north,
began towards the end of the 8th century, to leave their inhospitable
climate in search of the produce of more fortunate countries.
    The North-men made inroads on the coasts of France; and carrying
back immense booty, excited their compatriots to engage in the same
piratical voyages: and they were afterwards joined by numbers of neces-
sitous and daring adventurers from the coasts of Provence and Sicily.

Whom Dogon, Fier-a-bras, and Humfroi led
To conquest: while Trinacria to their power
Yielded her wheaten garland; and when thou,

In 844, these wandering innovators had a great number of vessels at
sea; and again visiting the coasts of France, Spain, and England, the fol-
lowing year they penetrated even to Paris: and the unfortunate Charles
the Bald [823–877], king of France, purchased at a high price, the
retreat of the banditti he had no other means of repelling.

These successful expeditions continued for some time; till Rollo
[c. 846–c. 930], otherwise Raoul, assembled a number of followers, and
after a descent on England, crossed the channel, and made himself
master of Rouen, which he fortified. Charles the Simple [879–929],
unable to contend with Rollo, offered to resign to him some of the
northern provinces, and to give him his daughter [Gisela] in marriage.
Neustria, since called Normandy, was granted to him, and afterwards
Brittany. He added the more solid virtues of the legislator to the fierce
valour of the conqueror—converted to Christianity, he established justice,
and repressed the excesses of his Danish subjects, till then accustomed
to live only by plunder. His name became the signal for pursuing those
who violated the laws; as well as the cry of Haro, still so usual in Nor-
mandy. The Danes and Francs produced a race of men celebrated for
their valour; and it was a small party of these that in 983, having been
on a pilgrimage to Jerusalem, arrived on their return at Salerno, and
found the town surrounded by Mahometans, whom the Salernians were
bribing to leave their coast. The Normans represented to them the base-
ness and cowardice of such submission; and notwithstanding the
inequality of their numbers, they boldly attacked the Saracen camp, and
drove the infidels to their ships. The prince of Salerno, astonished at
their successful audacity, would have loaded them with the marks of his
gratitude; but refusing every reward, they returned to their own country,
from whence, however, other bodies of Normans passed into Sicily
{Anciently called Trinacria}; and many of them entered into the service
of the emperor of the East, others of the Pope, and the duke of Naples
was happy to engage a small party of them in defence of his newly
founded dutchy. Soon afterwards three brothers of Coutance, the sons
of Tancred de Hauteville [980–1041], Guillaume Fier-a-bras [d. 1046],
Drogon [d. 1051], and Homfroi [d. 1057], joining the Normans estab-
lished at Aversa, became masters of the fertile island of Sicily; and
Robert Guiscard [1015–85] joining them, the Normans became sover-
eigns both of Sicily and Naples {Parthenope}. How William, the natural
son of Robert, duke of Normandy, possessed himself of England, is too
well known to be repeated here. William sailing from St. Valori, landed
in the bay of Pevensey; and at the place now called Battle, met the
English forces under Harold [II; r. 1066]: an esquire (ecuyer) called
Taillefer, mounted on an armed horse, led on the Normans, singing in a
thundering tone the war song of Rollo. He threw himself *(continued)*

130   Parthenope! within thy fertile bay
        Receiv'd the victors—

                    In the mailed ranks
        Of Normans landing on the British coast
        Rode Taillefer; and with astounding voice
        Thunder'd the war song daring Roland sang
135   First in the fierce contention: vainly brave,
        One not inglorious struggle England made—
        But failing, saw the Saxon heptarchy[1]
        Finish for ever.——Then the holy pile,[2]
        Yet seen upon the field of conquest, rose,
140   Where to appease heaven's wrath for so much blood,
        The conqueror bade unceasing prayers ascend,
        And requiems for the slayers and the slain.
        But let not modern Gallia° form from hence   *France*
        Presumptuous hopes, that ever thou again,
145   Queen of the isles! shalt crouch to foreign arms.
        The enervate sons of Italy may yield;
        And the Iberian, all his trophies torn
        And wrapp'd in Superstition's monkish weed,
        May shelter his abasement, and put on
150   Degrading fetters. Never, never thou!
        Imperial mistress of the obedient sea;
        But thou, in thy integrity secure,
        Shalt now undaunted meet a world in arms.

        England! 'twas where this promontory rears
155   Its rugged brow above the channel wave,
        Parting the hostile nations, that thy fame,
        Thy naval fame was tarnish'd, at what time

---

        among the English, and was killed on the first onset. In a marsh not far
        from Hastings, the skeletons of an armed man and horse were found a
        few years since, which are believed to have belonged to the Normans, as
        a party of their horse, deceived in the nature of the ground, perished in
        the morass.
1   The seven kingdoms of Anglo-Saxon England: Wessex, Sussex, Kent,
        Essex, East Anglia, Mercia, and Northumbria.
2   [Smith's note:] Battle Abbey was raised by the Conqueror [on the site of
        the Battle of Hastings], and endowed with an ample revenue, that
        masses might be said night and day for the souls of those who perished
        in battle.

Thou, leagued with the Batavian,[1] gavest to France
One day of triumph—triumph the more loud,
160   Because even then so rare. Oh! well redeem'd,
Since, by a series of illustrious men,
Such as no other country ever rear'd,
To vindicate her cause. It is a list
Which, as Fame echoes it, blanches the cheek
165   Of bold Ambition; while the despot feels
The extorted sceptre tremble in his grasp.

From even the proudest roll by glory fill'd,
How gladly the reflecting mind returns
To simple scenes of peace and industry,
170   Where, bosom'd in some valley of the hills
Stands the lone farm; its gate with tawny ricks
Surrounded, and with granaries and sheds,
Roof'd with green mosses, and by elms and ash
Partially shaded; and not far remov'd
175   The hut of sea-flints built; the humble home

---

1   [Smith's note:] In 1690, King William [III; r. 1689–1702] being then in
Ireland, Tourville, the French admiral [1642–1701], arrived on the coast
of England. His fleet consisted of seventy-eight large ships, and twenty-
two fire-ships. Lord Torrington, the English admiral [George Byng,
1663–1733], lay at St. Helens, with only forty English and a few Dutch
ships; and conscious of the disadvantage under which he should give
battle, he ran up between the enemy's fleet and the coast, to protect it.
The queen's council, dictated to by Russel [Edward Russell,
1653–1727], persuaded her to order Torrington to venture a battle. The
orders Torrington appears to have obeyed reluctantly: his fleet now con-
sisted of twenty-two Dutch and thirty-four English ships. Evertson, the
Dutch admiral [Cornelis Evertsen, 1642–1706], was eager to obtain
glory; Torrington, more cautious, reflected on the importance of the
stake. The consequence was, that the Dutch rashly sailing on were sur-
rounded, and Torrington, solicitous to recover this false step, placed
himself with difficulty between the Dutch and French;—but three
Dutch ships were burnt, two of their admirals killed, and almost all their
ships disabled. The English and Dutch declining a second engagement,
retired towards the mouth of the Thames. The French, from ignorance
of the coast, and misunderstanding among each other, failed to take all
the advantage they might have done of this victory. [The naval engage-
ment was known as the Battle of Beachy Head.]

Of one, who sometimes watches on the heights,[1]
When hid in the cold mist of passing clouds,
The flock, with dripping fleeces, are dispers'd
O'er the wide down; then from some ridged point
180 That overlooks the sea, his eager eye
Watches the bark° that for his signal waits   *boat or sailing vessel*
To land its merchandize:—Quitting for this
Clandestine traffic his more honest toil,
The crook abandoning, he braves himself
185 The heaviest snow-storm of December's night,
When with conflicting winds the ocean raves,
And on the tossing boat, unfearing mounts
To meet the partners of the perilous trade,
And share their hazard. Well it were for him,
190 If no such commerce of destruction known,
He were content with what the earth affords
To human labour; even where she seems
Reluctant most. More happy is the hind,°   *farm assistant*
Who, with his own hands rears on some black moor,
195 Or turbary,° his independent hut   *peat bog*
Cover'd with heather, whence the slow white smoke
Of smouldering peat arises——A few sheep,
His best possession, with his children share
The rugged shed when wintry tempests blow;
200 But, when with Spring's return the green blades rise
Amid the russet heath, the household live
Joint tenants of the waste throughout the day,
And often, from her nest, among the swamps,
Where the gemm'd sun-dew grows, or fring'd buck-bean,
205 They scare the plover,[2] that with plaintive cries
Flutters, as sorely wounded, down the wind.
Rude, and but just remov'd from savage life
Is the rough dweller among scenes like these,
(Scenes all unlike the poet's fabling dreams

---

1   [Smith's note:] The shepherds and labourers of this tract of country, a
    hardy and athletic race of men, are almost universally engaged in the
    contraband trade, carried on for the coarsest and most destructive
    spirits, with the opposite coast. When no other vessel will venture to sea,
    these men hazard their lives to elude the watchfulness of the Revenue
    officers, and to secure their cargoes.
2   [Smith's note:] Sun-dew.—Drosera rotundifolia. Buck-bean.—Menyan-
    thes trifoliatum. Plover.—Tringa vanellus.

210 Describing Arcady°)—But he is free;   *Arcadia*
     The dread that follows on illegal acts
     He never feels; and his industrious mate
     Shares in his labour. Where the brook is traced
     By crouding osiers,° and the black coot hides[1]   *willows*
215 Among the plashy reeds, her diving brood,
     The matron wades; gathering the long green rush
     That well prepar'd hereafter lends its light
     To her poor cottage, dark and cheerless else
     Thro' the drear hours of Winter. Otherwhile
220 She leads her infant group where charlock[2] grows
     "Unprofitably gay,"[3] or to the fields,
     Where congregate the linnet and the finch,
     That on the thistles, so profusely spread,
     Feast in the desert; the poor family
225 Early resort, extirpating with care
     These, and the gaudier mischief of the ground;
     Then flames the high rais'd heap; seen afar off
     Like hostile war-fires[4] flashing to the sky.
     Another task is theirs: On fields that shew
230 As angry Heaven had rain'd sterility,
     Stony and cold, and hostile to the plough,
     Where clamouring loud, the evening curlew runs[5]
     And drops her spotted eggs among the flints;
     The mother and the children pile the stones
235 In rugged pyramids;—and all this toil
     They patiently encounter; well content
     On their flock bed to slumber undisturb'd
     Beneath the smoky roof they call their own.
     Oh! little knows the sturdy hind, who stands
240 Gazing, with looks where envy and contempt

---

1 [Smith's note:] Coot.—Fulica aterrima.
2 Charlock is wild mustard and is poisonous (Curran, *Poems of Charlotte Smith*, 226n).
3 [Smith's note:] "With blossom'd furze, unprofitably gay." *Goldsmith.*
   [Oliver Goldsmith (c. 1730–74), "The Deserted Village" (1770), line 194. Goldsmith's poem was the iconic work on rural hardship and depopulation.]
4 [Smith's note:] The Beacons formerly lighted up on the hills to give notice of the approach of an enemy. These signals would still be used in case of alarm, if the Telegraph now substituted could not be distinguished on account of fog or darkness.
5 [Smith's note:] Curlew.—Charadrius œdienemus.

Are often strangely mingled, on the car
Where prosperous Fortune sits; what secret care
Or sick satiety is often hid,
Beneath the splendid outside: *He* knows not
245   How frequently the child of Luxury
Enjoying nothing, flies from place to place
In chase of pleasure that eludes his grasp;
And that content is e'en less found by him,
Than by the labourer, whose pick-axe smooths
250   The road before his chariot; and who doffs
What *was* an hat; and as the train pass on,
Thinks how one day's expenditure, like this,
Would cheer him for long months, when to his toil
The frozen earth closes her marble breast.

255   Ah! who *is* happy? Happiness! a word
That like false fire, from marsh effluvia born,[1]
Misleads the wanderer, destin'd to contend
In the world's wilderness, with want or woe
Yet *they* are happy, who have never ask'd
260   What good or evil means. The boy
That on the river's margin gaily plays,
Has heard that Death is there—He knows not Death,
And therefore fears it not; and venturing in
He gains a bullrush, or a minnow—then,
265   At certain peril, for a worthless prize,
A crow's, or raven's nest, he climbs the boll°   trunk
Of some tall pine; and of his prowess proud,
Is for a moment happy. Are *your* cares,
Ye who despise him, never worse applied?
270   The village girl is happy, who sets forth
To distant fair, gay in her Sunday suit,
With cherry colour'd knots, and flourish'd shawl,
And bonnet newly purchas'd. So is he
Her little brother, who his mimic drum
275   Beats, till he drowns her rural lovers' oaths
Of constant faith, and still increasing love;
Ah! yet a while, and half those oaths believ'd,
Her happiness is vanish'd; and the boy
While yet a stripling, finds the sound he lov'd

---

1   Will-o'-the-wisp. See Sonnet LXXXVI, p. 120, note 1.

280   Has led him on, till he has given up
      His freedom, and his happiness together.

      I once was happy, when while yet a child,
      I learn'd to love these upland solitudes,
      And, when elastic as the mountain air,
285   To my light spirit, care was yet unknown
      And evil unforeseen:—Early it came,
      And childhood scarcely passed, I was condemned,
      A guiltless exile, silently to sigh,
      While Memory, with faithful pencil, drew
290   The contrast; and regretting, I compar'd
      With the polluted smoky atmosphere
      And dark and stifling streets, the southern hills
      That to the setting Sun, their graceful heads
      Rearing, o'erlook the frith, where Vecta[1] breaks
295   With her white rocks, the strong impetuous tide,
      When western winds the vast Atlantic urge
      To thunder on the coast—Haunts of my youth!
      Scenes of fond day dreams, I behold ye yet!
      Where 'twas so pleasant by thy northern slopes
300   To climb the winding sheep-path, aided oft
      By scatter'd thorns: whose spiny branches bore
      Small woolly tufts, spoils of the vagrant lamb
      There seeking shelter from the noon-day sun;
      And pleasant, seated on the short soft turf,
305   To look beneath upon the hollow way
      While heavily upward mov'd the labouring wain,
      And stalking slowly by, the sturdy hind
      To ease his panting team, stopp'd with a stone
      The grating wheel.

                     Advancing higher still
310   The prospect widens, and the village church
      But little, o'er the lowly roofs around
      Rears its gray belfry,° and its simple vane;[2]   *bell tower*
      Those lowly roofs of thatch are half conceal'd

---

1 [Smith's note:] Vecta.—The Isle of Wight, which breaks the force of the
   waves when they are driven by south-west winds against this long and
   open coast. It is somewhere described as "Vecta shouldering the Western
   Waves." [Unable to trace this quotation. The Isle of Wight is located off
   the south coast of England.]
2 Weather vane.

By the rude arms of trees, lovely in spring,[1]
315 When on each bough, the rosy-tinctur'd bloom
Sits thick, and promises autumnal plenty.
For even those orchards round the Norman farms,
Which, as their owners mark the promis'd fruit,
Console them for the vineyards of the south,
Surpass not these.

320   Where woods of ash, and beech,
And partial copses, fringe the green hill foot,
The upland shepherd rears his modest home,
There wanders by, a little nameless stream
That from the hill wells forth, bright now and clear,
325 Or after rain with chalky mixture gray,
But still refreshing in its shallow course,
The cottage garden; most for use design'd,
Yet not of beauty destitute.[2] The vine
Mantles the little casement; yet the briar
330 Drops fragrant dew among the July flowers;
And pansies rayed, and freak'd and mottled pinks
Grow among balm, and rosemary and rue:
There honeysuckles flaunt, and roses blow
Almost uncultured: Some with dark green leaves
335 Contrast their flowers of pure unsullied white;
Others, like velvet robes of regal state
Of richest crimson, while in thorny moss
Enshrined and cradled, the most lovely, wear
The hues of youthful beauty's glowing cheek.
340 With fond regret I recollect e'en now
In Spring and Summer, what delight I felt
Among these cottage gardens, and how much
Such artless nosegays, knotted with a rush
By village housewife or her ruddy maid,
345 Were welcome to me; soon and simply pleas'd.

---

1 [Smith's note:] Every cottage in this country has its orchard; and I
imagine that not even those of Herefordshire, or Worcestershire, exhibit
a more beautiful prospect, when the trees are in bloom, and the "Pri-
mavera candida e vermiglia," ["Spring, all white and vermillion,"
Petrarch "Sonnet 310," *Petrarch's Lyric Poems*, trans. and ed. Robert M.
Durling (Cambridge, MA; Harvard UP, 1976), 488–89] is every where
so enchanting.
2 Cf. description of the "poor cottage," lines 118–21.

An early worshipper at Nature's shrine;[1]
I loved her rudest scenes—warrens, and heaths,
And yellow commons, and birch-shaded hollows,
And hedge rows, bordering unfrequented lanes
350 Bowered with wild roses, and the clasping woodbine
Where purple tassels of the tangling vetch[2]
With bittersweet, and bryony inweave,[3]
And the dew fills the silver bindweed's cups[4]—
I loved to trace the brooks whose humid banks
355 Nourish the harebell, and the freckled pagil;[5]
And stroll among o'ershadowing woods of beech,
Lending in Summer, from the heats of noon
A whispering shade; while haply there reclines
Some pensive lover of uncultur'd flowers,
360 Who, from the tumps[6] with bright green mosses clad,
Plucks the wood sorrel,[7] with its light thin leaves,
Heart-shaped, and triply folded; and its root
Creeping like beaded coral; or who there
Gathers, the copse's pride, anémones,[8]
365 With rays like golden studs on ivory laid
Most delicate: but touch'd with purple clouds,
Fit crown for April's fair but changeful brow.

---

1 Compare William Wordsworth's "I, so long / A worshipper of Nature"
passage in "Lines Written a Few Miles above Tintern Abbey, on Revisit-
ing the Banks of the Wye During a Tour, July 13, 1798" (1798), *Lyrical
Ballads 1798 and 1800*, ed. Michael Gamer and Dahlia Porter (Peterbor-
ough, ON: Broadview, 2008), beginning lines 152–53). *BH* contains a
number of Smithian echoes of Wordsworth's poem, including the
hedgerows in this passage (line 349) and the conversation between
brother and sister (lines 267–81).
2 [Smith's note:] Vetch.—Vicia sylvatica.
3 [Smith's note:] Bittersweet.—Solanum dulcamara. Bryony.—Bryonia
alba.
4 [Smith's note:] Bindweed.—Convolvulus sepium.
5 [Smith's note:] Harebell.—Hyacinthus non scriptus. Pagil.—Primula
veris.
6 Small rounded hills or mounds.
7 [Smith's note:] Oxalis acetosella.
8 [Smith's note:] Anemóne nemorosa.—It appears to be settled on late
and excellent authorities, that this word should not be accented on the
second syllable, but on the penultima. I have however ventured the more
known accentuation, as more generally used, and suiting better the
nature of my verse.

Ah! hills so early loved! in fancy still
I breathe your pure keen air; and still behold
370 Those widely spreading views, mocking alike
The Poet and the Painter's utmost art.
And still, observing objects more minute,
Wondering remark the strange and foreign forms
Of sea-shells; with the pale calcareous soil
375 Mingled, and seeming of resembling substance.[1]
Tho' surely the blue Ocean (from the heights
Where the downs westward trend, but dimly seen)
Here never roll'd its surge. Does Nature then
Mimic, in wanton mood, fantastic shapes
380 Of bivalves, and inwreathed volutes, that cling
To the dark sea-rock of the wat'ry world?
Or did this range of chalky mountains, once[2]
Form a vast bason, where the Ocean waves
Swell'd fathomless? What time these fossil shells,
385 Buoy'd on their native element, were thrown
Among the imbedding calx: when the huge hill
Its giant bulk heaved, and in strange ferment
Grew up a guardian barrier, 'twixt the sea
And the green level of the sylvan weald.

---

1 [Smith's note:] Among the crumbling chalk I have often found shells,
some quite in a fossil state and hardly distinguishable from chalk.
Others appeared more recent; cockles, muscles, and periwinkles, I well
remember, were among the number; and some whose names I do not
know. A great number were like those of small land snails. It is now
many years since I made these observations. The appearance of sea-
shells so far from the sea excited my surprise, though I then knew
nothing of natural history. I have never read any of the late theories of
the earth, nor was I ever satisfied with the attempts to explain many of
the phenomena which call forth conjecture in those books I happened
to have had access to on this subject. [Kevis Goodman suggests that for
Smith and her contemporaries the term "conjecture" would have evoked
a specific mode of "conjectural history," which worked from observed
particulars or known effects to invisible causes ("Conjectures on Beachy
Head: Charlotte Smith's Geological Poetics and the Ground of the
Present," *ELH* 81.3 (2014): 995–96).]
2 [Smith's note:] The theory here slightly hinted at, is taken from an idea
started by Mr. White. [Gilbert White (1720–93) was a pioneering British
naturalist. Smith is referring to his *The Natural History and Antiquities of
Selborne* (1789).]

390   Ah! very vain is Science's proudest boast,
      And but a little light its flame yet lends
      To its most ardent votaries; since from whence
      These fossil forms are seen, is but conjecture,
      Food for vague theories, or vain dispute,
395   While to his daily task the peasant goes,
      Unheeding such inquiry; with no care
      But that the kindly change of sun and shower,
      Fit for his toil the earth he cultivates.
      As little recks° the herdsman of the hill,   *understands*
400   Who on some turfy knoll, idly reclined,
      Watches his wether flock; that deep beneath
      Rest the remains of men, of whom is left[1]
      No traces in the records of mankind,
      Save what these half obliterated mounds
405   And half fill'd trenches doubtfully impart
      To some lone antiquary; who on times remote,
      Since which two thousand years have roll'd away,
      Loves to contemplate. He perhaps may trace,
      Or fancy he can trace, the oblong square
410   Where the mail'd legions, under Claudius, rear'd[2]
      The rampire,° or excavated fossé° delved;   *rampart / ditch or trench*
      What time the huge unwieldy Elephant
      Auxiliary reluctant, hither led,[3]

---

1 [Smith's note:] These Downs are not only marked with traces of
   encampments, which from their forms are called Roman or Danish; but
   there are numerous tumuli [barrows, or burial mounds] among them.
   Some of which having been opened a few years ago, were supposed by a
   learned antiquary to contain the remains of the original natives of the
   country.
2 [Smith's note:] That the legions of Claudius [the Roman Emperor
   Claudius (10 BCE–54 CE)] were in this part of Britain appears certain.
   Since this emperor received the submission of Cantii, Atrebates, Ireno-
   bates, and Regni, in which latter denomination were included the people
   of Sussex.
3 [Smith's note:] In the year 1740, some workmen digging in the park at
   Burton in Sussex, discovered, nine feet below the surface, the teeth and
   bones of an elephant; two of the former were seven feet eight inches in
   length. There were besides these, tusks, one of which broke in removing
   it, a grinder not at all decayed, and a part of the jaw-bone, with bones of
   the knee and thigh, and several others. Some of them remained very
   lately at Burton House, the seat of John Biddulph, Esq. Others were in
   possession of the Rev. Dr. Langrish, minister of Petworth   *(continued)*

From Afric's forest glooms and tawny sands,
415 First felt the Northern blast, and his vast frame
Sunk useless; whence in after ages found,
The wondering hinds, on those enormous bones
Gaz'd; and in giants dwelling on the hills[1]
Believed and marvell'd—

                Hither, Ambition, come!
420 Come and behold the nothingness of all
For which you carry thro' the oppressed Earth,
War, and its train of horrors—see where tread
The innumerous hoofs of flocks above the works
By which the warrior sought to register
425 His glory, and immortalize his name—

---

at that period, who was present when some of these bones were taken
up, and gave it as his opinion, that they had remained there since the
universal deluge. The Romans under the Emperor Claudius probably
brought elephants into Britain. Milton, in the Second Book of his
History, in speaking of the expedition, says that "He like a great eastern
king, with armed elephants, marched through Gallia" [Milton, *The
History of Britain* (1670); see Jacqueline Labbe (ed.), *Works of Charlotte
Smith*, vol. 14 (London: Pickering and Chatto, 2007), 248–49n94]. This
is given on the authority of Dion Cassius, in his Life of the Emperor
Claudius [as part of Dio Cassius's (155–235 CE) *Roman History*]. It has
therefore been conjectured, that the bones found at Burton might have
been those of one of these elephants, who perished there soon after its
landing; or dying on the high downs, one of which, called Duncton Hill,
rises immediately above Burton Park, the bones might have been
washed down by the torrents of rain, and buried deep in the soil. They
were not found together, but scattered at some distance from each
other. The two tusks were twenty feet apart. I had often heard of the ele-
phant's bones at Burton, but never saw them; and I have no books to
refer to. I think I saw, in what is now called the National Museum at
Paris, the very large bones of an elephant, which were found in North
America: though it is certain that this enormous animal is never seen in
its natural state, but in the countries under the torrid zone of the old
world. I have, since making this note, been told that the bones of the
rhinoceros and hippopotamus have been found in America.

1 [Smith's note:] The peasants believe that the large bones sometimes
found belonged to giants, who formerly lived on the hills. The devil also
has a great deal to do with the remarkable forms of hill and vale: the
Devil's Punch Bowl, the Devil's Leaps, and the Devil's Dyke, are names
given to deep hollows, or high and abrupt ridges, in this and the neigh-
bouring county.

The pirate Dane, who from his circular camp[1]
Bore in destructive robbery, fire and sword
Down thro' the vale, sleeps unremember'd here;
And here, beneath the green sward, rests alike
430   The savage native, who his acorn meal[2]
Shar'd with the herds, that ranged the pathless woods;
And the centurion, who on these wide hills
Encamping, planted the Imperial Eagle.[3]
All, with the lapse of Time, have passed away,
435   Even as the clouds, with dark and dragon shapes,
Or like vast promontories crown'd with towers,
Cast their broad shadows on the downs: then sail
Far to the northward, and their transient gloom
Is soon forgotten.

                But from thoughts like these,
440   By human crimes suggested, let us turn
To where a more attractive study courts
The wanderer of the hills; while shepherd girls
Will from among the fescue bring him flowers,[4]
Of wonderous mockery; some resembling bees
445   In velvet vest, intent on their sweet toil,[5]
While others mimic flies, that lightly sport[6]
In the green shade, or float along the pool,
But here seem perch'd upon the slender stalk,

---

1   [Smith's note:] The incursions of the Danes were for many ages the
    scourge of this island.
2   [Smith's note:] The Aborigines of this country lived in woods, unshel-
    tered but by trees and caves; and were probably as truly savage as any of
    those who are now termed so.
3   Standard of the Roman Empire.
4   [Smith's note:] The grass called Sheep's Fescue (Festuca ovina) clothes
    these Downs with the softest turf.
5   [Smith's note:] Ophrys apifera, Bee Ophrys, or Orchis, found plentifully
    on the hills, as well as the next.
6   [Smith's note:] Ophrys muscifera.—Fly Orchis. [Swedish botanist Carl]
    Linnaeus [1707–78], misled by the variations to which some of this
    tribe are really subject, has perhaps too rashly esteemed all those which
    resemble insects, as forming only one species, which he terms Ophrys
    insectifera. See English Botany. [Labbe notes that here Smith quotes
    verbatim from James Edward Smith and James Sowerby, *English Botany;*
    or, Coloured Figures of British plants, with their Essential Characters, Syn-
    onyms, and Places of Growth, 36 vols. (London: J. Davis, 1790–1814),
    1.64 (Labbe, *Works of Charlotte Smith* 14.249 n101).]

And gathering honey dew. While in the breeze
450   That wafts the thistle's plumed seed along,
Blue bells wave tremulous.[1] The mountain thyme[2]
Purples the hassock of the heaving mole,
And the short turf is gay with tormentil,[3]
And bird's foot trefoil, and the lesser tribes
455   Of hawkweed;[4] spangling it with fringed stars.—
Near where a richer tract of cultur'd land
Slopes to the south; and burnished by the sun,
The guardian of the flock, with watchful care,[5]
Repels by voice and dog the encroaching sheep—
460   While his boy visits every wired trap[6]
That scars the turf; and from the pit-falls takes
The timid migrants, who from distant wilds,[7]
Warrens, and stone quarries, are destined thus
To lose their short existence. But unsought

---

1   [Smith's note:] Blue bells (Campanula rotundifolia).
2   [Smith's note:] Mountain thyme—Thymus serpyllum. "It is a common
    notion, that the flesh of sheep which feed upon aromatic plants, particu-
    larly wild thyme, is superior in flavour to other mutton. The truth is,
    that sheep do not crop these aromatic plants, unless now and then by
    accident, or when they are first turned on hungry to downs, heaths, or
    commons; but the soil and situations favourable to aromatic plants,
    produce a short sweet pasturage, best adapted to feeding sheep, whom
    nature designed for mountains, and not for turnip grounds and rich
    meadows. The attachment of bees to this, and other aromatic plants, is
    well known." Martyn's Miller. [Thomas Martyn, *The Gardener's and
    Botanist's Dictionary ... by the Late Philip Miller ... To Which Are Now
    Added a Complete Enumeration and Description of All Plants* (1797–1807)
    (Curran, *Poems of Charlotte Smith* 236n).]
3   [Smith's note:] Tormentil—Tormentilla reptans.
4   [Smith's note:] Trefoil.—Trifolium ornithopoides. Hawkweed.—Hiera-
    cium, many sorts.
5   [Smith's note:] The downs, especially to the south, where they are less
    abrupt, are in many places under the plough; and the attention of the
    shepherds is there particularly required to keep the flocks from
    trespassing.
6   [Smith's note:] Square holes cut in the turf, into which a wire noose is
    fixed, to catch Wheatears. Mr. White says, that these birds (Motacilla
    œnanthe) are never taken beyond the river Adur, and Beding Hill; but
    this is certainly a mistake.
7   [Smith's note:] These birds are extremely fearful, and on the slightest
    appearance of a cloud, run for shelter to the first rut, or heap of stones,
    that they see.

465   By Luxury yet, the Shepherd still protects
        The social bird, who from his native haunts[1]
        Of willowy current, or the rushy pool,
        Follows the fleecy croud, and flirts and skims,
        In fellowship among them.

                              Where the knoll
470   More elevated takes the changeful winds,
        The windmill rears its vanes; and thitherward
        With his white load,[2] the master travelling,
        Scares the rooks rising slow on whispering wings,
        While o'er his head, before the summer sun
475   Lights up the blue expanse, heard more than seen,
        The lark sings matins;° and above the clouds   *morning prayers*
        Floating, embathes his spotted breast in dew.
        Beneath the shadow of a gnarled thorn,
        Bent by the sea blast,[3] from a seat of turf
480   With fairy nosegays strewn, how wide the view![4]
        Till in the distant north it melts away,
        And mingles indiscriminate with clouds:
        But if the eye could reach so far, the mart
        Of England's capital, its domes and spires
485   Might be perceived—Yet hence the distant range
        Of Kentish hills,[5] appear in purple haze;
        And nearer, undulate the wooded heights,
        And airy summits,[6] that above the mole

---

1   [Smith's note:] The Yellow Wagtail.—Motacilla flava. It frequents the banks of rivulets in winter, making its nest in meadows and corn-fields. But after the breeding season is over, it haunts downs and sheepwalks, and is seen constantly among the flocks, probably for the sake of the insects it picks up. In France the shepherds call it *La Bergeronette*, and say it often gives them, by its cry, notice of approaching danger.

2   Grain being brought to the mill to be ground into flour.

3   [Smith's note:] The strong winds from the south-west occasion almost all the trees, which on these hills are exposed to it, to grow the other way.

4   [Smith's note:] So extensive are some of the views from these hills, that only the want of power in the human eye to travel so far, prevents London itself being discerned. Description falls so infinitely short of the reality, that only here and there, distinct features can be given.

5   [Smith's note:] A scar of chalk in a hill beyond Sevenoaks in Kent, is very distinctly seen of a clear day.

6   [Smith's note:] The hills above Dorking in Surry; over almost the whole extent of which county the prospect extends.

Rise in green beauty; and the beacon'd ridge
490 Of Black-down shagg'd with heath,[1] and swelling rude
Like a dark island from the vale; its brow
Catching the last rays of the evening sun
That gleam between the nearer park's old oaks,
Then lighten up the river, and make prominent
495 The portal, and the ruin'd battlements[2]
Of that dismantled fortress; rais'd what time
The Conqueror's successors fiercely fought,
Tearing with civil feuds the desolate land.
But now a tiller of the soil dwells there,
500 And of the turret's loop'd and rafter'd halls
Has made an humbler homestead—Where he sees,
Instead of armed foemen, herds that graze
Along his yellow meadows; or his flocks
At evening from the upland driv'n to fold—

505 In such a castellated[3] mansion once
A stranger chose his home; and where hard by
In rude disorder fallen, and hid with brushwood
Lay fragments gray of towers and buttresses,
Among the ruins, often he would muse—
510 His rustic meal soon ended, he was wont
To wander forth, listening the evening sounds
Of rushing milldam, or the distant team,
Or night-jar, chasing fern-flies:[4] the tir'd hind

---

1 [Smith's note:] This is an high ridge, extending between Sussex and
Surry. It is covered with heath, and has almost always a dark appear-
ance. On it is a telegraph [a beacon].
2 [Smith's note:] In this country there are several of the fortresses or
castles built by Stephen of Blois, in his contention for the kingdom, with
the daughter of Henry the First, the empress Matilda [the battle for the
English crown fought between 1135 and 1154]. Some of these are now
converted into farm houses.
3 Built like a castle, with turrets and battlements.
4 [Smith's note:] Dr. Aikin remarks, I believe, in his essay "On the Appli-
cation of Natural History to the Purposes of Poetry," how many of our
best poets have noticed the same circumstance, the hum of the Dor
Beetle (Scarabæus stercorarius,) among the sounds heard by the evening
wanderer. [In *An Essay on the Application of Natural History to Poetry*
(London: J. Johnson, 1777), 7–8 (Curran, *Poems of Charlotte Smith*
239n).] I remember only one instance in which the more remarkable,
though by no means uncommon noise, of the Fern Owl, or Goatsucker,

Pass'd him at nightfall, wondering he should sit
515 On the hill top so late: they from the coast
Who sought bye paths with their clandestine load,
Saw with suspicious doubt, the lonely man
Cross on their way: but village maidens thought
His senses injur'd; and with pity say
520 That he, poor youth! must have been cross'd in love—
For often, stretch'd upon the mountain turf
With folded arms, and eyes intently fix'd
Where ancient elms and firs obscured a grange,
Some little space within the vale below,
525 They heard him, as complaining of his fate,
And to the murmuring wind, of cold neglect
And baffled hope he told.—The peasant girls
These plaintive sounds remember, and even now
Among them may be heard the stranger's songs.

---

530   Were I a Shepherd on the hill
            And ever as the mists withdrew
        Could see the willows of the rill
        Shading the footway to the mill
            Where once I walk'd with you—

535   And as away Night's shadows sail,
            And sounds of birds and brooks arise,
        Believe, that from the woody vale

---

is mentioned. It is called the Night Hawk, the Jar Bird, the Churn Owl,
and the Fern Owl, from its feeding on the Scarabæus solstitialis, or
Fern Chafer, which it catches while on the wing with its claws, the
middle toe of which is long and curiously serrated, on purpose to hold
them. It was this bird that was intended to be described in the Forty-
second Sonnet (Smith's Sonnets [note by 1807 ed.]). I was mistaken in
supposing it as visible in November; it is a migrant, and leaves this
country in August. I had often seen and heard it, but I did not then
know its name or history. It is called Goatsucker (Caprimulgus), from a
strange prejudice taken against it by the Italians, who assert that it
sucks their goats; and the peasants of England still believe that a
disease in the backs of their cattle, occasioned by a fly, which deposits
its egg under the skin, and raises a boil, sometimes fatal to calves, is the
work of this bird, which they call a Puckeridge. Nothing can convince
them that their beasts are not injured by this bird, which they therefore
hold in abhorrence.

I hear your voice upon the gale
        In soothing melodies;

540   And viewing from the Alpine height,
            The prospect dress'd in hues of air,
        Could say, while transient colours bright
        Touch'd the fair scene with dewy light,
            'Tis, that *her* eyes are there!

545   I think, I could endure my lot
            And linger on a few short years,
        And then, by all but you forgot,
        Sleep, where the turf that clothes the spot
            May claim some pitying tears.

550   For 'tis not easy to forget
            One, who thro' life has lov'd you still,
        And you, however late, might yet
        With sighs to Memory giv'n, regret
            The Shepherd of the Hill.

        —————

555 Yet otherwhile it seem'd as if young Hope
    Her flattering pencil gave to Fancy's hand,
    And in his wanderings, rear'd to sooth his soul
    Ideal bowers of pleasure—Then, of Solitude
    And of his hermit life, still more enamour'd,
560 His home was in the forest; and wild fruits
    And bread sustain'd him. There in early spring
    The Barkmen[1] found him, e'er the sun arose;
    There at their daily toil, the Wedgecutters[2]
    Beheld him thro' the distant thicket move.
565 The shaggy dog following the truffle hunter,[3]
    Bark'd at the loiterer; and perchance at night
    Belated villagers from fair or wake,

1   [Smith's note:] As soon as the sap begins to rise, the trees intended for
    felling are cut and barked. At which time the men who are employed in
    that business pass whole days in the woods.
2   [Smith's note:] The wedges used in ship-building are made of beech
    wood, and great numbers are cut every year in the woods near the
    Downs.
3   [Smith's note:] Truffles are found under the beech woods, by means of
    small dogs trained to hunt them by the scent.

While the fresh night-wind let the moonbeams in
Between the swaying boughs, just saw him pass,
570 And then in silence, gliding like a ghost
He vanish'd! Lost among the deepening gloom.—
But near one ancient tree, whose wreathed roots
Form'd a rude couch, love-songs and scatter'd rhymes,
Unfinish'd sentences, or half erased,
575 And rhapsodies like this, were sometimes found—

————

Let us to woodland wilds repair
  While yet the glittering night-dews seem
To wait the freshly-breaking air,
  Precursive of the morning beam,
580 That rising with advancing day,
Scatters the silver drops away.

An elm, uprooted by the storm,
  The trunk with mosses gray and green,
Shall make for us a rustic form,
585   Where lighter grows the forest scene;
And far among the bowery shades,
Are ferny lawns and grassy glades.

Retiring May to lovely June
  Her latest garland now resigns;
590 The banks with cuckoo-flowers[1] are strewn,
  The woodwalks blue with columbines,
And with its reeds, the wandering stream
Reflects the flag-flower's[2] golden gleam.

There, feathering down the turf to meet,
595   Their shadowy arms the beeches spread,
While high above our sylvan seat,
  Lifts the light ash its airy head;
And later leaved, the oaks between
Extend their bows of vernal green.

---

1 [Smith's note:] Cuckoo-flowers.—Lychnis dioica. Shakespeare describes
the Cuckoo buds as being yellow. [*Love's Labour's Lost* 5.2.871.] He
probably meant the numerous Ranunculi, or March marigolds (Caltha
palustris) which so gild the meadows in Spring; but poets have never
been botanists. The Cuckoo flower is the Lychnis floscuculi.
2 [Smith's note:] Flag-flower.—Iris pseudoacorus.

600   The slender birch its paper rind
            Seems offering to divided love,
        And shuddering even without a wind
            Aspins, their paler foliage move,
        As if some spirit of the air
605   Breath'd a low sigh in passing there.

        The Squirrel in his frolic mood,
            Will fearless bound among the boughs;
        Yaffils[1] laugh loudly thro' the wood,
            And murmuring ring-doves tell their vows;
610   While we, as sweetest woodscents rise,
        Listen to woodland melodies.

        And I'll contrive a sylvan room
            Against the time of summer heat,
        Where leaves, inwoven in Nature's loom,
615   Shall canopy our green retreat;
        And gales that "close the eye of day"[2]
        Shall linger, e'er they die away.

        And when a sear and sallow hue
            From early frost the bower receives,
620   I'll dress the sand rock cave for you,
            And strew the floor with heath and leaves,
        That you, against the autumnal air
        May find securer shelter there.

        The Nightingale will then have ceas'd
625   To sing her moonlight serenade;
        But the gay bird with blushing breast,[3]
            And Woodlarks still will haunt the shade,[4]

---

1   [Smith's note:] Yaffils.—Woodpeckers (picus); three or four species in
    Britain.
2   [Smith's note:] "And liquid notes that close the eye of day." *Milton.*
    ["O Nightingale" (1645), line 5. See Appendix B1, p. 238.] The idea
    here meant to be conveyed is of the evening wind, so welcome after a
    hot day of Summer, and which appears to sooth and lull all nature into
    tranquillity.
3   [Smith's note:] The Robin (Motacilla rubecula) which is always heard
    after other songsters have ceased to sing.
4   [Smith's note:] The Woodlark (Alauda nemorosa) sings very late.

And by the borders of the spring
Reed-wrens will yet be carolling[1]

630 The forest hermit's lonely cave
        None but such soothing sounds shall reach,
    Or hardly heard, the distant wave
        Slow breaking on the stony beach;
    Or winds, that now sigh soft and low,
635 Now make wild music as they blow.

    And then, before the chilling North
        The tawny foliage falling light,
    Seems, as it flits along the earth,
        The footfall of the busy Sprite,
640 Who wrapt in pale autumnal gloom,
    Calls up the mist-born Mushroom.

    Oh! could I hear your soft voice there,
        And see you in the forest green
    All beauteous as you are, more fair
645   You'ld look, amid the sylvan scene,
    And in a wood-girl's simple guise,
    Be still more lovely in mine eyes.

    Ye phantoms of unreal delight,
        Visions of fond delirium born!
650 Rise not on my deluded sight,
        Then leave me drooping and forlorn
    To know, such bliss can never be,
    Unless loved like me.

    ———————

    The visionary, nursing dreams like these,
655 Is not indeed unhappy. Summer woods
    Wave over him, and whisper as they wave,
    Some future blessings he may yet enjoy.
    And as above him sail the silver clouds,
    He follows them in thought to distant climes,
660 Where, far from the cold policy of this,
    Dividing him from her he fondly loves,
    He, in some island of the southern sea,

1 [Smith's note:] Reed-wrens (Motacilla arundinacea) sing all the summer
and autumn, and are often heard during the night.

May haply build his cane-constructed bower[1]
Beneath the bread-fruit, or aspiring palm,
665 With long green foliage rippling in the gale.
Oh! let him cherish his ideal bliss—
For what is life, when Hope has ceas'd to strew
Her fragile flowers along its thorny way?[2]
And sad and gloomy are his days, who lives
Of Hope abandon'd!

670   Just beneath the rock
Where Beachy overpeers the channel wave,
Within a cavern mined by wintry tides
Dwelt one,[3] who long disgusted with the world
And all its ways, appear'd to suffer life
675 Rather than live; the soul-reviving gale,
Fanning the bean-field, or the thymy heath,
Had not for many summers breathed on him;
And nothing mark'd to him the season's change,
Save that more gently rose the placid sea,
680 And that the birds which winter on the coast
Gave place to other migrants; save that the fog,
Hovering no more above the beetling cliffs
Betray'd not then the little careless sheep[4]
On the brink grazing, while their headlong fall

---

1 [Smith's note:] An allusion to the visionary delights of the new discov-
ered islands [the various islands of the Pacific, visited by Captain James
Cook (1728–79) in his late-eighteenth-century voyages], where it was
first believed men lived in a state of simplicity and happiness; but where,
as later enquiries have ascertained, that exemption from toil, which the
fertility of their country gives them, produces the grossest vices; and a
degree of corruption that late navigators think will end in the extirpation
of the whole people in a few years.
2 This echoes Sonnet LXXII, line 14, as well as the sentiments and
imagery of many of Smith's other sonnets.
3 [Smith's note:] In a cavern almost immediately under the cliff called
Beachy Head, there lived, as the people of the country believed, a man
of the name of Darby, who for many years had no other abode than this
cave, and subsisted almost entirely on shell-fish. He had often adminis-
tered assistance to ship-wrecked mariners; but venturing into the sea on
this charitable mission during a violent equinoctial storm, he himself
perished. As it is above thirty years since I heard this tradition of Parson
Darby (for so I think he was called): it may now perhaps be forgotten.
4 [Smith's note:] Sometimes in thick weather the sheep feeding on the
summit of the cliff, miss their footing, and are killed by the fall.

685   Near the lone Hermit's flint-surrounded home,
       Claim'd unavailing pity; for his heart
       Was feelingly alive to all that breath'd;
       And outraged as he was, in sanguine youth,
       By human crimes, he still acutely felt
       For human misery.

690   Wandering on the beach,
       He learn'd to augur° from the clouds of heaven,   *divine or predict*
       And from the changing colours of the sea,
       And sullen murmurs of the hollow cliffs,
       Or the dark porpoises,[1] that near the shore
695   Gambol'd and sported on the level brine
       When tempests were approaching: then at night
       He listen'd to the wind; and as it drove
       The billows with o'erwhelming vehemence
       He, starting from his rugged couch, went forth
700   And hazarding a life, too valueless,
       He waded thro' the waves, with plank or pole
       Towards where the mariner in conflict dread
       Was buffeting for life the roaring surge;
       And now just seen, now lost in foaming gulphs,
705   The dismal gleaming of the clouded moon
       Shew'd the dire peril. Often he had snatch'd
       From the wild billows, some unhappy man
       Who liv'd to bless the hermit of the rocks.
       But if his generous cares were all in vain,
710   And with slow swell the tide of morning bore
       Some blue swol'n cor'se to land; the pale recluse
       Dug in the chalk a sepulchre—above
       Where the dank sea-wrack mark'd the utmost tide,
       And with his prayers perform'd the obsequies
       For the poor helpless stranger.

715   One dark night
       The equinoctial wind blew south by west,
       Fierce on the shore;—the bellowing cliffs were shook
       Even to their stony base, and fragments fell
       Flashing and thundering on the angry flood.
720   At day-break, anxious for the lonely man,
       His cave the mountain shepherds visited,

---

1 [Smith's note:] Delphinus phocœna.

Tho' sand and banks of weeds had choak'd their way—
He was not in it; but his drowned cor'se
By the waves wafted, near his former home
725 Receiv'd the rites of burial. Those who read
Chisel'd within the rock, these mournful lines,
Memorials of his sufferings, did not grieve,
That dying in the cause of charity
His spirit, from its earthly bondage freed,
730 Had to some better region fled for ever.

SELECTED ADDITIONAL POEMS

From *Elegiac Sonnets* Volume One

Elegy[1]

"DARK gathering clouds involve the threatening skies,
   The sea heaves conscious of the impending gloom,
Deep, hollow murmurs from the cliffs arise;
   They come!—the Spirits of the Tempest come!

5 Oh, may such terrors mark the approaching night
      As reign'd on that these streaming eyes deplore!
   Flash, ye red fires of heaven! with fatal light,
      And with conflicting winds ye waters! roar.

   Loud and more loud, ye foaming billows! burst;
10   Ye warring elements! more fiercely rave,
   Till the wide waves o'erwhelm the spot accurst
      Where ruthless Avarice finds a quiet grave!"

   Thus with clasp'd hands, wild looks, and streaming hair,
      While shrieks of horror broke her trembling speech,
15 A wretched maid—the victim of Despair,
      Survey'd the threatening storm and desart beech:

   Then to the tomb where now the father slept
      Whose rugged nature bade her sorrows flow,
   Frantic she turn'd—and beat her breast and wept,
20   Invoking vengeance on the dust below.

   "Lo! rising there above each humbler heap,
      Yon cypher'd stones *his* name and wealth relate,

---

1 [Smith's note:] This elegy is written on the supposition that an indigent
   young woman had been addressed by the son of a wealthy yeoman, who
   resenting his attachment, had driven him from home, and compelled
   him to have recourse for subsistence to the occupation of a pilot, in
   which, in attempting to save a vessel in distress, he perished.
       The father dying, a tomb is supposed to be erected to his memory in
   the church-yard mentioned in Sonnet the 44th ["Written at the Church
   Yard at Middleton in Sussex"]. And while a tempest is gathering, the
   unfortunate young woman comes thither; and courting the same death
   as had robbed her of her lover, she awaits its violence, and is at length
   overwhelmed by the waves.

Who gave his son—remorseless—to the deep,
    While I, his living victim, curse my fate.

25 Oh! my lost love! no tomb is placed for thee,
    That may to strangers' eyes thy worth impart!
Thou hast no grave but in the stormy sea!
    And no memorial but this breaking heart!

Forth to the world, a widow'd wanderer driven,
30   I pour to winds and waves the unheeded tear,
Try with vain effort to submit to Heaven,
    And fruitless call on him—'who cannot hear.'[1]

Oh! might I fondly clasp him once again,
    While o'er my head the infuriate billows pour,
35 Forget in death this agonizing pain,
    And feel his father's cruelty no more!

Part, raging waters! part, and shew beneath,
    In your dread caves, his pale and mangled form;
Now, while the Demons of Despair and Death
40   Ride on the blast, and urge the howling storm!

Lo! by the lightning's momentary blaze,
    I see him rise the whitening waves above,
No longer such as when in happier days
    He gave the enchanted hours—to me and love.

45 Such, as when daring the enchased sea,
    And courting dangerous toil, he often said
That every peril, one soft smile from me,
    One sigh of speechless tenderness o'erpaid.

But dead, disfigured, while between the roar
50   Of the loud waves his accents pierce mine ear,
And seem to say——Ah, wretch! delay no more,
    But come, unhappy mourner!—meet me here.

---

1 [Smith's note:] "I fruitless mourn to him who cannot hear, / And weep
the more because I weep in vain." Gray's exquisite Sonnet; in reading
which it is impossible not to regret that he wrote only one. [Thomas
Gray (1716–71), "Sonnet on the Death of Mr Richard West" (1742),
lines 13–14. See Appendix A1.]

Plate 5.   Elegy

Corbould del.   Heath sculp.t

Published Jan.y 1.1789.by T. Cadell Strand.

Yet, powerful Fancy! bid the phantom stay,
    Still let me hear him!—'Tis already past!
55 Along the waves his shadow glides away,
    I lose his voice amid the deafening blast!

    Ah! wild Illusion, born of frantic Pain!
    He hears not, comes not from his watery bed!
    My tears, my anguish, my despair are vain,
60   The insatiate Ocean gives not up its dead!

    'Tis not his voice!—Hark! the deep thunders roll!
    Upheaves the ground—the rocky barriers fail!
    Approach, ye horrors that delight my soul!
    Despair, and Death, and Desolation, hail!"

65 The Ocean hears—The embodied waters come—
    Rise o'er the land, and with resistless sweep
    Tear from its base the proud aggressor's tomb,
    And bear the injured to eternal sleep!

Thirty-eight

Addressed to Mrs H——Y[1]

    IN early youth's enclouded scene,
    The brilliant morning of eighteen,
    With health and sprightly joy elate
        We gazed on life's enchanting spring,
5   Nor thought how quickly time would bring
    The mournful period—Thirty-eight.

    Then the starch maid, or matron sage,
    Already of that sober age,
    We view'd with mingled scorn and hate;
10   In whose sharp words, or sharper face,
        With thoughtless mirth we loved to trace
    The sad effects of—Thirty-eight.

---

1 This poem is address to Eliza Hayley (1750–97), the wife of William
   Hayley (1745–1820), to whom Smith dedicated the first edition of *ES*.
   On William Hayley, see p. 51, note 1.

Till saddening, sickening at the view,
We learn'd to dread what Time might do;
15 And then preferr'd a prayer to Fate
    To end our days ere that arrived;
    When (power and pleasure long survived)
We met neglect and—Thirty-eight.

But Time, in spite of wishes, flies,
20 And Fate our simple prayer denies,
And bids us Death's own hour await:
    The auburn locks are mix'd with grey,
    The transient roses fade away,
But Reason comes at—Thirty-eight.

25 Her voice the anguish contradicts
That dying vanity inflicts;
Her hand new pleasures can create,
    For us she opens to the view
    Prospects less bright—but far more true,
30 And bids us smile at—Thirty-eight.

No more shall *Scandal*'s breath destroy
The social converse we enjoy
With bard or critic tête à tête;—
    O'er Youth's bright blooms her blights shall pour,
35   But spare the improving friendly hour
That Science gives to—Thirty-eight.

Stripp'd of their gaudy hues by Truth,
We view the glitt'ring toys of youth,
And blush to think how poor the bait
40   For which to public scenes we ran,
    And scorn'd of sober Sense the plan
Which gives content at—Thirty-eight.

Tho' Time's inexorable sway
Has torn the myrtle[1] bands away,
45 For other wreaths 'tis not too late,
    The amaranth's[2] purple glow survives,

---

1 Myrtle is associated with love, and with Venus, the Goddess of love.
2 See Sonnet XX, in which Smith also associates amaranth, a mythical
   flower with petals that never fade, with friendship.

And still Minerva's° olive lives   *goddess of wisdom*
On the calm brow of—Thirty-eight.

With eye more steady we engage
50 To contemplate approaching age,
And life more justly estimate;
    With firmer souls, and stronger powers,
    With reason, faith, and friendship ours,
    We'll not regret the stealing hours
55 That lead from Thirty—even to Forty-eight.

From *Elegiac Sonnets* Volume Two

The Dead Beggar
An Elegy[1]

Addressed to a LADY, who was affected at seeing the Funeral of
a nameless Pauper, buried at the Expence of the Parish,
in the Church-Yard at Brighthelmstone, in November 1792

SWELLS then thy feeling heart, and streams thine eye
   O'er the deserted being, poor and old,
Whom cold, reluctant, Parish Charity
   Consigns to mingle with his kindred mold?

5 Mourns't thou, that *here* the time-worn sufferer ends
   Those evil days still threatening woes to come;
Here, where the friendless feel no want of friends,
   Where even the houseless wanderer finds an home?

What tho' no kindred croud in sable forth,
10   And sigh, or seem to sigh, around his bier;
Tho' o'er his coffin with the humid earth
   No children drop the unavailing tear?

---

1 [Smith's note:] I have been told that I have incurred blame for having
used in this short composition, terms that have become obnoxious to
certain persons. Such remarks are hardly worth notice; and it is very
little my ambition to obtain the suffrage of those who suffer party preju-
dice to influence their taste; or of those who desire that because they
have themselves done it, every one else should be willing to sell their
birth-rights, the liberty of thought, and of expressing thought, for the
promise of a mess of pottage [stew]. [A reference to line 20 of the poem,
"vindicates the insulted rights of Man." This language echoes the title of
Thomas Paine's *Rights of Man* (1791) and Mary Wollstonecraft's treatise
A Vindication of the Rights of Men (1790).]
    It is surely not too much to say, that in a country like ours, where
such immense sums are annually raised for the poor, there ought to be
some regulation which should prevent any miserable deserted being
from perishing through want, as too often happens to such objects as
that on whose interment these stanzas were written.
    It is somewhat remarkable that a circumstance exactly similar is the
subject of a short poem called the Pauper's Funeral, in a volume lately
published by Mr. Southey [Robert Southey (1774–1843), *Poems* (1797),
47–48].

Rather rejoice that *here* his sorrows cease,
    Whom sickness, age, and poverty oppress'd;
15 Where Death, the Leveller, restores to peace
    The wretch who living knew not where to rest.

Rejoice, that tho' an outcast spurn'd by Fate,
    Thro' penury's rugged path his race he ran;
In earth's cold bosom, equall'd with the great,
20   Death vindicates the insulted rights of Man.

Rejoice, that tho' severe his earthly doom,
    And rude, and sown with thorns the way he trod,
Now, (where unfeeling Fortune cannot come)
    He rests upon the mercies of his GOD.

The Female Exile[1]

Written at Brighthelmstone in Nov. 1792

NOVEMBER's chill blast on the rough beach is howling,
    The surge breaks afar, and then foams to the shore,
Dark clouds o'er the sea gather heavy and scowling,
    And the white cliffs re-echo the wild wintry roar.

5 Beneath that chalk rock, a fair stranger reclining,
    Has found on damp sea-weed a cold lonely seat;
Her eyes fill'd with tears and her heart with repining,
    She starts at the billows that burst at her feet.

There, day after day, with an anxious heart heaving,
10   She watches the waves where they mingle with air;
For the sail which, alas! all her fond hopes deceiving,
    May bring only tidings to add to her care.

---

1 [Smith's note:] This little Poem, of which a sketch first appeared in
blank verse in a Poem called "The Emigrants" [lines 1.200–32], was
suggested by the sight of the group it attempts to describe—a French
lady and her children. The drawing from which the print is taken I owe
to the taste and talents of a lady, whose pencil has bestowed the highest
honor this little book can boast. [The drawing was done in response to
Smith's poem by Henrietta (Harriet) Duncannon, countess of Bessbor-
ough (1761–1821). For Smith's response to the drawing see her letter in
Appendix C1.]

Loose stream to wild winds those fair flowing tresses,
    Once woven with garlands of gay Summer flowers;
15 Her dress unregarded, bespeaks her distresses,
    And beauty is blighted by grief's heavy hours.

Her innocent children, unconscious of sorrow,
    To seek the gloss'd shell, or the crimson weed stray;
Amused with the present, they heed not to-morrow,
20   Nor think of the storm that is gathering to day.[1]

The gilt, fairy ship, with its ribbon-sail spreading,
    They launch on the salt pool the tide left behind;
Ah! victims—for whom *their* sad mother is dreading
    The multiplied miseries that wait on mankind!

25 To fair fortune born, she beholds them with anguish,
    Now wanderers with her on a once hostile soil,
Perhaps doom'd for life in chill penury to languish,
    Or abject dependence, or soul-crushing toil.

But the sea-boat, her hopes and her terrors renewing,
30   O'er the dim grey horizon now faintly appears;
She flies to the quay, dreading tidings of ruin,
    All breathless with haste, half expiring with fears.

Poor mourner!—I would that my fortune had left me
    The means to alleviate the woes I deplore;
35 But like thine my hard fate has of affluence bereft me,
    I can warm the cold heart of the wretched no more!

---

1 Pastor Fido echoes this image in his poem "On Passing the RETREAT
    of CHARLOTTE SMITH, *near* Chichester, in Sussex." See Appendix
    E3.

Engraved by J. Neagle from a Drawing by the Right Hon. the Countess of Besborough

The gilt fairy Ship, with its ribbon sail spreading,
They launch on the salt Pool the tide left behind.
Ah, Victims for whom their sad Mother is dreading,
The multiplied Miseries that wait on Mankind!

Published May 25.ᵗʰ 1797, by Cadell and Davies, Strand

From *Beachy Head* (1807)

Flora[1]

REMOTE from scenes, where the o'erwearied mind
Shrinks from the crimes and follies of mankind,
From hostile menace, and offensive boast,
Peace, and her train of home-born pleasures lost;
5   To fancy's reign, who would not gladly turn,
And lose awhile, the miseries they mourn
In sweet oblivion? Come then, Fancy! deign,
Queen of ideal pleasure, once again,
To lend thy magic pencil, and to bring
10 Such lovely forms, as in life's happier spring,
On the green margin of my native Wey,
Before mine infant eyes were wont to play,
And with that pencil, teach me to describe
The enchanting goddess of the flowery tribe,
15 Whose first prerogative it is to chase
The clouds that hang on languid beauty's face;[2]
And, while advancing suns and tepid showers,
Lead on the laughing Spring's delicious hours,
Bid the wan maid the hues of health assume,
20 Charm with new grace, and blush with fresher bloom.

The vision comes!—While slowly melt away,
Night's hovering shades before the eastern ray,
Ere yet declines the morning's humid star,
Fair Fancy brings her; in her leafy car
25 Flora descends, to dress the expecting earth,
Awake the germs,° and call the buds to birth;   *seeds*
Bid each hybernacle[3] its cell unfold,
And open silken leaves, and eyes of gold!

Of forest foliage of the firmest shade
30 Enwove by magic hands, the car was made;

---

1 Ancient Italian goddess of flowers and fertility.
2 [Smith's note:] "The spleen is seldom felt where Flora reigns— / The lowering eye, the petulance, the frown / And sullen sadness, that do shade, distort, / And mar the face of Beauty, when no cause / For such immeasurable grief appears, / These Flora banishes." Cowper. [William Cowper (1731–1800), *The Task* (1785), 1.455–58. Smith substitutes the word "woe" in Cowper for "grief."]
3 The winter covering of a plant bud.

Oak, and the ample Plane, without entwined,
And Beech and Ash the verdant concave lin'd;
The Saxifrage,[1] that snowy flowers emboss,
Supplied the seat; and of the mural moss
35 The velvet footstool rose, where lightly rest,
Her slender feet in Cypripedium° drest.   *orchids*
The tufted rush,[2] that bears a silken crown,
The floating feathers of the thistle's down,
In tender hues of rainbow lustre dyed,
40 The airy texture of her robe supplied,
And wild convolvuli,[3] yet half unblown,
Form'd, with their wreathing buds, her simple zone,
Some wandering tresses of her radiant hair,
Luxuriant floated on the enamour'd air;
45 The rest were by the Scandix'[4] points confin'd
And graced a shining knot, her head behind—
While, as a sceptre of supreme command,
She waved the Anthoxanthum[5] in her hand.
Around the goddess, as the flies that play,
50 In countless myriads in the western ray,
The sylphs[6] innumerous throng; whose magical powers
Guard the soft buds, and nurse the infant flowers;
Round the sustaining stems weak tendrils bind,
And save the pollen from dispersing wind;
55 From suns too ardent, shade their transient hues,
And catch in odorous cups translucent dews.
The ruder tasks of others are, to chase
From vegetable life the insect race,
Break the polluting thread the spider weaves,
60 And brush the aphis[7] from th' unfolding leaves.

---

1 [Smith's note:] Saxifraga hypniodes.—Moss Saxifrage, commonly called
   Ladies' Cushion.
2 [Smith's note:] Eriophorum angustifolium.
3 [Smith's note:] Convolvulus arvensis—a remarkably pretty plant, but no
   favourite with the husbandman.
4 [Smith's note:] Scandix pecten—Venus' comb, or Shepherd's needle.
5 [Smith's note:] Anthoxantham odoratum—Vernal Meadow Grass. It is
   to this grass that hay owes its fine odour.
6 A fairy-like being that inhabits the air.
7 [Smith's note:] Aphis, or Aphides—These are the "myriads brushed
   from Russian wilds;" the blights, cankers, lice or vermin, to use
   common phrases, that so often disfigure, and destroy the fairest veg-
   etable productions.

For conquest arm'd these pigmy warriors wield
The thorny lance, and spread the hollow shield
Of lichen[1] tough; or bear, as silver bright,
Lunaria's[2] pearly circlet, firm and light.
65   On the helm'd head the crimson foxglove[3] glows,
Or Scutellaria[4] guards the martial brows,
While the Leontodon[5] its plumage rears,
And o'er the casque° in waving grace appears;   *helmet*
With stern undaunted eye, one warlike chief
70   Grasps the tall club from Arum's[6] blood-dropt leaf;
This, with the Burdock's[7] hooks annoys his foes,
The purple thorn that borrows from the Rose.
In honeyed nectarines couched, some drive away
The forked insidious earwig from his prey;
75   Fearless the scaled libellula[8] assail,
Dart their keen lances at the encroaching snail;
Arrest the winged ant, on pinions light,
And strike the headlong beetle in his flight.
Nor less assiduous round their lovely queen,
80   The lighter forms of female fays° are seen;   *fairies*
Rich was the purple vest Floscella wore,
Spun of the tufts the Tradescantia[9] bore;
The Cistus'[10] flowers minute her temple graced,
And threads of Yucca[11] bound her slender waist.

---

1 [Smith's note:] Lichen—Of these many have the forms of shields, when in fructification.

2 [Smith's note:] Lunaria annua—Moonward, usually called Honesty.

3 [Smith's note:] Digitalis purpurea.

4 [Smith's note:] Scutellaria galericulata—small skull-cap.

5 [Smith's note:] Leontodon officinalis—Common Dent-de-lion.

6 [Smith's note:] Arum maculatum—Vulgarly Cuckoo pint, or Lords and Ladies.

7 [Smith's note:] Arctium lappa.

8 [Smith's note:] The Dragon-fly, or as it is called in the southern countries, the Horse-stinger, though it preys only on other insects. Several sorts of these are seen about water; but its introduction here is a poetical licence, as it does not feed on, or injure flowers.

9 [Smith's note:] Tradescantia virginica—The silk-like tuft within this plant appears to the eye composed of very fine filaments; but on examining one of these small silky threads through a microscope, it looks like a string of Amethysts.

10 [Smith's note:] Cistus helianthemum. Dwarf Cistus.

11 [Smith's note:] Yucca filamentosa.

85 From the wild bee,[1] whose wond'rous labour weaves,
    In artful folds the rose's fragrant leaves,
    Was borrow'd fair Petalla's light cymar;
    And the Hypericum,[2] with spangling star,
    O'er her fair locks its bloom minute enwreath'd;
90 Then, while voluptuous odours round her breath'd,
    Came Nectarynia; as the arrowy rays
    Of lambent° fire round pictur'd seraphs blaze,   *glowing*
    So did the Passiflora's[3] radii shed,
    Cerulean° glory o'er the sylphid's head,   *azure or deep blue*
95 While round her form, the pliant tendrils twined,
    And clasp'd the scarf that floated on the wind.
    More grave the para-nymph Calyxa drest;
    A brown transparent spatha[4] formed her vest;
    The silver scales that bound her raven hair,
100 Xeranthemum's[5] unfading clayx bear;
    And a light sash of spiral Ophrys[6] press'd
    Her filmy tunic, on her tender breast.
    But where shall images or words be found
    To paint the fair ethereal forms, that round
105 The queen of flowers attended? and the while
    Bask'd in her eyes, and wanton'd in her smile.
    Now towards the earth the gay procession bends,
    Lo! from the buoyant air, the car descends;
    Anticipating then the various year,
110 Flowers of all hues and every month appear,
    From every swelling bulb its blossoms rise;
    Here, blow the Hyacinths of loveliest dyes,
    Breathing of heaven; and there, her royal brows

---

1   [Smith's note:] Apis centuncularis. This insect weaves, or rather cements
    rose leaves together, to form its cell.
2   [Smith's note:] An elegant shrub, of which Cowper thus speaks: "Hyper-
    icum all bloom, so thick a swarm / Of flowers, like flies clothing her
    slender rods, / That scarce a leaf appears" [*The Task* 5.165–67]. It seems
    admirably adapted to a fairy garland.
3   [Smith's note:] Passiflora cerulea.
4   [Smith's note:] The sheath from which many flowers spring, such as the
    Narcissis, &c.
5   [Smith's note:] The scales of one species of the Xeranthemum are par-
    ticularly elegant.
6   [Smith's note:] Ophrys spiralis—Ladies traces.
    The following lines describing well known flowers, notes would be
    superfluous.

Begemmed with pearl, the Crown imperial shews;
115 Peeps the blue Gentian, from the soft'ning ground,
Jonquils and Violets, shed their odours round;
The Honeysuckle rears his scallop'd horn;
A snow of blossoms whiten on the thorn.
Here, like the fatal fruit to Paris given,
120 That spread fell feuds throughout the fabled heaven,
The yellow Rose her golden globe displays;
There lovelier still, among the spiny sprays
Her blushing rivals glow with brighter dyes,
Than paints the summer sun on western skies.
125 And the scarce tinged, and paler Rose unveil
Their modest beauties to the sighing gale.
Thro' the deep woodland's wild uncultur'd scene,
Spreads the soft influence of the floral queen;
See a fair pyramid the Chesnut rear,
130 Its crimson tassels on the Larch appear;
The Fir, dark native of the sullen North,
Owns her soft sway; and slowly springing forth
On the rough Oak are buds minute unfurl'd,
Whose giant produce may command the world!
135 Each forest thicket feels the balmy air,
And plants that love the shade are blowing there.
Rude rocks with Filices° and Bryums° smile,   *ferns / mosses*
And wastes are gay with Thyme and Chamomile.
Ah! yet prolong the dear delicious dream,
140 And trace her power along the mountain stream.
See! from its rude and rocky source, o'erhung
With female fern,[1] and glossy adder's-tongue[2]
Slowly it wells, in pure and chrystal drops,
And steals soft-gliding, thro' the upland copse;
145 Then murmuring on, along the willowy sides,
The reed-bird whispers,[3] and the Halcyon hides;[4]
While among sallows° pale, and birchen bowers,   *a type of willow*
Embarks in Fancy's eye the queen of flowers.

---

1 [Smith's note:] Polypodium filix fœmina.
2 [Smith's note:] Asplenium scolopendrium.
3 [Smith's note:] Motacilla salicaria. The Reed Sparrow, or Willow Wren.
   A bird that in a low and sweet note imitates several others, and sings all
   night.
4 [Smith's note:] Alcedo hispida—The Kingfisher, or halcyon, one of the
   most beautiful of English birds.

O'er her light skiff, of woven bull-rush made,
150　The Water lily[1] lends a polish'd shade;
While Galium[2] there, of pale and silver hue,
And Epilobiums[3] on the banks that grew,
From her soft couch; and as the Sylphs divide,
With pliant arms, the still increasing tide,
155　A thousand leaves among the stream unfold;
Amid its waving swords, in flaming gold
The Iris[4] towers; and here the Arrowhead[5]
And water Crowfoot,[6] more profusely spread
Spangle the quiet current; higher there,
160　As conscious of her claims, in beauty rare,
Her rosy umbels rears the flow'ring Rush,[7]
While with reflected charms the waters blush.
The naiad° now, the year's fair goddess leads,　　*river or stream sprite*
Through richer pastures and more level meads
165　Down to the sea; where even the briny sands
Their product offer to her glowing hands;
For there, by sea-dews nurs'd and airs marine,
The Chelidonium[8] blows; in glaucous[9] green,
Each refluent° tide the thorn'd Eryngium[10] laves,°　　*ebbing / washes*
170　And its pale leaves seem tinctured by the waves;
And half-way up the cliff, whose rugged brow
Hangs o'er the ever toiling surge below,
Springs the light Tamarisk[11]—The summit bare,
Is tufted by the Statice;[12] and there,

1　[Smith's note:] Nymphæ alba.
2　[Smith's note:] Galium palustre—White Ladies' bedstraw.
3　[Smith's note:] Epilobiums—Willow herbs, various species.
4　[Smith's note:] Iris palustris—Yellow Iris.
5　[Smith's note:] Sagittaria sagittifolia.
6　[Smith's note:] Ranunculus aquaticus.
7　[Smith's note:] Butomus umbellatus. The only native of England of the class Enneandria. ·
8　[Smith's note:] Chelidonium glaucium. The horned or sea Poppy.
9　Pale grey or bluish green. The term can also refer to the whitish bloom that covers some plants.
10　[Smith's note:] Eryngium maritimum—Sea Holly.
11　[Smith's note:] Tamarix gallica. This elegant plant is not very uncommon on cliffs in the West of England, and was in 1800 to be found on an high rock to the eastward of the town of Hastings in Sussex.
12　[Smith's note:] Statics armeria—Sea Pink, Sea Lavender, commonly called Thrift, is frequently used for borders of flower-beds. It covers some of the most sterile cliffs.

175   Crush'd by the fisher, as he stands to mark
     Some distant signal or approaching bark,
     The Saltwort's[1] starry stalks are thickly sown,
     Like humble worth, unheeded and unknown!
     From depths where corals spring from chrystal caves,
180   And break with scarlet branch, the eddying waves,
     Where Algae[2] stream, as change the flowing tides,
     And where, half flower, half fish, the Polyp[3] hides,
     And long tenacious bands of sea-lace twine
     Round palm-shaped leaves impearl'd with coralline,
185   Enamour'd Fancy now the sea-maids calls,
     And from their grottos dim, and shell-paved halls,
     Charm'd by her voice, the shining train emerge,
     And buoyant float above the circling surge;
     Green Byssus,[4] waving in the sea-born gales,
190   Form'd their thin mantles, and transparent veils,
     Panier'd in shells or bound with silver strings,
     Of silken pinna;[5] each her trophy brings
     Of plants, from rocks and caverns submarine,
     With leathery branch, and bladder'd buds between;
195   There, its dark folds the pucker'd laver spread,
     With trees in miniature of various red;
     There flag-shaped olive-leaves, depending hung,
     And fairy fans from glossy pebbles sprung;

---

1 [Smith's note:] Salsola kali. This plant when burnt affords a fossile alkali, and is used in the manufacture of glass. The best is brought from the Mediterranean, and forms a considerable article of commerce. It is very frequent on the cliffs on the Sussex coast.

2 [Smith's note:] The algæ include all the sea plants, and some other aquatics.

3 [Smith's note:] The Polypus or Sea Anemone. Coralline is, if I do not misunderstand the only book I have to consult, a shelly substance, the work of sea insects, adhering to stones and to sea-weeds.

4 [Smith's note:] Flos aquæ—Paper byssus; a semitransparent substance floating on the waves.

5 [Smith's note:] The Pinna, or Sea Wing, is contained in a two-valved shell. It consists of fine long silk-like fibres. The Pinna on the coast of Provence, and Italy, is called the Silk-worm of the Sea. Stockings and gloves of exquisite fineness have been made of it. See note 27, to the Economy of Vegetation. [Erasmus Darwin (1731–1802), *Economy of Vegetation* (Part One of *The Botanic Garden*, 1791), p. 72–73. For Darwin, see Appendix A9.]

    The subsequent lines attempt a description of Sea Plants, without any correct classification.

Then her terrestrial train the nereids° meet,   *sea nymph*
200 And lay their spoils saline at Flora's feet.
O! fairest of the fabled forms! that stream,
Dress'd by wild Fancy, thro' the poet's dream,
Still may thy attributes of leaves and flowers,
Thy garden's rich, and shrub-o'ershadow'd bowers,
205 And yellow meads, with Spring's first honours bright,
The child's gay heart, and frolic step invite;
And, while the careless wanderer explores,
The umbrageous° forest, or the rugged shores,   *shady*
Climbs the green down, or roams the broom-clad waste,
210 May Truth, and Nature, form his future taste!
Goddess! on youth's bless'd hours thy gifts bestow;
Bind the fair wreath on virgin-beauty's brow,
And still may Fancy's brightest flowers be wove
Round the gold chains of hymeneal° love.   *marital*
215 But most for those, by Sorrow's hands oppress'd,
May thy beds blossom, and thy wilds be dress'd;
And where by Fortune and the world forgot,
The mourner droops in some sequester'd spot,
("Sad luxury to vulgar minds unknown,"[1])
220 O'er blighted happiness for ever gone,
Yet the dear image seeks not to forget,
But woos his grief, and cherishes regret;
Loving, with fond and lingering pain, to mourn
O'er joys and hopes that never will return;—
225 Thou, visionary power! mayst bid him view
Forms not less lovely, and as transient too;
And while they soothe the wearied pilgrim's eyes,
Afford an antepast° of Paradise.   *foretaste*

Saint Monica[2]

AMONG deep woods is the dismantled scite°   *site*
Of an old Abbey, where the chaunted° rite,   *chanted*
By twice ten brethren of the monkish cowl,
Was duly sung; and requiems for the soul

---

1 Thomas Tickell (1685–1740), "To the Right Honourable Earl of
Warwick, on the Death of Mr. Addison" (1721), line 34.
2 Saint Monica (332–387) was the mother of Saint Augustine of Hippo
(354–430), who wrote about her in his *Confessions* (Book IX). Her feast
day of 4 May fell on Smith's birthday.

5   Of the first founder: For the lordly chief,
     Who flourish'd paramount of many a fief,
     Left here a stipend yearly paid, that they,
     The pious monks, for his repose might say
     Mass and orisons to Saint Monica.

10 Beneath the falling archway overgrown
     With briars, a bench remains, a single stone,
     Where sat the indigent, to wait the dole
     Given at the buttery;° that the baron's soul   *pantry*
     The poor might intercede for; there would rest,
15 Known by his hat of straw with cockles drest,[1]
     And staff and humble weed[2] of watchet° gray,   *light blue*
     The wandering pilgrim; who came there to pray
     The intercession of Saint Monica.

     Stern Reformation[3] and the lapse of years
20 Have reft the windows, and no more appears
     Abbot or martyr on the glass anneal'd;
     And half the falling cloisters are conceal'd
     By ash and elder: the refectory wall
     Oft in the storm of night is heard to fall,
25 When, wearied by the labours of the day,
     The half awaken'd cotters, starting say,
     "It is the ruins of Saint Monica."

     Now with approaching rain is heard the rill°   *small stream*
     Just trickling thro' a deep and hollow gill[4]

---

1 According to Stuart Curran, "A hat with a cockle-shell attached to it signified that the pilgrim had visited the shrine of St. James of Campostella in Spain" (*Poems of Charlotte Smith*, 299n).

2 Clothing, dress.

3 When Henry VIII (r. 1509–47) broke away from the Catholic Church in the sixteenth century, abbeys were abandoned, and many of them were sacked. Most eventually fell into ruin.

4 [Smith's note:] Gill is a word understood in many parts of England, and more particularly in the North, to mean an hollow watercourse, or an hollow overshadowed with coppice and brush wood, such as frequently occur in hilly countries. It has the same meaning as Gully, a deep trench in the earth, so frequent in the West Indies, where the tropic rains tear away the earth and make hollows, which in process of time become overgrown with trees, and the resort of monkeys and other animals.

30 By osiers,° and the alder's crowding bush,   *willows*
    Reeds, and dwarf elder, and the pithy rush,
    Choak'd and impeded: to the lower ground
    Slowly it creeps; there traces still are found
    Of hollow squares, embank'd with beaten clay,
35 Where brightly glitter'd in the eye of day
    The peopled waters of Saint Monica.

    The chapel pavement, where the name and date,
    Or monkish rhyme, had mark'd the graven plate,
    With docks and nettles now is overgrown;
40 And brambles trail above the dead unknown—
    Impatient of the heat, the straggling ewe
    Tinkles her drowsy bell, as nibbling slow
    She picks the grass among the thistles gray,
    Whose feather'd seed the light air bears away,
45 O'er the pale relicks of Saint Monica.

    Reecho'd by the walls, the owl obscene
    Hoots to the night; as thro' the ivy green
    Whose matted tods° the arch and buttress bind,[1]   *clumps*
    Sobs in low gusts the melancholy wind:
50 The Conium[2] there, her stalks bedropp'd with red,
    Rears, with Circea, neighbour of the dead;
    Atropa[3] too, that, as the beldams° say,   *old women*
    Shews her black fruit to tempt and to betray,
    Nods by the mouldering shrine of Monica.

55 Old tales and legends are not quite forgot.
    Still Superstition hovers o'er the spot,
    And tells how here, the wan and restless sprite,
    By some way-wilder'd peasant seen at night,
    Gibbers and shrieks,[4] among the ruins drear;

---

1 [Smith's note:] A judicious friend objected to this expression as obscure;
   but it has the authority of Spencer. "At length within an *Ivy tod* / There
   shrouded was the little God." *Sheperd's Calender*. Ecl. 3. [Edmund
   Spenser (c. 1552–99), *The Shepheardes Calender* (1579), Eclogue 3, lines
   67–68.] And I think I could quote other poets as having used it.
2 [Smith's note:] Conium masculatum.
3 [Smith's note:] Atropa belladonna.
4 [Smith's note:] The word Gibber has been also objected to; but besides
   that it appears to me very expressive, I have for its use the example of

60 And how the friar's lanthorn° will appear   *lantern*
   Gleaming among the woods, with fearful ray,
   And from the church-yard take its wavering way,
   To the dim arches of Saint Monica.

   The antiquary comes not to explore,
65 As once, the unrafter'd roof and pathless floor;
   For now, no more beneath the vaulted ground
   Is crosier, cross, or sculptur'd chalice found,
   Nor record telling of the wassail ale,[1]
   What time the welcome summons to regale,
70 Given by the matin peal on holiday,
   The villagers rejoicing to obey,
   Feasted, in honour of Saint Monica.

   Yet often still at eve, or early morn,
   Among these ruins shagg'd with fern and thorn,
75 A pensive stranger from his lonely seat
   Observes the rapid martin, threading fleet
   The broken arch: or follows with his eye,
   The wall-creeper[2] that hunts the burnish'd fly;
   Sees the newt basking in the sunny ray,[3]
80 Or snail that sinuous winds his shining way,
   O'er the time-fretted walls of Monica.

   He comes not here, from the sepulchral stone
   To tear the oblivious pall that Time has thrown,
   But meditating, marks the power proceed
85 From the mapped lichen, to the plumed weed,

Shakspeare: "—the sheeted dead / Did squeal and *gibber* in the streets of
Rome." Hamlet. [*Hamlet* 1.1.115–16; Smith substitutes "squeal" for
Shakespeare's "squeak."]

1 Spiced or mulled wine drunk during celebrations for Christmas Eve and
  Twelfth Night.
2 [Smith's note:] Certhia muraria—This bird frequents old towers,
  castles, and walls; feeding on insects.
3 [Smith's note:] Lacerta vulgaris—This reptile in its complete state lives
  among rubbish and old walls. It is the Wall Newt of Shakespeare, as part
  of the food of poor Tom: "The wall newt and the water newt, / With rats
  and mice and such small deer, / Have been Tom's food for many a year."
  [*King Lear* 3.4.119–27. Freely quoted.] And is commonly known by the
  name of Evett or Eft; and from its ugliness is held in abhorrence, and is
  supposed to be venomous, though perfectly harmless.

From thready mosses to the veined flower,
The silent, slow, but ever active power
Of Vegetative Life, that o'er Decay
Weaves her green mantle, when returning May
90 Dresses the ruins of Saint Monica.

Oh Nature! Ever lovely, ever new,
He whom his earliest vows has paid to you
Still finds, that life has something to bestow;
And while the dark Forgetfulness they go,
95 Man, and the works of man; immortal Youth,
Unfading Beauty, and eternal Truth,
Your Heaven-indited volume will display,
While Art's elaborate monuments decay,
Even as these shatter'd aisles, deserted Monica!

From *The Miscellaneous Prose Works of Sir Walter Scott, Bart:
Biographical Memoirs* (1829)[1]

To My Lyre

Such as thou art, my faithful Lyre,
For all the great and wise admire,
   Believe me, I would not exchange thee,
Since e'en adversity could never
5   Thee from my anguish'd bosom sever,
   Or time or sorrow e'er estrange thee.
Far from my native fields removed,
From all I valued, all I loved;
   By early sorrows soon beset,
10 Annoy'd and wearied past endurance,
With drawbacks,[2] bottomry,[3] ensurance,
   With samples drawn, and tare and tret:[4]
With Scrip,[5] and Omnium,[6] and Consols,[7]
With City Feasts and Lord Mayors' Balls,
15   Scenes that to me no joy afforded;
For all the anxious Sons of Care,
From Bishopsgate to Temple Bar,[8]
   To my young eyes seem'd gross and sordid.
Proud city dames, with loud shrill clacks,
20 ("The wealth of nations on their backs,")

---

1 Catherine Ann Dorset (1750–1817), Smith's sister, published a biogra-
phy of the writer that appeared in Sir Walter Scott's (1771–1832)
volume of biographical memoirs. "To My Lyre" was included in this
biography. For more information see p. 161, note 1.
2 Refund or remittance on goods for export.
3 Money borrowed by the owner of a ship that uses the ship as
collateral.
4 A tret is an allowance for waste, after deduction of tare (the weight of a
container deducted from gross weight to obtain the weight of an empty
container). These are all terms that would have been familiar to mer-
chants.
5 Certificate or a receipt used to redeem a credit.
6 The total of items in any stock or fund.
7 Consolidated annuities, a form of government bond.
8 Bishopsgate is one of the key financial districts of London, while the
area around Temple Bar is one of the key legal districts of the city.

Their clumsy daughters and their nieces,
Good sort of people! and well meaners,
But they could not be my congeners,
    For I was of a different species.
25 Long were thy gentle accents drown'd,
Till from Bow-bells[1] detested sound
    I bore thee far, my darling treasure;
And unrepining left for thee
Both Calepash and Callipee,[2]
30   And sought green fields, pure air, and leisure.
Who that has heard thy silver tones—
Who that the Muse's influence owns,
    Can at my fond attachment wonder,
That still my heart should own thy pow'r?
35 Thou! who hast soothed each adverse hour,
    So thou and I will never sunder.
In cheerless solitude, bereft
Of youth and health, thou still art left,
    When hope and fortune have deceived me;
40 Thou, far unlike the summer friend,
Didst still my falt'ring steps attend,
    And with thy plaintive voice relieved me.
And as the time ere long must come
When I lie silent in the tomb,
45   Thou wilt preserve these mournful pages;
For gentle minds will love my verse,
And Pity shall my strains rehearse,
    And tell my name to distant ages.

---

1 The Smiths lived near St-Mary-le-Bow church in Cheapside, East
   London, in the early part of their marriage.
2 Cuts of turtle meat considered to be delicacies.

Appendix A: Key Precursors and Contemporaries

[In addition to the works of contemporaries included in this appendix, in Appendix B a number of sonnets by John Milton (1608–74) can be found in the body of the essay by John Thelwall (1764–1834), including Milton's "O Nightingale," which was a touchstone for later poets, including Smith. In Appendix E there is also a sample of the poetry that appeared about Smith in contemporary newspapers and magazines.]

1. Thomas Gray, "Sonnet on the Death of Mr Richard West" (1742), *Poems by Mr. Gray* (Dublin: William Sleater, 1775), 166

[Thomas Gray (1716–71) wrote this sonnet in 1742 on the death of his friend Richard West (1716–42) at the age of 25. Not published until 1775, it was a relatively recent work when Smith began writing and it helped to establish the potential of the sonnet as an elegiac form. Smith frequently references Gray, and her poems have direct thematic resonances with this sonnet, as well as with Gray's "Ode on a Distant Prospect of Eton College" (1747) and his "Elegy Written in a Country Churchyard" (1750).]

> In vain to me the smiling mornings shine,
>   And redd'ning Phoebus lifts his golden fire:[1]
> The birds in vain their amorous descant° join;   *song*
>   Or chearful fields resume their green attire:
> 5 These ears, alas! for other notes repine,
>   A different object do these eyes require.
> My lonely anguish melts no heart but mine;
>   And in my breast the imperfect joys expire.
> Yet morning smiles the busy race to chear,
> 10   And new-born pleasure brings to happier men:
> The fields to all their wonted tribute bear:
>   To warm their little loves the birds complain:
> I fruitless mourn to him, that cannot hear,
>   And weep the more, because I weep in vain.
>   EPITAPH

---

1 The sun. In Greek mythology the sun god Phoebus Apollo was also god of poetry, music, and healing. "[G]olden fire" echoes Phoebus Apollo's golden lyre, the source of his power.

2. From William Cowper, *The Task, A Poem in Six Books. To Which are Added, by the same Author, an Epistle to Joseph Hill, Esq. Tirocinium, or a Review of Schools, and the History of John Gilpin* (London: J. Johnson, 1785)

[Smith dedicated *The Emigrants* to William Cowper (1731–1800), and his use of blank verse influenced her own writing. In her dedication to Cowper she describes *The Task* as a work that "honoured Liberty," alluding to the passage from Book 5 that follows. She suggests that it "seems to foretell" the fall of the Bastille of 1789, specifically "the demolition of regal despotism in France." On Cowper, *The Task*, and Cowper's response to *The Emigrants*, see p. 127, note 1.]

From Book 5 *The Winter Morning Walk*, lines 363–448

    Whose freedom is by suff'rance, and at will
Of a superior, he is never free.
365 Who lives, and is not weary of a life
Exposed to manacles, deserves them well.
The state that strives for liberty, though foiled
And forced t' abandon what she bravely sought,
Deserves at least applause for her attempt,
370 And pity for her loss. But that's a cause
Not often unsuccessful; pow'r usurp'd
Is weakness when oppos'd; conscious of wrong
'Tis pusillanimous and prone to flight.
But slaves that once conceive the glowing thought
375 Of freedom, in that hope itself possess
All that the contest calls for; spirit, strength,
The scorn of danger, and united hearts
The surest presage of the good they seek.[1]

    Then shame to manhood, and opprobrious more
380 To France, than all her losses and defeats
Old or of later date, by sea or land,
Her house of bondage worse than that of old

---

1 [Cowper's note:] The author hopes that he shall not be censured for unnecessary warmth upon so interesting a subject. He is aware that it is become almost fashionable to stigmatize such sentiments as no better than empty declamation. But it is an ill symptom, and peculiar to modern times.

Which God avenged on Pharaoh,[1]—the Bastile.
Ye horrid tow'rs, th' abode of broken hearts,
385 Ye dungeons and ye cages of despair,
That monarchs have supplied from age to age
With music such as suits their sov'reign ears,
The sighs and groans of miserable men!
There's not an English heart that would not leap
390 To hear that ye were fall'n at last, to know
That ev'n our enemies, so oft employed
In forging chains for us, themselves were free.
For he that values liberty, confines
His zeal for her predominance within
395 No narrow bounds; her cause engages him
Wherever pleaded. 'Tis the cause of man.
There dwell the most forlorn of human kind
Immured though unaccused, condemn'd untried,[2]
Cruelly spared, and hopeless of escape.
400 There like the visionary emblem seen
By him of Babylon,[3] life stands a stump,
And filletted about with hoops of brass,
Still lives, though all its pleasant boughs are gone.
To count the hour-bell and expect no change;
405 And ever as the sullen sound is heard,
Still to reflect that though a joyless note
To him whose moments all have one dull pace,
Ten thousand rovers in the world at large
Account it music; that it summons some
410 To theatre or jocund feast or ball;
The wearied hireling finds it a release
From labor; and the lover that has chid
Its long delay, feels ev'ry welcome stroke
Upon his heart-strings trembling with delight—
415 To fly for refuge from distracting thought
To such amusements as ingenious woe
Contrives, hard-shifting and without her tools—

---

1 Cowper's comparison refers to Egypt, the Israelites' enslavement there, and
   God's subsequent punishment, according to Exodus, of the Pharoah and his
   hosts by drowning in the Red Sea (James Sambrook, ed., *The Task and Selected
   Other Poems*, by William Cowper [London: Longman, 1994], 178n).
2 Under "lettres de cachet," warrants bearing the royal seal, many prisoners
   were incarcerated in the Bastille and elsewhere without trial or opportunity
   for defence or appeal.
3 See Daniel 4:1–26 (Sambrook, *The Task* 179n).

To read engraven on the mouldy walls,
In stagg'ring types, his predecessor's tale,
420 A sad memorial, and subjoin his own—
To turn purveyor to an overgorged
And bloated spider, till the pamper'd pest
Is made familiar, watches his approach,
Comes at his call, and serves him for a friend—
425 To wear out time in numb'ring to and fro
The studs that thick emboss his iron door,
Then downward and then upward, then aslant
And then alternate, with a sickly hope
By dint of change to give his tasteless task
430 Some relish, till the sum exactly found
In all directions, he begins again
Oh comfortless existence! hemm'd around
With woes, which who that suffers, would not kneel
And beg for exile, or the pangs of death?
435 That man should thus encroach on fellow man,
Abridge him of his just and native rights,
Eradicate him, tear him from his hold
Upon th' endearments of domestic life
And social, nip his fruitfulness and use,
440 And doom him for perhaps an heedless word
To barrenness and solitude and tears,
Moves indignation. Makes the name of king,
(Of king whom such prerogative can please)
As dreadful as the Manichean God,[1]
445 Adored through fear, strong only to destroy.

'Tis liberty alone that gives the flow'r
Of fleeting life its lustre and perfume,
And we are weeds without it.

3. William Bowles, "Sonnet IX. To the River Itchin, near Winton," *Sonnets, Written Chiefly on Picturesque Spots, During a Tour*, 2nd ed. (Bath: R. Cruttwell, 1789)

[William Bowles's (1762–1850) sonnets, originally published as *Fourteen Sonnets, Elegiac and Descriptive* (1789), share Smith's elegiac focus on loss and nature. Samuel Taylor Coleridge (1772–1834) deduced the rules of the English sonnet from the two poets, but, possibly in an

---

1 A reference to the ancient religion of Manichaeism, which was associated with dualism and is here used as a derogatory term for a principle of evil.

effort to separate himself from a potentially female tradition, implicitly signalled a preference for Bowles. This championing was influential on later critics and, until renewed attention was paid to Smith, Bowles was often credited with having begun the sonnet revival of the final decades of the century. For Coleridge's "Introduction to the Sonnets," see Appendix B3.]

Itchin, when I behold thy banks again,
    Thy crumbling margin, and thy silver breast,
    On which the self-same tints still seem to rest,
Why feels my heart the shiv'ring sense of pain?
5   Is it—that many a summer's day has past
Since, in life's morn, I carol'd on thy side?
Is it—that oft, since then, my heart has sigh'd,
    As Youth, and Hope's delusive gleams, flew fast?
Is it—that those, who circled on thy shore,
10 Companions of my youth, now meet no more?
    Whate'er the cause, upon thy banks I bend
Sorrowing, yet feel such solace at my heart,
    As at the meeting of some long-lost friend,
    From whom, in happier hours, we wept to part.

4. Jane West, "On the Sonnets of Mrs. Charlotte Smith," from *Miscellaneous Poems, and a Tragedy* (York: W. Blanchard, 1791), 94–95

[Jane West (1758–1852) was a prolific writer of poetry, novels, conduct literature, essays, and plays, whose anonymously published novel *A Gossip's Story* (1796) was the main source for Jane Austen's *Sense and Sensibility* (1811).[1] West was far more conservative in her political and religious views than Smith. Although this poem reflects West's admiration of her famous contemporary, these ideological differences are evident.]

The widow'd turtle, mourning for her love,
    Breathes the soft plaintive melody of woe:
And streams, that gently steal along the grove,
    In murmurs dear to melancholy flow.

---

1   Paula R. Feldman, "Jane West," *British Women Poets of the Romantic Era: An Anthology* (Baltimore and London: Johns Hopkins UP, 1997), 792.

5 Yet to thy strains, sweet nymph of Arun's vale,
       Harsh is the turtle's note, and harsh the stream,
   Ev'n when their echos die upon the gale,
       Or catch attention by the lunar beam.

   Thy strains soul-harrowing melting pity hears,
10   Yet fears to break thy privacy of pain,
   She blots thy page with sympathetic tears,
       And while she mourns thy wrongs enjoys thy strain.

   Hast thou indeed no solace? does the earth
       Afford no balm thy anguish to relieve?
15 Still must thou feel the pain of suff'ring worth,
       Taught by refinement but to charm and grieve.

   Oh! if despair directs thy pensive eyes
       To where death terminates terrestrial woes,
   May faith from thence exhault them to the skies,
20   Where glory's palm for suffering virtue grows.

   There may thy lyre, whose sweetly magic pow'rs
       From pain'd attention forc'd applauding tears,
   With hallelujahs fill the eternal bowers,
       The theme prolonging through eternal years.

5. From [Frances Burney,] *Brief Reflections Relative to the Emigrant French Clergy: Earnestly Submitted to the Humane Consideration of the Ladies of Great Britain* (London: T. Cadell, 1793), 1–4, 6–7

[*The Emigrants* was only one of a number of pieces published about the situation of the French emigrants in 1793. Other writing included pamphlets by Smith's contemporaries, the novelist Frances Burney (1752–1840) and the moral campaigner Hannah More (1745–1833) (see Introduction, p. 33, note 1). The following excerpt from Burney's pamphlet demonstrates the extent to which Smith was participating in circulating ideas about the necessity for a kind of female sympathy in this debate.]

The astonishing period of political history upon which our days have fallen, robs all former times of wonder, wearies expectation, sickens even hope! while the occurrences of every passing minute have such prevalence over our minds, that public affairs assume the interest of private feelings, affect domestic peace, and occupy not merely the most retired part of mankind, but even mothers, wives, and children with solicitude irresistible.

Yet the amazement which has been excited, though stupendous, though terrific, by the general events that in our neighbour kingdom have convulsed all order, and annihilated tranquility, is feeble, is almost null, compared with that produced by the living contrast of virtue and of guilt exhibited in the natives of one and the same country; virtue, the purest and most disinterested, emanating from the first best cause, religion; and guilt, too heinous for any idea to which we have hitherto given description.

The emigrant FRENCH CLERGY, who present us with the bright side of this picture, are fast verging to a situation of the most necessitous distress; and, notwithstanding the generous collections repeatedly raised, and the severest economy unremittingly exercised in their distribution, if something further is not quickly obtained, all that has been done will prove of no avail, and they must soon end their hapless career, not by paying the debt to nature, but by famine.

That the kingdom at large, in its legislative capacity, will ere long take into consideration a more permanent provision for these pious fugitives, there is every reason to infer from the national interest, which has universally been displayed in their cause. To preserve them in the mean time is the object of present application.

So much has already so bountifully been bestowed in large donations, that it seems wanting in modesty, if not in equity, to make further immediate demands upon heads of houses, and masters of families.

Which way, then, may these destitute wanderers turn for help? To their own country they cannot go back; it is still in the same state of lawless iniquity which drove them from it, still under the tyrannical sway of the sanguinary despots of the Convention.[1]

What then remains? Must their dreadful hardships, their meek endurance, their violated rights, terminate in the death of hunger?

No! there is yet a resource; a resource against which neither modesty nor equity plead; a resource which, on the contrary, had every moral propensity, every divine obligation, in its favour: this resource is FEMALE BENEFICENCE.

★★★★★

The minutest scrutinizer into the rights of charity cannot here start one objection that a little consideration will not supersede. No votaries

---

1 See Introduction, pp. 30–32.

of pleasure, ruined by extravagance and luxury, forfeit pity in censure by imploring your assistance; no slaves of idleness, no dupes of ambition, invite reproof for neglected concerns in soliciting your liberality. The objects of this petition are reduced, indeed, from affluence to penury, but the change has been wrought through the exaltation of their souls, not through the depravity of their conduct.[1] Whatever may be their calls upon our tenderness, their claims to every thinking mind, are still higher to our admiration. Driven from house and home, despoiled of dignities and honours, abandoned to the seas for mercy, to chance for support, many old, some infirm, all impoverished? with mental strength alone allowed them for coping with such an aggregate of evil! Weigh, weigh but a moment their merits and their sufferings, and what will not be sooner renounced than the gratification of serving so much excellence. It is to *itself* the liberal heart does justice in doing justice to the oppressed; they are its own happiest feelings which it nourishes, in nourishing the unfortunate.

6. **Mary Robinson, "Sonnet XLIII,"** *Sappho and Phaon: In a series of Legitimate Sonnets, with Thoughts on Poetical Subjects, and Anecdotes of the Grecian Poetess* **(1796), reprinted from** *Selected Poems*, **ed. Judith Pascoe (Peterborough, ON: Broadview, 2000), 179**

[Smith's contemporary Mary Robinson (1758–1800) produced a 64-sonnet sequence, *Sappho and Phaon* (1796) in the voice of the classical Grecian poetess Sappho, detailing her passionate (but doomed) love for the boatman Phaon. In contrast to the majority of Smith's *Elegiac Sonnets*, Robinson's sequence explicitly takes as its model the Italian (Petrarchan) form. The following sonnet from *Sappho and Phaon* demonstrates a sexual passion that is notably absent from Smith's sonnets. For an excerpt from Robinson's preface to *Sappho and Phaon*, in which she engages in the debate about the sonnet, see Appendix B2, and for Robinson's sonnet addressed to Smith after Smith's son was wounded at Dunkirk, see Appendix E5. For Smith's uneasiness about being associated with Robinson because of her personal life, see Smith's letter in Appendix C1a, p. 246, note 1.]

---

1   Cf. Smith's more ambivalent description of different members of the French clergy in *Em* 1.113–53.

WHILE from the dizzy precipice I gaze,
　　The world receding from my pensive eyes,
　　High o'er my head the tyrant eagle flies,
Cloth'd in the sinking sun's transcendent blaze!
5　The meek-ey'd moon, 'midst clouds of amber plays
　　As o'er the purpling plains of light she hies,°　　　*hurries or hastens*
　　Till the last stream of living lustre dies,
And the cool concave owns her temper'd rays!
　　So shall this glowing, palpitating soul,
10　Welcome returning Reason's placid beam,
　　While o'er my breast the waves Lethean[1] roll,
To calm rebellious Fancy's fev'rish dream;
　　Then shall my Lyre disdain love's dread control,
And loftier passions, prompt the loftier theme!

7. From William Wordsworth, *The Prelude, 1798–99*, ed. Stephen Parrish (Ithaca, NY: Cornell UP, 1977), First Part, lines 1–66

[Wordsworth's (1770–1850) blank verse poem *The Prelude* was not published until 1850, after the poet's death. It would eventually stretch to fourteen books, but he wrote a shorter, two-part version much earlier, during the period in which his work was very much in conversation with Smith's. The first part, the opening of which is presented here, discusses the formative implications of childhood and meditates on the role of Nature. See Introduction, p. 36.]

　　　　　　　Was it for this
　　That one, the fairest of all rivers, loved
　　To blend his murmurs with my Nurse's song,
　　And from his alder shades, and rocky falls,
5　And from his fords and shallows, sent a voice
　　That flowed along my dreams? For this didst thou
　　O Derwent, travelling over the green plains
　　Near my "sweet birthplace,"[2] didst thou, beauteous Stream
　　Make ceaseless music through the night and day,

1　Referring to the river Lethe, the river of oblivion or forgetfulness in Greek mythology. See *ES*, Sonnet V, p. 60.
2　The river Derwent passed close to Wordsworth's birthplace in Cockermouth. The quotation draws attention to this phrase in Samuel Taylor Coleridge's *Frost at Midnight* (1798), line 33.

10 Which with its steady cadence tempering
    Our human waywardness, composed my thoughts
    To more than infant softness, giving me,
    Among the fretful dwellings of mankind,
    A knowledge, a dim earnest of the calm,
15 Which Nature breathes among the fields and groves?
        Beloved Derwent! fairest of all streams!
    Was it for this that I, a four year's child,
    A naked Boy, among thy silent pools
    Made one long bathing of a summer's day?
20 Basked in the sun, or plunged into thy streams,
    Alternate, all a summer's day, or coursed
    Over the sandy fields, and dashed the flowers
    Of yellow grunsel,° or when crag and hill,   *ragwort*
    The woods, and distant Skiddaw's lofty height
25 Were bronzed with a deep radiance, stood alone,
    A naked Savage in the thunder shower?
        And afterwards, 'twas in a later day
    Though early, when upon the mountain-slope
    The frost and breath of frosty wind had snapped
30 The last autumnal crocus, 'twas my joy
    To wander half the night among the cliffs
    And the smooth hollows, where the woodcocks ran
    Along the moonlight turf. In thought and wish,
    That time, my shoulder all with springes° hung,   *snares*
35 I was a fell destroyer. Gentle powers!
    Who give us happiness and call it peace!
    When scudding on from snare to snare I plied
    My anxious visitation, hurrying on,
    Still hurrying hurrying onward, how my heart
40 Panted; among the scattered yew-trees, and the crags
    That looked upon me, how my bosom beat
    With expectation. Sometimes strong desire,
    Resistless, overpowered me, and the bird
    Which was the captive of another's toils
45 Became my prey; and when the deed was done
    I heard among the solitary hills
    Low breathings coming after me, and sounds
    Of undistinguishable motion, steps
    Almost as silent as the turf they trod.
50   Nor less in spring-time, when on southern banks
    The shining sun had from his knot of leaves
    Decoyed the primrose-flower, and when the vales
    And woods were warm, was I a rover then

In the high places, on the lonesome peaks,
55 Among the mountains and the winds. Though mean
And though inglorious were my views,[1] the end
Was not ignoble. Oh, when I have hung
Above the raven's nest, by knots of grass,
Or half-inch fissures in the slipp'ry rock,
60 But ill sustained, and almost, as it seemed,
Suspended by the blast which blew amain,
Shouldering the naked crag, oh at that time,
While on the perilous ridge I hung alone,
With what strange utterance did the loud dry wind
65 Blow through my ears! the sky seemed not a sky
Of earth, and with what motion moved the clouds!

8. Anne Bannerman, "Sonnet VII," from *Poems by Anne Bannerman* (Edinburgh: Mundell & Son, 1800), 105, 110

[Anne Bannerman (1765–1829) was another of the many women writers influenced by Smith. A Scottish poet, her volume of poems included "Sonnets from Petrarch, Ossian, etc.," and ten sonnets based on Johann Wolfgang von Goethe's (1749–1832) *Werther* (1774), much in the manner of Smith (see *ES* Sonnets XXI–XXV and p. 71, note 3). The following sonnet comes from Bannerman's Werter sequence and is keyed into the same scene as Smith's Sonnet XXII.]

SONNET VII[2]

Pierc'd by the rugged thorn, I burst my way
  Thro' tangled thickets, which oppose in vain;
Would that my streaming blood might now allay
  My soul's deep agony and fever'd brain!

---

1 That is, to steal raven's eggs.
2 [Bannerman's note:] I break my way through copses, amongst thorns and briers, which tear me to pieces, and I feel a little relief. Sometimes I lie stretched on the ground, overcome with fatigue, and dying with thirst; sometimes, late in the night, when the moon shines upon my head, I lean against a bending tree in some sequestered forest, and quite worn out and exhausted, I steep till break of day.
  The dismal cell, the sackcloth, the girdle, with sharp points of iron, would be indulgence and luxury in comparison of what I now suffer.

WERTER, Let. XXXV
[Goethe, *The Sorrows of Werter: A German Story*
(London: J. Dodsley, 1779), 1.153–54]

5   Oft, when the shudd'ring damps my frame benumb,
      Shines on my blasted head th' unclouded moon;
      Till, faint with anguish, and with thirst o'ercome,
      Amid the silence of the night's pale noon,

      I sink exhausted till the dawn of morn!
10   O God! the darkest dungeon which entombs
      The living victim, or the racking steel
      By the last tears of groaning nature worne,
      Were ease to what my ebbing life consumes,
      Were bliss and luxury to what I feel!

9. From Erasmus Darwin, *The Temple of Nature; or, the Origin of Society: A Poem, with Philosophical Notes* (London: J. Johnson, 1803)

[Erasmus Darwin (1731–1802), grandfather of Charles Darwin (1809–82), was a physician and natural philosopher who established the popularity of the heavily footnoted "philosophical poem" in the 1790s, combining poetry and science. In addition to footnotes, Darwin also included with his works lengthy endnotes. Like Smith's in *Beachy Head*, Darwin's view of nature was one of ceaseless change inextricably bound up with human history. In this extract from his final scientific poem, he also refers readers to his important medical treatise *Zoonomia; or, Laws of Organic Life* (1794–96), which incorporated early ideas of the theory of evolution, and his two-book poem *The Botanic Garden* (1791), one of the most popular and controversial poems of the 1790s.]

Canto I. Production of Life

295   V. "Organic life beneath the shoreless waves[1]
      Was born, and nurs'd in Ocean's pearly caves;

---

1 [Darwin's note:] The earth was originally covered with water, as appears from some of its highest mountains, consisting of shells cemented together by a solution of part of them, as the limestone rocks of the Alps; Ferber's Travels [*Travels through Italy in the Years 1771 and 1772* (1776)]. It must be therefore concluded, that animal life began beneath the sea.

    Nor is this unanalogous to what still occurs, as all quadrupeds and mankind in their embryon state are aquatic animals; and thus may be said to resemble gnats and frogs. The fetus in the uterus has an organ called the placenta, and fine extremities of the vessels of which permeate the arteries of the uterus, and the blood of the fetus becomes thus oxygenated from the passing stream of the material arterial blood; exactly as is done by the gills of fish from the stream of water, which they occasion to pass through them.

First forms minute,[1] unseen by spheric glass,
Move on the mud, or pierce the watery mass;
These, as successive generations bloom,
300   New powers acquire, and larger limbs assume;
Whence countless groups of vegetation spring,
And breathing realms of fin, and feet, and wing.

    "Thus the tall Oak, the giant of the wood,
Which bears Britannia's thunders on the flood;
305   The Whale, unmeasured monster of the main,
The lordly Lion, monarch of the plain,
The Eagle soaring in the realms of air,
Whose eye undazzled drinks the solar glare,
Imperious man, who rules the bestial crowd,
310   Of language, reason, and reflection proud,
With brow erect, who scorns this earthy sod,
And styles himself the image of his God;
Arose from rudiments of form and sense,
An embryon point,[2] or microscopic ens!

315   "Now in vast shoals beneath the brineless tide,[3]
On earth's firm crust testaceous[4] tribes reside;
Age after age expands the peopled plain,

But the chicken in the egg possesses a kind of aerial respiration, since the extremities of its placental vessels terminate on a membranous bag, which contains air, at the broad end of the egg; and in this the chick in the egg differs from the fetus in the womb, as there is in the egg no circulating maternal blood for the insertion of the extremities of its respiratory vessels, and in this also I suspect that the eggs of birds differ from the spawn of fish; which latter is immersed in water, and which has probably the extremities of its respiratory organ inserted into the soft membrane which covers it, and is in contact with the water.

1 [Darwin's note:] See Additional Note I, on Spontaneous Vitality.

2 [Darwin's note:] The arguments, showing that all vegetables and animals arose from such a small beginning, as a living point or living fibre, are detailed in Zoonomia, Sect. XXXIX.4.9 on Generation.

3 [Darwin's note:] As the salt of the sea has been gradually accumulating, being washed down into it from the recrements of animal and vegetable bodies, the sea must originally have been as fresh as river water; and as it is not saturated with salt, must become annually saline. The sea-water about our island contains at this time from about one twenty-eighth to one thirtieth part of sea salt, and about one eightieth of magnesian salt; Brownrigg on Salt. [William Brownrigg (1711–1800), *On the Art of Making Common Salt* (1748).]

4 Hard-shelled, that is crustaceous.

The tenants perish, but their cells remain;
Whence coral walls[1] and sparry[2] hills ascend
320　From pole to pole, and round the line extend.

10. John Keats, "Sonnet VII: When I have fears that I may cease to be," *Life, Letters and Literary Remains of John Keats* (London: Edward Moxon, 1848), 2:386

[John Keats (1795–1821) was one of the second generation of Romantic poets most influenced by Smith. This sonnet, written in 1817 but published posthumously, owes much to the style, language, and imagery of *Elegiac Sonnets*.]

WHEN I have fears that I may cease to be
　　Before my pen has glean'd my teeming brain,
Before high piled books, in charact'ry,
　　Hold like rich garner the full-ripen'd grain;
5　When I behold, upon the night's starr'd face,
　　Huge cloudy symbols of a high romance,
And think that I may never live to trace
　　Their shadows, with the magic hand of chance;
And when I feel, fair creature of an hour!
10　　That I shall never look upon thee more,
Never have relish in the faery power
　　Of unreflecting love!—then on the shore
Of the wide world I stand along, and think
Till Love and Fame to nothingness do sink.

1　[Darwin's note:] An account of the structure of the earth is given in Botanic Garden, Vol. I. Additional Notes, XVI. XVIII. XIX. XX. XXIII. XXIV.
2　Abounding in spar, a general term for a number of crystalline minerals.

Appendix B: Contemporary Writing on Smith and the Sonnet

1. John Thelwall, "An Essay on the ENGLISH SONNET; illustrated by a comparison between the Sonnets of MILTON and those of CHARLOTTE SMITH," *Universal Magazine* (December 1792): 408–14

[In this lengthy essay, the radical writer John Thelwall (1764–1834) responds to a (possibly imaginary) critic's contention that Charlotte Smith's sonnets are illegitimate because they do not conform to the stricter rhyme schemes characteristic of earlier examples of the genre, including those by John Milton (1608–74). He concludes by asserting the superiority of Smith's sonnets over those of Milton. We have reproduced this essay in full because it is not as readily available elsewhere as the other texts presented in this appendix. We have also reproduced the sonnets from Milton that Thelwall quotes, as valuable contextual material for Smith's work. However, we have not reproduced the Smith sonnets quoted in the essay as they are available in this edition.]

FEW things are more painful to a generous mind, engaged in the pursuits of literature, than to observe the pedantic prejudices in favour of the models of established writers, by which the wings of aspiring genius are shackled, and the efforts of modern invention censured and restrained. This, however, is a mortification that must frequently occur to every one who, surveying for himself the region of letters, observes how the honours of criticism are conferred. The prerogative of name triumphs over the natural distinctions of merit; improvement is decried as heretical innovation; and, in the court of Parnassus,[1] as in those of law, *to be right*, in opposition to precedent, is frequently *to be wrong*.

[The essay then remarks that this is particularly the case with regard to poetry, before going on to discuss Homer, who "rose to the unequalled height of epic poetry, because his imagination was unclogged by the chains of former precedent."]

But leaving this bold imagination to the experiment of some happier age, when poetic genius shall be nourished by more liberal personage, I will venture to observe, that, in the more humble walks of

---

1 The world of literature and poetry.

poetry, (notwithstanding all the empiricism of pedantic critics) there are some who, quitting the dull path of precedent, have presumed, with daring irregularity, to surpass the celebrated writers, for improving upon whose models they have been censured.

Among the foremost of these is to be reckoned the pathetic and elegant Charlotte Smith, whose *illegitimate* sonnets (for the spiritual court of criticism has thought proper to bastardise them) display a more touching melancholy, a more poetical simplicity, nay I will venture to say, a greater vigour and correctness of genius, than any other English poems that I have ever seen, under the same denomination: and I certainly do not mean to except the sonnets of Milton.

Yet I remember to have heard some professed critics express a very different opinion upon this subject; and that, too, upon no better argument than their nonconformity to certain arbitrary regulations, "more honoured (according to my judgement, at least) in the breach than the observance."

To criticism of this kind I was by no means disposed to listen with silent attention. But what was my surprise when I heard one of these "mighty lords of literary sway," after dwelling for a considerable time upon the praises of one of those minor wits, whose passive obedience to the dogmas of the critical divan had secured his approbation, conclude his panegyric by observing, that "his Sonnet was in Milton's best style; which was certainly the highest of all possible praise."

Whether this be the case or not, let those decide who have perused Milton's Sonnets with pleasure: for my part, I confess, I read them as a task; unwilling to be entirely ignorant of any of the beauties of the author of those many sublime and wonderful passages that dignify the Paradise Lost, under whatever pile of dullness or pedantry, those more obscure beauties might be hid.

But the critic I am speaking of was not content with adding the *cloud* of his incense to the effulgence of a reputation too established to be injured even by injudicious praise; he must also cloud, with as ill-founded censure, the rising splendour of our poetical Aurora,[1] and criticise what he appeared to want taste to enjoy.

"Little elegies," said he, "consisting of four stanzas and a couplet, are not more *sonnets* than they are *epic poems*." "Be it so then," replied I, "call them epic poems if you will. The time is coming, I hope when we shall estimate things, not by their titles, but their merits." "But," continued he, "the sonnet is of a particular and arbitrary construction; it partakes of the nature of blank verse, by the lines running into each other at proper intervals."— "Why not write them in blank verse then? For I appeal to every reader of poetry, whether this is the description

1   Roman Goddess of the dawn.

of a kind of versification ever agreeable in English rhyme, except, indeed, in poems of some length, where it is occasionally introduced, with great success, to relieve the ear from that satiety, which the uniform harmony of the couplet might else produce?" But mark the pedantry of the rule that follows.

"Each line," continued he, "of the first eight, rhymes *four times*, and the order in which these rhymes should fall is *decisive.*"

Independent of the difficulty of this (for labour, with this critic, is a requisite ingredient of beauty) it is not enough that all the graces of form are bestowed by nature, and those of motion and gesture by a polished cultivation, hour upon hour must be devoted to the toilet, that the hand of art may be conspicuous in the finishing.—Independent, I say, of the difficulty in this, in a language whose rhymes do not flow with that copious facility, which distinguishes the Italian terminations, let me again appeal to the ear of the reader, and ask him, whether even some of the most beautiful stanzas in Spenser (in which only one of the rhymes is repeated to the fourth, and another to the third time) do not tire the ear by this frequent recurrence of similar sounds, and whether even the exquisite poem of Beattie[1] does not sometimes lose more than it gains by the restraints of this form of versification?

"Of Milton's English sonnet," pursued the critic, "only that to Oliver Cromwell ends with a couplet; but that single instance is a sufficient precedent."—"Bravo!" said I, "does not this smatter a little of the authoritative wisdom of the Roman law, when every hasty judgment of a sottish or tyrannical emperor, became a precedent for the regulation of future judgments? In my humble opinion, the sonnet terminating with a couplet, would not have been a whit less beautiful, even though Milton had omitted this single instance."

"The style of the sonnet," continued the critic, disdaining to reply to so licentious an observation, "should be nervous; and where the subject will properly bear elevation, *sublime*; with which simplicity of language is by no means incompatible. If the subject is familiar and domestic, the style should, though affectionate, be vigorous; though plain, energetic."

With these observations I so perfectly coincide, that I have only quoted them, to shew that all the *essential* qualities required by this hypercritic are to be found in the sonnets, which it was the business of his criticism to decry. What, for example, can be more nervous or sublime than the following sonnet from the novel of *Emmeline*?[2]

---

1 James Beattie (1735–1803) was a Scottish poet and philosopher.
2 Smith published the sentimental novel *Emmeline, or the Orphan of the Castle* in 1788.

[Quotes Sonnet XL in full]

And as for the sonnet on familiar subjects, how enchanting is the ninth of this writer—

"Blest is yon shepherd on the turf reclined," &c.

And the twenty-seventh.

Sighing I see yon little troop at play, &c.

But can the imagination conceive a more charming association of all the requisites called for by the critic, than in the following?

[Quotes Sonnet XI in full]

Nor is it any serious objection to the excellence of this sonnet, that some of the images are borrowed from other poets; since the selection and arrangement sufficiently prove the taste and judgment of the writer, and her claim to imagination is sufficiently substantiated by what she had added, of equal merit, of her own.

The amiable solicitude with which Mrs. Smith has been careful to quote the passages she has made use of, is an argument of the liberality of her mind, as well as the frequent tributes of applause, she has paid to the genius of contemporary and departed writers; a liberality that should have secured her from the harsh treatment of puny critics. But the cold austerity of pedantry is insensible to all such appeals of candour. There seems, however, to be a passage, in Young's "Night Thoughts," which has escaped the attention of Mrs. Smith, to which the first line at least of this sonnet has some obligations:—

Tir'd Nature's soft restorer! balmy Sleep! &c.

But to proceed with the conversation: my critic expatiated on what he called the great models of perfection for the sublime and for the domestic sonnet. In this display of critical acumen, I found that he wandered sometimes into the regions of obscurity; for, with whatever attention I regarded his eloquent declamation, I found it is not easy to develop his meaning, I considered, however, that a little obscurity in these subjects, either in the writer or the speaker is not amiss. It gives an air of mystery to the oracular fiat; that perplexes the judgment of the hearer, and induces him to implicit submission, that he may avoid the trouble of unravelling the meaning.

"The great models of perfection for the sublime and domestic sonnet."—*Domestic sonnet!*—I shall never get past this word. I have heard of domestic virtues, domestic enjoyments, domestic animals, domestic utensils &c. but never of the domestic sonnet before. When we hear a critic talking of domestic poetry, would we not suppose he alluded to some art of cookery in rhyme?—But, "The models," continued my critic, "for the sublime and for the domestic sonnet are Milton's 'To the Soldier to spare his Dwelling place,' and 'To Mr. Lawrence.'"

Let us bring them before the reader, then, that he may know what perfection is.

SONNET VIII.

When the Assault was intended in the City.

Captain or colonel, or knight in arms,
  Whose chance on these defenceless doors may seize,
  If deed of honour *did thee ever please*,
Guard them, and him within *protect from harms*.
He can requite thee, for he knows the charms
  That call fame on such gentle acts as these,
  And he can spread thy name o'er lands and seas,
Whatever clime the sun's bright circle warms.
  Lift not thy spear against the muse's bower:
The great Emathion conquerer[1] did spare
  The house of Pindarus,[2] when temple and tower
Went to the ground: and the repeated air
  Of sad Electra's[3] poet had the power
To save th' Athenian walls from ruin bare.

Such is the sonnet adduced by my very critic; and I must confess, that notwithstanding that it is not entirely free from "certain hardnesses," on which he expatiated much, a noble sonnet it is; yet cer-

---

1 Emathia is a district of Macedonia. The "Emathion conquerer" is Alexander the Great (356–323 BCE).
2 Pindar (518–438 BCE) was the greatest lyric poet of Ancient Greece. His family house in Thebes was spared by Alexander the Great when that city was destroyed by the Macedonians in 335 BCE.
3 In Greek mythology, Electra was the daughter of Agamemnon and Clytemnestra and the sister of Orestes. She persuaded her brother to kill their mother and their mother's lover Aegisthus in revenge for the murder of their father.

tainly not equal in sublimity of expression, either to that of Charlotte Smith above quoted, or that "Written in the Church yard of Middleton on the coast of Sussex," by the same lady.

[Quotes Sonnet XLIV in full]

Perhaps it is not saying too much to declare, that in the narrow compass of these fourteen lines, are included all the requisites of good poetry; vivid painting, numerous harmony, sublimity of thought and expression, and pathos of sentiment. What, in particular, can surpass the thought of breaking the silent sabbath of the grave? But to return to Milton, whose other model of perfection, I find, is his

SONNET XX.

To Mr. Laurence

"Laurence, of virtuous father virtuous son,
   Now that the fields are dank, and ways are mire,
   Where shall we sometimes meet, and by the fire
Help waste a sullen day, what may be won
From the hard season gaining? Time will run
   On smoother, till Favonius[1] re-inspire
   The frozen earth, and clothe in fresh attire
The lily and the rose, that neither sow'd nor spun.
What neat repast shall feast us, light and choice,
   Of Attic taste, with wine, whence we may rise
To hear the lute well touched, or artful voice.
Warble immoral notes and Tuscan air?
He who of those delights can judge, and spare
   To interpose them oft is not unwise."

Nobody will be bold enough to say, that there are not some beautiful thoughts, and some good versification in this sonnet. Yet, surely, there is nothing in it that Mrs. Smith need despair to rival. It is true, that in the melancholy effusions of this charming writer, it would be difficult to find a sonnet that admits a fair comparison with the present; but of the eight, that are epistolary in her collection, I know of no one that need blush to stand by the side of it; though there are some of them which would certainly have been more pleasing to an English ear, but for the officious criticisms that seduced Mrs. Smith,

---

1 The west wind, associated with springtime.

in some of her latter compositions, to the adoption of the Italian model.

But to take up the comparison of fair and liberal grounds, allowing what is due to the different biases of the receptive genius of each, let the admirer of Milton's sonnets bring forward two of his composition, upon any subjects whatever, that can compare with the following of Mrs. Smith.

[Quotes Sonnets IV and XXXVI in full]

Ignorance may perhaps admire the learning, but common sense will say little for the taste, of the man who should refuse to be pleased with these, because they are not what he chuses to term *the true sonnet*. The meaning of the word sonnet is nothing more than *a little song*, or *little poem*; and if we permit the critics to prescribe the number of lines which it is to consist of, it is certainly too much to submit to them also the exact succession of the rhymes. This ought surely to be left to the genius of the writer; or at least to that of the language.

"But Oh!" says the critic, "this is making the art of poetry too easy. The sonnet is certainly the most difficult" (he might have added the most affected) "species of composition; but difficulty well subdued is excellence." Since when? I should be glad to know. I humbly conceive that if the mind of the reader is elevated and delighted with any production of genius, it is a matter of small consequence to him, what was the degree of trouble or facility with which that production was composed: otherwise the more costive the brain of the poet, the greater ought to be the delight of the reader; though I believe in general it will be exactly the reverse.

"Mrs. Smith," continued the admirer of Milton, "says she has been told, that the *regular* sonnet suits not the nature or genius of our language. Surely this assertion cannot be demonstrated, and therefore was not worthy of attention."

"Very true," replied I, sarcastically; "we certainly cannot *demonstrate* a negative. But the presumption being very strong, let us listen to your demonstration of the opposite fact."

"With all my heart," continued he, with much exultation: "Out of eighteen English sonnets written by Milton, four only are bad. The rest, though they are not all free from certain hardnesses, have a pathos, and a greatness in their simplicity, sufficient to endear the legitimate sonnet to every reader of *just taste*; they possess a *characteristic grace*, which can never belong to three elegiac stanzas closing with a couplet."

"Perhaps by a reader of *just taste*," said I, "you mean nothing more than a reader with just such a taste as your own; and understanding you in that sense, I certainly shall not contradict you. And as for the grace that is *characteristic* of the *legitimate* sonnet, never belonging to the *illegitimate* sonnet, this, I flatter myself, is a matter of little consequence, provided we can prove the latter to have a grace of a *better character*; which I think I shall do by the following quotations."

MILTON'S SONNET I

To the Nightingale.

"O Nightingale, that on yon bloomy spray
    Warblest at eve, when all the woods are still,
    Thou with fresh hope the lover's heart dost fill,
While the jolly hours lead on propitious May.
Thy liquid notes that close the eye of day,   ·
    First heard before the shallow cuckoo's bill,
    Portend success in love; O if Jove will
Have link'd that amorous power to thy soft lay,
    Now timely sing, ere the rude bird of hate
Foretell my hopeless doom in some grove nigh;
    As thou from year to year hast sung too late
For my relief, yet hadst no reason why:
    Whether the muse, or love call thee his mate,
Both them I serve, and of their train am I."

To which I will contrast

CHARLOTTE SMITH'S SONNET VII

On the Departure of the Nightingale.

[Quotes Sonnet VII in full]

Now putting the *just taste* and *characteristic graces* of the critic entirely out of the question, let me appeal to any lover of poetry, which of these sonnets fills his mind, his fancy, his ear, with the sweetest associations of sentiment, imagery, and harmony? Which flows with the easiest and most attractive grace, the true sonnet-like versification of Milton, or the elegiac stanza of Charlotte Smith? Nay, and what more than all exposes the disadvantages of the regular sonnet, is, that in almost all of the sonnets of Milton, the last six lines, for which there is more licence, and which indeed are left entirely to the taste of the writer, are eminently superior to the eight that precede.

I shall conclude with observing, that as it was my sole design to vindicate the freedom of English verse from the pedantic chains of the Italian sonnet, and not to decry the merit of a writer, whom every lover of poetry must bow down to with veneration, I have uniformly treated the immortal Milton with the utmost candour, quoting none but his best sonnets, that the question might be treated in the fairest and most conclusive manner. Whoever shall cast his eye over the little poems of that great master of the epic lyre, or even refer to the worst of them quoted by Dr. Johnson, with his usual kindness, in illustration of the word sonnet, in his dictionary, will be convinced, that if I had a heart base enough to attempt to injure the reputation of this awful poet, I might have made a different selection. But the whole region of poetry is not to be seized with one grasp. Every province has its separate competitors. Over the epic field, Milton, of all British bards, triumphs without a rival, Shakespeare in the dramatic, and in the sonnet, Charlotte Smith.

    J.T.

2. **From Mary Robinson, "Preface" to** *Sappho and Phaon: In a series of Legitimate Sonnets, with Thoughts on Poetical Subjects, and Anecdotes of the Grecian Poetess* **(1796), reprinted from** *Selected Poems*, **ed. Judith Pascoe (Peterborough, ON: Broadview, 2000), 144–49**

[Here Smith's contemporary Mary Robinson (1758–1800), in the preface to her own sonnet sequence, engages in the debate about the "legitimate sonnet." Robinson cites Smith in order to move beyond Samuel Johnson's (1709–84) assertion that no "man of eminence" has attempted the form since Milton and she associates the form in particular with women writers. For an example of one of Robinson's own sonnets, see Appendix A6.]

PREFACE

It must strike every admirer of poetical compositions, that the modern sonnet, concluding with two lines, winding up the sentiment of the whole, confines the poet's fancy, and frequently occasions an abrupt termination of a beautiful and interesting picture; and that the ancient, or what is generally denominated, the LEGITIMATE SONNET,[1] may be carried on in a series of sketches, composing, in

---

1 By the term "legitimate sonnet," Robinson is referring to the Petrarchan sonnet. See p. 18, note 3.

parts, one historical or imaginary subject, and forming in the whole a complete and connected story.

[Robinson then discusses and (like Thelwall above) quotes in full Milton's "Sonnet To the Nightingale" (1645) as an example of a legitimate sonnet.]

Dr Johnson describes a Sonnet, as "a short poem, consisting of fourteen lines, of which the rhymes are adjusted by a particular rule." He further adds, "It has not been used by any man of any eminence since MILTON."[1]

Sensible of the extreme difficulty I shall have to encounter, in offering to the world a little wreath, gathered in that path, which, even the best poets have thought it dangerous to tread; and knowing that the English language is, of all others, the least congenial to such an undertaking, (for, I believe, that the construction of this kind of sonnet was originally in the Italian, where the vowels are used almost every other letter,) I only point out the track where more able pens may follow with success; and where the most classical beauties may be adopted, and drawn forth with peculiar advantage.

Sophisticated sonnets are so common, for every rhapsody of rhyme, from six lines to sixty comes under that denomination, that the eye frequently turns from this species of poem with disgust. Every schoolboy, every romantic scribbler, thinks a sonnet a task of little difficulty. From this ignorance in some, and vanity in others, we see the monthly and diurnal publications abounding with ballads, odes, elegies, epitaphs, and allegories, the non-descript ephemera from the heated brains of self-important poetasters, all ushered into notice under the appellation of SONNET!

I confess myself such enthusiastic votary of the Muse, that any innovation which seems to threaten even the least of her established rights, makes me tremble, lest that chaos of dissipated pursuits which has too long been growing like an overwhelming shadow, and menacing the lustre of intellectual light, should, aided by the idleness of some, and the profligacy of others, at last obscure the finer mental powers, and reduce the dignity of talents to the lowest degradation.

---

1   [Robinson's note:] Since the death of Doctor Johnson a few ingenious and elegant writers have composed sonnets, according to the rules described by him: of their merits the public will judge, and the *literati* decide. The following quotations are given as the opinions of living authors, respecting the legitimate sonnet. [Here Robinson quotes the opening paragraph of Smith's Preface to the first edition of *ES* (see p. 53) and from William Kendall. Johnson defined the sonnet in his *Dictionary of the English Language* (1755).]

[Robinson goes on to discuss poetry in general as a "national orna-ment," citing Milton, Alexander Pope (1688–1744), Edmund Spenser (c. 1552–99), and William Collins (1721–59), and quoting at length from William Cowper (1731–1800).]

I cannot conclude these opinions without paying tribute to the talents of my illustrious countrywomen; who, unpatronized by courts, and unprotected by the powerful, persevere in the paths of literature, and ennoble themselves by the unperishable lustre of MENTAL PRE-EMINENCE.

3. From Samuel Taylor Coleridge, "Introduction to the Sonnets," *Poems*, 2nd ed. (London, 1797), 71–72

[In the introduction to the sonnets section in his book, Samuel Taylor Coleridge (1732–1834) sets out his influential definition of the sonnet as "a small poem, in which some lonely feeling is developed." It is clear that Coleridge's account of the sonnet is strongly influenced by Smith's sonnets, and he cites Smith, along with her contemporary William Bowles (1762–1850), as an innovator in the genre. For an example of one of Bowles's sonnets, and Coleridge's championing of him, see Appendix A3.]

The composition of the Sonnet has been regulated by Boileau in his Art of Poetry, and since Boileau, by William Preston, in the elegant preface to his Amatory Poems:[1] the rules, which they would establish, are founded on the practice of Petrarch. I have never yet been able to dis-cover either sense, nature, or poetic fancy in Petrarch's poems; they appear to me all one cold glitter of heavy conceits and metaphysical abstractions. However, Petrarch, although not the inventor of the Sonnet, was the first who made it popular; and his countrymen have taken *his* poems as the model. Charlotte Smith and Bowles are they who first made the Sonnet popular among the present English: I am justified therefore by analogy in deducing its laws from *their* compositions.

The Sonnet then is a small poem, in which some lonely feeling is developed. It is limited to a *particular* number of lines, in order that the reader's mind having expected the close at the place in which he finds it, may rest satisfied; and that so the poem may acquire, as it were, a

---

1 Nicholas Boileau (1636–1711), *L'Art poétique* (1674); William Preston (1753–1807) was an Irish poet and dramatist. Coleridge is referring here to Preston's recent preface "To the reader" in the "Sonnets, Love Elegies and Amatory Poems" section of volume one of *The Poetical Works of William Preston, Esq.* (Dublin, 1793).

Totality,—in plainer phrase, may become a *Whole.* It is confined to fourteen lines, because as some particular number is necessary, and that particular number must be a small one, it may as well be fourteen as any other number. When no reason can be adduced against a thing, Custom is a sufficient reason for it. Perhaps, if the Sonnet were comprized in less than fourteen lines, it would become a serious Epigram; if it extended to more, it would encroach on the province of the Elegy. Poems in which no lonely feeling is developed, are not Sonnets because the Author has chosen to write them in fourteen lines: they should rather be entitled Odes, or Songs, or Inscriptions [...].

In a Sonnet then we require a development of some lonely feeling, by whatever cause it may have been excited; but those Sonnets appear to me the most exquisite, in which moral Sentiments, Affections, or Feelings, are deduced from, and associated with, the scenery of Nature. Such compositions generate a habit of thought highly favourable to delicacy of character. They create a sweet and indissoluble union between the intellectual and the material world. Easily remembered from their briefness, and interesting alike to the eye and the affections, these are the poems which we can "lay up in our heart, and our soul," and repeat them "when we walk by the way, and when we lie down, and when we rise up." Hence, the Sonnets of BOWLES derive their marked superiority over all other Sonnets; here they domesticate with the heart, and become, as it were, a part of our identity.

Appendix C: Selections from Smith's Letters Relating to Her Poetry

1. From Charlotte Smith, *The Collected Letters of Charlotte Smith*, ed. Judith Stanton (Bloomington: Indiana UP, 2003), 266–68, 48–50, 741–42

a. Charlotte Smith to William Davies[1]

[Oxford, 25 April 1797]

To Mr Davies.

Sir,

I received the parcel last night but not till so late an hour that I could not do any thing to day more than writing the enclos'd to the Printer & sending this Copy of the list of Subscribers, which I beg the favor of you to correct by your own if any where deficient & then send to the Dutchess of Devonshire[2] who is <u>now at Chiswick</u>—with a Note to this effect:

> "Messrs Caddell & Davies respectfully acquaint the Dutchess of Devonshire that they have receiv'd from Mrs Charlotte Smith the enclos'd list of Subscribers to the 2nd Vol of Sonnets &c who mentions that Grace [*sic*] has she believes several names to add for most of which Mrs CS. has received the Subscription money. As the Book will now in a few days be compleated, it is necessary to prepare the list for the press. Wherefore at Mrs Smiths desire, Messrs C. & D. take the liberty of begging of her Grace to do them the honor to add such names as are omitted, & it will be an additional obligation if her Grace will be pleased to send it as soon as may be convenient."

---

1 William Davies (d. 1820) was one of Smith's long-time publishers. As well as all editions of *ES* to appear in Smith's lifetime, Davies, together with Thomas Cadell Sr. and Thomas Cadell Jr., published *The Emigrants* and a number of her novels. This letter was written on the publication of the first two-volume edition of *ES* and contains a detailed discussion of the illustrations. It demonstrates the extent to which Smith was involved in the publication process.

2 Georgiana Cavendish, Duchess of Devonshire (1757–1806).

Unless this is done, I am afraid I shall never get the list completed, & tho I care very little about its being so much inferior in both rank & numbers to the first (the reason of which I know perfectly well & by no means am sorry for), Yet there are some among the Dutchess's friends whom I very particularly wish to have, & whose names are in my opinion the first in this Country.[1] Be so good as to give your attention to this as soon as possible. I should imagine a day might very soon be fix'd for the Publication—I return the last proof to the Printer & propose sending up every thing but the preface by a conveyance that Offers on Thursday to Mr Low, who is sending Copies of the book he publish'd for me to one of my absent sons by a Gentleman going to Canada, & I send a pacquet at the same time of Letters &c for Leiut Lionel Smith to the care of Mr Lowe. Therefore the delay will not occasion you double expence, & I will write to Low to beg he will send you the pacquet, or You may send for it On Thursday after the arrival of the Oxford Coaches. The Preface I send to Mr Hayley to correct who will return it to you—

I am now to speak of the proofs, & let me before I forget it say that I was disappointed at not having Lady Bessboroughs & the other two drawings sent down with the proofs.[2] Pray let me have them with the next pacquet without fail. I cannot say (because I cannot say the thing that is not) that I am satisfied with either of Mr Heaths engravings.[3] It seems to me that the expression of the Lunatic is quite changd & instead of a Madman the figure is that of a fool with a black Wig on, & his mantle looks like a piece of a ploughed field flying in the Air. It is of no use to complain now, for I know it cannot be alterd & if Mr Heath did it, as assuredly he did, to the best of his comprehension, I may perhaps be merely fastidious & fancy perfection which is not to be found in engraving on so small a scale, except with French Engravers, who certainly do execute small plates with an elegance &

---

1 Publishing by subscription allowed authors access to money in advance of publication. It was, therefore, a way of providing financial relief to authors (like Smith) who might be having financial difficulties. However, as the subscribers to a volume were typically listed at the beginning of an edition, it also allowed authors to display the rank and influence of their admirers. Smith viewed her long list of subscribers to *ES* (the first subscription edition of the book had 817 subscribers) as a testament to her own social standing.

2 Among the illustrations added to the 1797 edition was the one by Henrietta (Harriet) Duncannon (1761–1821), countess of Bessborough, which accompanied Smith's poem "The Female Exile" (see p. 202). She was the younger sister of the Duchess of Devonshire.

3 James Heath (1757–1834). Smith is here discussing the image that accompanies Sonnet LXX.

delicacy that we have not yet reached. I have two small plates done in France that have perhaps set my expectations too high. Do not therefore say any thing to Mr Heath for he will hate me, & it will be of no use.

As to the single female figure, Mr Corbould[1] originally faild in comprehending my idea which perhaps was for want of my expressing myself clearly. But my notion which I meant to give him was that of a River Nymph—The fat girl he produced was any thing but such an ideal Sylphish representation. She is now a little subdued but still not a river Nymph, nor the Naiad of a Stream or any thing like one, but the figure is now simple & pretty, and the Landscape, tho a little too dark, very much what it ought to be in general, & upon the whole I shall take the figure for the Phoebe of "the Forest Boy" instead of what I had intended it for—the closing Poem—As it will not badly represent her melancholy Musing—

By the brook where it winds thro' the Copse of Arbeal

But I wish that, if it can be done without much trouble, ~~that~~ a little more of sorrowful, mournful expression may be given to her Countenance ~~& I will add another~~ which may I believe be done with a single stroke of the Graver about the mouth or perhaps brows.

Allow me also to remark that the Water wants effect: it is almost mingled with the rock near the ~~left~~ right margin, & the piece of ground on which her feet rest looks too much like a twelf cake,[2] it is so extremely regular. The trees too on the left margin in the first distance are very shelly, not to say wiggy[3]—A very little trouble only (as I suppose) is necessary to break the straightness of the fore ground & give a little more freedom to the Trees in the second distance. I do not mean those on the rock over her head. If there is any wish of spoiling the face, it is better to let it go as it is—

The Plate from Lady Bessborough's drawing is beautiful—& sweetly done, particularly the little Girl standing. But there is something odd in the face of the figure. It seems as if the nose was so long that the Lady was forced to go without either Mouth or chin. Can it be so in the Drawing?

This puts me in mind to beg you would add to the note to the Dtss, as follows:

---

1 Richard Corbould (1757–1831) was a painter who provided a number of illustrations for *ES*, Volumes One and Two.
2 A large cake used for the festivities of Twelfth Night. It had a bean or coin on top to determine who was the "king" or "queen" of the feast.
3 Presumably, Smith means "wig-like."

Messrs C. & D. beg the favor of being inform'd whether they may put Lady Bessboroughs name to the Plate of "the Female Exile," & if so, hope to be honourd with her Ladyship's instructions how it is to be engraved at the bottom—

I beleive from the fifth plates taken off up to the 30th or thereabouts are the best. You will I am persuaded reserve some of the best for the Dutchess, Lady B— & others of my immediate friends.

When a few have been taken off, the prints will lose something of the blackness they now have—

As I have no Letters to day on my money matters, I suppose I am not to have the money, at least not without going to Town for it.

         I am, Sir, yr Obed & Oblig'd Sert, Charlotte Smith.

Oxford, April 25 1797

In answer to your Question whether I wd have my name at the bottom of the Portrait, I had rather not. There seems to be no occasion for it, & it will be no advantage. I hope You will take such precautions as are in your power to prevent its being exhibited in Magazines "with anecdotes of this admir'd Authoress" like Mrs Mary Robinson[1] & other Mistresses whom I have no passion for being confounded with, & also that you will prevent the Poems getting into Newspapers or being printed "with beauties of Poetry, or elegant selections,"[2] which to my certain knowledge have done an infinite deal of harm to the first Vol as to its sale—

I beg the favor of you to buy for me & send down by the next pacquet Southeys Poems—[3]

I wish you would ask Mr Hayley if any name sd be put (to the portrait) of the Painter. Mr Condé[4] will of course put his if he thinks it

---

1 Mary Robinson (1758–1800) was an actress and one-time mistress of the Prince of Wales who went on to become, alongside Smith, one of the most famous authors of the period. Although both women championed the radical causes and shared friends and acquaintances, Smith was eager to distance herself from Robinson and from her scandalous private life. See Appendices A6 and E5 for examples of Robinson's sonnets and Appendix B2 for her praise of Smith's work.

2 These types of books, titled *Elegant Extracts* or *Elegant Selections*, compiled extracts from the works of various poets, often classifying them by type ("Sacred and Moral," "Didactic, Descriptive, Narrative and Pathetic," etc.). Authors would have made very little, if any, money from being published in such collections.

3 Robert Southey (1774–1843), *Poems*, 2nd ed. (1797).

4 Pierre Condé (1767/68–1840) was a printmaker and miniature painter. He engraved the new frontispiece portrait for the 1797 volume of *Elegiac Sonnets*.

worth while, but I am afraid of offending Mr Romney[1] if I do the other witht asking him, or let it go unask'd.

b. Charlotte Smith to Joel Barlow[2]

Brighthelmstone Novr 3rd
1792

I am extremely flatterd, Dear Sir, by your early and very obliging attention to my Letter & indeed have great reason to quarrel with Dr Warner[3] for neglecting an appointment which would have been the means of introducing me to your acquaintance. I read with great satisfaction the "Advice to the Priveledged Orders" and have been, as well as some of my most judicious and reasoning friends here, very highly gratified by the lesser tract, Your Letter to the National Convention.[4] Which cannot I think fail of having great effect not only where it is address'd, but on those who at present consider themselves as less immediately interested in the questions it discusses. I really pity the advocates for despotism.

They are so terribly mortified at the late events in France, and as they had never any thing to say that had even the semblance of reason and now are evidently on the wrong side of the question both in Theory and Practice, it is really pitiable to hear the childish shifts and miserable evasions to which they are reduced.

I am however sensibly hurt at the hideous picture which a friend of mine, himself one of the most determined Democrates I know, has given of the situation of the Emigrants. He has follow'd the progress of the retreating Army in their reterog[r]ade motion, and describes the condition of the French exiles as being more deplorable even than

---

1 George Romney (1734–1802) was a painter and a friend of Smith's patron, William Hayley (1745–1820). His portrait of Smith provided the model for Condé's frontispiece.

2 Joel Barlow (1754–1812) was an American radical who moved between London and Paris between 1790 and 1792. Book I of *The Emigrants* bears the same date as this letter and is written out of this moment.

3 John Warner (1736–1800) was the chaplain to the British ambassador in Paris and was a mutual acquaintance of both Smith and Barlow.

4 The two influential tracts by Barlow that Smith alludes to here are *Advice to the Privileged Orders, in the Several States of Europe, Resulting from the Necessity and Propriety of a General Revolution in the Principle of Government* (1792–93) and *A Letter to the National Convention of France on the Defects of the Constitution of 1791, and the Extent of the Amendments Which Ought to Be Applied* (1792).

their crimes seem to deserve. The magnitude of the Revolution is such as ought to make it embrace every great principle of Morals, & even in a Political light (with which I am afraid Morals have but little to do), it seems to me wrong for the Nation entirely to exile and abandon these Unhappy Men.[1] How truly great would it be, could the Convention bring about a reconciliation. They should suffer the loss of a very great part of their property & all their power. But they should still be considered as Men & Frenchmen, and tho I would not kill the fatted Calf,[2] They should still have a plate of Bouille[3] at home if they will take it & not be turned out indiscriminately to perish in foreign Countries and to carry every where the impression of the injustice and ferocity of the French republic—That glorious Government will soon be so firmly establish'd that five and twenty thousand emigrants or three times the number cannot affect its stability. The people will soon feel the value of what they have gain'd and will not be shaken by their efforts in arms from without, or their intrigues within (even if they were to intrigue), & many of them have probably sufferd enough to be glad of returning on almost any terms. Their exile includes too that of a very great number of Women and Children who must be eventually not only a national loss but on whom, if the Sins of the Father are visited, it will be more consonant to the doctrine of scripture than of reason.

I not only wish that an amnesty was pass'd for these ill advisd Men, but that their wretched victim Louis Capet[4] was to be dismiss'd with his family and an ample settlement made upon him & his posterity so long as they do not disturb the peace of the Republic. I do not understand of what use it can be to bring to trial an Officer for whom the whole nation determines it has no farther occasion. To punish him for the past seems as needless [as] to make him an example for the future, for, if no more Kings are suffer'd, it will avail nothing to shew the ill consequence of being a bad one by personal punishment inflicted on the unfortunate Man who could not help being born the Grandson of Louis 15th—Surely it would be great to shew the world that, when a people are determind to dismiss their King, he becomes indeed a phantom & cannot be an object of fear, & I am persuaded there are on all sides much stronger

---

1 In April 1792 a law had been passed declaring much property forfeit, and moves were being made to banish emigrants in perpetuity. See Introduction, p. 32. Around this time Smith's eldest daughter Anna Augusta met the by-then destitute emigrant Alexandre Marc-Constant de Foville, whom she would go on to marry.

2 To produce one's best food to celebrate. From the parable of the prodigal son, as told by Jesus in the Bible (Luke 15:11–32).

3 Bouillon (French): a soup prepared with broth.

4 A familiar name for the French monarch, Louis XVI (r. 1774–92), who was then in captivity with his family.

reasons for dismissing than for destroying him. On this occasion, the Republic should perhaps imitate the magnaminity of Uncle Toby, "Go poor devil! why should we hurt thee? There is surely room enough in the World for Us and thee!"[1] It is making this unhappy individual of too much consequence to suppose that his life Can be demanded for the good of people. And when he was reduced to the condition of an affluent private Gentleman, & even that affluence depending on the Nation, I cannot conceive that he would do any harm, but wd sink into total insignificance & live a memento of the dependence of Kings, not on hereditary and divine right, but on the will of the people—

Will you have the goodness to send the Poem by Mr Fingal[2] to Bells, Bookseller Opposite the end of Bond Street in Oxford Street, who will on Teusday or Wednesday forward to me a pacquet of Books—I will carefully return it when I have done with it by the same conveyance. I am afraid I shall not be in Town this Winter as my friend with whom I staid last year in Henrietta Street is gone to Lisbon.[3] But if I should see London for a short time it will give me infinite pleasure to wait on Mrs Barlow by whose favourable opinion I am much flatter'd as well as to have an opportunity of assuring you personally of the esteem with which I am,

Sir
your most oblig'd & obedt Sert,
Charlotte Smith

c. Charlotte Smith to Joseph Johnson[4]

[Tilford] Saturday, July 12th
1806

Dear Sir,

Your letter to day gave me great satisfaction. If <u>you</u> are satisfied that the verses are worth any thing, I am perfectly convinced that they would make a ~~short~~ small volume and sell to advantage; it seems to me

---

1   Tristram Shandy's Uncle Toby, who says this to a fly (Laurence Sterne, *The Life and Opinions of Tristram Shandy, Gentleman* [1760], ed. Ian Watt [Boston: Houghton Mifflin, 1965], 121).

2   Likely American poet John Trumbull's (1750–1831) *M'Fingal* (1782) (*CL* 51n7).

3   Henrietta O'Neill (1758–93), author of "Ode to the Poppy," which Smith included in the 1797 edition of *ES*.

4   Joseph Johnson (1738–1809) was an influential London publisher who published a number of radical thinkers, including Mary Wollstonecraft (1759–97). He published Smith's *Conversations Including Poetry* (1804) as well as her posthumous works, *Beachy Head: with other poems* (1807) and *The Natural History of Birds* (1807).

that the volume should be printed uniformly with the other two because the probability is that those who are in possession of the other two Volumes will purchase this, & as, of the latter editions, I have reason to beleive some thousands have been sold, this circumstance only would secure the sale of enough to pay the expence of printing, which, for such volumes as these (without plates) I have been informed is not great. It seems to be the fashion of the day to print the notes at the end; sometimes with a (V.N.).[1] In this instance they would be rather numerous because of historical, biograph[ic]al, & local facts relative to Beechy & the Coast & the extraordinary story of <u>Parson Darby</u>, a Man who, disgusted with the World, lived many years as tradition tells in a cave of the Cliff by Beachy head & was lost in attempting to save some Shipwreck'd Seamen.[2] The poems too which relate to natural history will want notes.

My wish was to have made such a bargain with Cadell & Davies, thro your interposition, as would have put an handsome Sum into your hands in liquidation of my <u>debt</u>, which is my first <u>object</u>, & secondly, to have done what they themselves propos'd or at least Mr Davies during some correspondence on this matter last year—that is, to publish a collection of all the Poems I have written which, on my mature judgement, appear worth retaining (expunging all the <u>adulatory</u> lines particularly— As the only means by which I can testify my regard for having ever written them, & I will give those Authors, who have complimented <u>me</u> & if I chose to do like Miss Seward,[3] I could come prancing with several cantering (and canting) outriders of this sort, among whom is the present most reverend Bishop of Glocester, then indeed only the Revd Mr Huntingford, a third Master at Win Col[4])—I say I will give those Authors who, whether in public or in little <u>elegant effusions</u> have complimented <u>me</u>, leave to blot out, annihilate, expunge, & obliterate <u>every civil thing they ever said.</u> Who ever lived for twenty years without seeing abundant cause to alter their opinions of the charming creatures who seem'd once so very delightful?

---

1   *Vide notam* (Latin: "see note").
2   See notes to *BH* in this edition, p. 188, note 3.
3   Smith and Anna Seward (1742–1809) were rival sonneteers, and there was no love lost between them (see p. 41). Smith is referring here to Seward's book *Original Sonnets, on Various Subjects* (1799), in which Seward includes two poems praising her poetry: T. Park's "To Miss Seward: On reading her centenary of Sonnets" and "Verses by the Rev. H.F. Carey, on reading the following paraphrases." Smith evidently thought this practice reflected conceit on Seward's behalf.
4   According to Stanton, the Reverend George Isaac Huntingford (1748–1832) was made bishop of Gloucester in 1802 (*CL* 743n5). Smith clearly counts him among her supporters.

Bref [*sic*]: If you will have the goodness to propose this plan to Mr Davies, he might perhaps think it worth while to attend to it, & act upon it in a way that may appear satisfactory. I have written to him & told him that you, who were so good as to be my Treasurer, intended talking to him on this business, but that you doubted there being enough—A doubt however I am clear may be done away, But that if he still thought the purchase of no more value that he seem'd to think it last year, I would print on my own account, & on this experiment, I am not at all afraid of venturing, nor at all doubtful of the success, & Yet for reasons I will not again hint at, it really is of importance to me to have the book come out very soon.[1] I am told that I need only remind certain people of me in this way to obtain a Company for my Youngest Son if his life is spared and that I shall get something done for the very deserving young Man who is engaged to Harriet & who has suffered by a brother a great loss of fortune.[2] Besides which, it would raise my spirits, often sinking into absolute despondence, when my bays seem blighted & Misses amatory verses seem to put me by.

Will you therefore set on foot this little volume? It should be made as much like the two others as can be because the purchasers of those will in all probability buy this. Messrs Cadell & Davies have I beleive some copies left tho when I have sent strangers there twice to buy sets for me, they have sold the 8th and 9th Edition whereas the 1st volume is in the 10th. By the way, the notes to those want re-writing. They are sad nonsense here & there. No indeed I do not doubt your gallantry, or what is better your benevolence & good nature, but in truth, I did think you treated Ladies literature a little like the late James Dodsley who, when I offerd him my Sonnets in 1783, said, "What I suppose now this is all loving stuff about Shepherds and Shepherdesses, & little lambs, & all that."[3]

Lord Egremont[4] has given no orders abt my dividend, but the Bankers will condescend to pay 30£. Next month I am entitled to

---

1 Smith, as always, desperately needed the money that she would make from this volume.

2 Smith's youngest son, George Augustus Frederick Smith (1785–1806) was an adjutant in the army. In the army, promotions needed to be bought (commissioned), and George did not have the funds to move out of his company (regiment). As a result of being unable to move regiments, he was shipped out to the West Indies, where he died of yellow fever on 16 September 1806.

3 James Dodsley (1724–97), a London publisher and bookseller. Dodsley was William Hayley's publisher, which may have been why Smith sent her collection to him in the first instance.

4 See XVIII, p. 68, note 3.

receive 3000£ a part of my own fortune back. It was bought in just at the peace of Amiens, & I lose 18£ a year. I have a great mind to sell it out & place it on Landed security. It is my childrens after my death, but why should I lose 18£ a year which wd almost pay my property tax. I am, Dear Sir,

yr oblig'd & grateful Sert, Charlotte Smith

I will return the <divds> in the course of the week.

Appendix D: Selected Reviews of Smith's Major Poems

[Here we provide a number of key reviews for Smith's major poems. All texts have been transcribed from facsimile versions available through Proquest's *British Periodicals Online* database.]

1. From Review of *Elegiac Sonnets*, *Monthly Review* 71 (November 1784): 368–71

The Poetess apologizes, in her Preface, that her Sonnets are not of the legitimate kind. We cannot, however, agree with her. That recurrence of the rhyme which, in conformity to the Italian model, some writers so scrupulously observe, is by no means essential to this species of composition, and it is frequently as inconvenient as it is unnecessary. The English language can boast of few good Sonnets. They are in general harsh, formal, and uncouth: faults entirely owing to the pedantic and childish affectation of interchanging the rhymes, after the manner of the Italians. The slightest attention to the peculiarities of the respective languages might evince the propriety of the copy, in this point, deviating from the original.

Plaintive tenderness and simplicity characterise the Sonnets before us.

[Quotes Sonnet I in full along with "The Origin of Flattery"]

2. From Review of *Elegiac Sonnets*, *Gentleman's Magazine* 56 (April 1786): 333–34

It has been suggested by a valuable correspondent, that we cannot adopt a more elegant decoration than a few sonnets by this pathetic poetess. To the number of those originally published by her, she has now made an addition of twenty new ones. We cannot, however forbear expressing a hope that the misfortunes she so often hints at, are all imaginary. We must have perused her very tender and exquisite effusions with diminished pleasure, could we have supposed her sorrows to be real.—It would be hard indeed if a lady, who has so much contributed to the delight of others, should feel any want of happiness herself.

[Quotes Sonnets V, IX, and XXXVI in their entirety]

A very trifling compliment is paid to Mrs. Smith when it is observed how much her Sonnets exceed those of *Shakespeare* and *Milton*. She has undoubtedly conferred honour on a species of poetry which most of her predecessors in this country have disgraced.—The pieces, however, which are the genuine offspring of her own fancy, are by far the most interesting in her whole collection. The wretched suicide *Werter* is too much flatterd by her notice; and the strains of *Petrarch* are more talked of than imitated, even in the country that produced them.

As Mrs. *Smith*, in her XXXIXth Sonnet, addressed to some Female Friend, has declared herself an unfit Votary of "Laughing Thalia," why will she not undertake the cause of her "Pensive Sister," by producing a tragedy?[1]

3. From Review of *The Emigrants*, *European Magazine* 24 (July 1793): 41–45

THIS Poem is preceded by a Preface to Mr. Cowper, the celebrated author of "The Task," to whom it is highly complimentary, both as a Patriot and a Poet.[2] The authoress takes this opportunity of deploring the national antipathy which exists between her own country and France, "and which," she says, "has been increased of late in England by confounding the original muse (of Liberty) with the wretched catastrophes that have followed its ill management; the attempts of public virtue with the outrages that guilt and folly have committed in its disguise. The very name of Liberty has not only lost the charm it used to have in British ears, but many who have written or spoken in its defence have been stigmatized as promoters of anarchy and enemies to the prosperity of their country. Perhaps even the author of 'The Task,' with all his goodness and tenderness of heart, is in the catalogue of those who are reckoned to have been too warm in the cause which it was once the glory of Englishmen to avow and defend."

The following extract from the Preface, also, it would be very unfair to suppress, as it will throw great light upon the Emigrants, and bring the reader more acquainted with the authoress, who, by a liberty usually allowed to the servants of the Muses, is the subject of a part of her Poem; and whom we can discover almost at the bottom of every page, as we may the portrait of some of the most renowned painters in the corner of their most favourite pictures.

[Quotes Preface in part, from "A Dedication usually consists of ... so long existed to the injury of both."]

---

1   See Sonnet XXIX, p. 76.
2   On Smith's dedication to Cowper and her use of the term "Liberty," see
    p. 129, note 1, and p. 127, note 1.

The reader, being now acquainted with the design of these Poems, is placed in a situation to form a truer judgement of the execution and success. The high reputation already acquired by Mrs. Smith, in the judgement of all persons of taste and sentiment, by her "Elegiac Sonnets," makes it unnecessary for us to make any other enquiry than whether she has sustained or increased it by the present effusions of her Muse? and we shall without hesitation acquit ourselves of our obligation to give a verdict, by fairly assigning it as our opinion, that "The Emigrants," whatever be their merits, which we acknowledge to be very great, and of which we shall presently extract some of the most striking instances, are not entitled to that peculiar and exclusive admiration which the Sonnets have so justly acquired. "Colin was born to complain"; but whether it be that blank verse fatigues by its monotony, unless relieved by variety, and the dignity of the Epic Muse, or offends by the length of the periods, when there is too much attention employed to interrupt the monotony; we do not think it is the proper measure in which to complain—at least to do nothing else but complain.[1]

The whole Poem may be considered as a soliloquy pronounced by the authoress; and being a tissue of reflections arising from one object, varied by scarce any episodes, and admitting of no relief but from different description, it does not sufficiently keep alive the attention, though it is frequently roused by interesting passages and beautiful imagery. It consists of brilliant parts, but does not present a perfect "*ensemble*." There is very little in the whole which does not deserve its share of praise, though the *whole* has but a disputable pretension to the applause of strict criticism and severe discernment.

[The review then offers a detailed criticism of the poetical style of *The Emigrants* enumerating upon its defects and "beauties" and quoting from the poem at length in order to support its analysis.]

The bounds of our Review forbid us to follow Mrs. Smith in those digressions which allude to her own situation or feelings; we think we have spoken sufficiently in praise of her Poems, and that our admiration of her talents is by this time so unequivocal, that we shall not be thought desirous to detract from their merit, when we suggest, that "The Emigrants" would have been more interesting had she selected

---

1   The reviewer may here mean to allude, also, to the poetic genre of Complaint, in which the poet complains or laments. This popular Renaissance genre was based on the expression of seemingly interminable sorrow, in contrast to Elegy, which aimed to express sorrow and then move on.

characteristic personages, in whose fate, virtues, and misfortunes, we could have felt a distinct interest as we read them. As it is, no particular character, or even species of misfortune, is suffered to dwell long enough upon the mind to produce any very great and concentrated degree of anxiety and interest. We pity *all* too much to suffer acutely for *any* one.

Defendit numerus junctæque umbone phalanges.[1]

If numbers and society can extinguish the sense of shame on the one hand by division, on the other they are able to reduce and diminish compassion to almost an insensible point, by multiplying objects with equal claims upon the feelings; for the sense of pity itself becomes obtuse and dull by too frequent use or too much dilatation.

4. From Review of *The Emigrants*, *Monthly Review, or Literary Journal* 12 (December 1793): 375–76

WHATEVER is capable of exciting the generous emotions of sympathy is a proper subject of poetry, whose office is to afford pleasure by presenting interesting objects to the imagination. The sufferings of the French emigrants certainly furnish a subject of this kind; and poetry, like charity, will dwell only on such circumstances as are best fitted to excite its proper feelings. In the poem before us, Mrs. Smith has judiciously confined her attention to those particulars in the case of the emigrants, which have excited sympathy in the minds of the humane of all parties; and she describes their condition with that propriety and tenderness, which those who are acquainted with her former productions will be prepared to expect. The style of the poem is seldom highly poetical, and sometimes is even nearly prosaic; yet the general effect is truly pleasing; and there are passages which do credit to the elegant pen that wrote the justly admired Elegiac Sonnets.

[Transcribes Book 2, lines 17–35 and Book 2, lines 127–50]

We heartily adopt the author's wish, expressed in the dedication of her poem to Mr. Cowper, "that this painful exile (of the emigrants) may finally lead to the extirpation of that reciprocal hatred so unworthy of great and enlightened nations; that it may tend to humanize both countries, by convincing each that good qualities exist in the

---

1 An allusion to Juvenal's Satire I, "Their numbers and their compact array protect them."

other; and may at length annihilate the prejudices that have so long existed to the injury of both."

5. From Review of *Beachy Head*, *British Critic* 30 (August 1807): 170–74

MOST sincerely do we lament the death of Mrs. Charlotte Smith. We acknowledged in her a genuine child of genius, a most vivid fancy, refined taste, and extraordinary sensibility. We could not, indeed, always accord with her in sentiment. With respect to some subjects beyond her line of experience, reading, and indeed talent, she was unfortunately wayward and preposterous;[1] but her poetic feeling and ability have rarely been surpassed by any individual of her sex. Her sonnets in particular will remain models of that species of composition; and, as Johnson remarked of Gray's Elegy in a Country Church-yard, had she always written thus, it were vain to blame and useless to praise her. It remains to take notice of these posthumous poems. The first is on Beachy Head, and in blank verse. Blank verse is of late becoming a favourite style of composition. We are inclined to suspect that this proceeds either from idleness, or from a conscious want of powers. But a vast deal more is required in blank verse than youthful poets may at first imagine. We are by no means satisfied with the regular and correct structure of the verse, we require both classical taste, strong poetical fancy, a judicious arrangement, and melodious rhythm.

Mrs. Smith has demonstrated this in her first poem, that she could adorn any branch of poetry upon which she chose to exercise her powers. This poem is distinguished by great vigour, and, by what was the characteristic of the author's mind, a sweet and impressive tenderness of melancholy. It is a very charming composition. We would not disgrace our page by any hypercritical cavil[2] on little oversights and inaccuracies, but confidently appeal to the subjoined specimen in vindication of the praise which we have given to the poem.

[Quotes from "Beachy Head," lines 258–312, and then briefly discusses three other poems from the volume: "The Truant Dove," "The Lark's Nest," and "The Swallow." "The Swallow" is then quoted in full. The review then goes on to very briefly list the rest of the poems in the volume.]

---

1   The conservative *British Critic* is most likely referring to Smith's more radical engagements with the revolutionary debate, in particular in her novel *Desmond* (1792).
2   Trivial or annoying objection.

We take our leave of this author with unfeigned regret and sympathy. Her life was embittered by sorrow and misfortune, this gave an unavoidable tinge to her sentiments, which, from the gay and the vain, and the unfeeling, may excite a sneer of scorn and contempt; but in the bosoms of those who, like Charlotte Smith, with refined feelings, improved by thought and study, and reflection, have been compelled, like her, to tread the thorny paths of adversity, will prompt the generous wish, that fortune had favoured her with more complacency; and will induce the disposition to extenuate such portions of her productions, as sterner judgment is unable to approve.

Appendix E: Poetry about Smith Appearing in Newspapers and Magazines

[Poetry about Charlotte Smith regularly appeared in the newspapers (see Introduction, p. 41). Texts have been transcribed from the fac-simile editions of the newspapers and periodicals available through the *17th and 18th Century Burney Collection Newspapers* Online database and Proquest's *British Periodicals Online* database. Where this is not the case, we have indicated the text's source in the headnote.]

1. Anonymous, "Sonnet to Mrs. Smith," *European Magazine* 10 (August 1786): 125

'Tis said, and I myself have so believ'd
"Fiction's the properest field for Poesy";
Tho' few have car'd th' assertion to deny,
As few there are who have not been deceiv'd:
5 For sure than thine more sweet no strains can flow,
Than thine no tenderer plaints the heart can move,
More rouse the soul to sympathetic love;
And yet—sad source! They spring from REAL woe.
Oh! may again kind Heav'n thy hopes illume!
10 Again may peace thy gentlest bosom bless!
May hours far happier smooth thy rude distress,
And thou life's dear enjoyments reassume!
Tho' ah! So sweet, so pensive sweet, thy grief,
Compassion's self might almost grudge relief.

2. D., "SONNET to Mrs. Smith, on reading her Sonnets lately published," *European Magazine* (May 1786): 366

NOT the sweet bird, who thro' the nights of May
    Pours the sad story of her hapless love
To the touch'd heart, such tender things can say,
    Or with such plaintive eloquence can move!
5 Base were those grovelling minds, those breasts of stone,
    Who taught *thee* grief nor time nor hope can heal:
Hours may they know unpitied and alone;
    When *their own* woes shall make the wretches feel.
Oh! could or fame or friendship aught impart
10   To cure the cruel wounds thy peace has known

For others sorrows, still thy tender heart
Should softly melt;—but never for thine own!
Till pitying all—and ev'n thy foes forgiven,
Thy candid spirit—seeks its native heaven.

Chichester, May 8, 1786.

3. Pastor Fido, "On passing the RETREAT of CHARLOTTE SMITH, *near* Chichester, in Sussex," *World* (7 August 1788)

O! SACRED be this *calm sequester'd* SEAT,
    And blest the Spot that claims so soft a Care!
Sacred, that gives to VIRTUE a retreat;
    And blest, that shields a *persecuted* fair!

5   I past the Spot:—'twas rustic and recluse,
    The Roof was lowly, and the Fields were rude,
Where liv'd, who VIRTUE lov'd, who Lov'd the MUSE;
    There flown for safety and solitude.

Beneath the Covert of an aged Tree,
10   Whose Foliage wide o'erspread the daisi'd Green,
Her lowly Head reclining on her Knee;
    She sate alone—unwilling to be seen.

She seem'd as tho' her All on Earth were flown,
    Nor car'd she now for all that Earth could bring,
15 Nor mov'd her Eyes to greet the cheering Sun,
    To smile on NATURE, or salute the SPRING.

And all around, upon the tender Grass,
    Her *little children* play'd in Gambol's Fair:
Unconscious they of Woes they have to pass,
20   Regret unknowing, and devoid of Care.

And as around they led the devious Dance,
    Or Flow'rets pick'd, or join'd in Frolicks near;
Oft would her Eyes enjoy a thoughtless Glance,
    She oft would Smile—and Smiling drop a Tear.

25 I saw her face, it pierc'd me to the Soul,
    DEJECTION on her *brow* was seated high;
Wan CARE her lovely Cheeks had ravag'd foul,
    And *bitter Anguish* beam'd within her Eye.

I heard her Voice, and it was Music still,
30   And who *unmov'd at such sweet sounds* could be;
Lost now the Sprightlier Notes, the rapt'rous thrill,
        But tun'd to Tones of Plaintive Malady.

"Play on, (she cried) unmindful of your fate,
        For why should INFANCY a pang sustain?
35   May Heav'n your joys prolong to latest date,
        And give a pleasure for my every pain.

For me, what now avails that NATURE *blest*,
        That genius warm'd that Taste enrich'd my Mind;
Can these the wayward strokes of Fate Arrest?
40   Or move a HUSBAND, *faithless and unkind*?

Nought now remains but all the live-long day,
        To waste my hours in Woe and Sorrows pale;
And still at Night, to take my lonely way,
        And by the *Moon-beams* woo the NIGHTINGALE."

4. "Ticklepitcher," "Ode to Charlotte Smith," *Morning Post* (16 December 1789)

CHARLOTTE, my dear! I'm really hurt,
To see you throw about your dirt,
And give yourself such dreadful labour,
To soil and vilify your neighbour.
5   Bless me! you hardly can be known,
When seated on your critic throne,
Attended by that worthy man
HAYLEY;[1] and SEWARD[2] smiling thro' her fan.
        When late your Sonnets I perused,
10   Without a joke I was *amused*,
And when you said the moon at night
Was very pale, and gave a light,
And that the nightingales would sing,
I own I rather lik'd the thing.
15   I was as pleas'd as pleas'd could be,

---

1   William Hayley, to whom *ES* was dedicated.
2   Anna Seward (1742–1809), also known as the "Swan of Litchfield," was a
    poet and friend of William Hayley (1745–1820). Ironically, she was not an
    admirer of Smith's poetry (see Introduction, p. 41).

To see the "*sea-bird quit the sea*,"
And when you said how billows roll,
I lov'd "*the mournful purpose of your soul.*"
And when you stood "*upon a rock,*
20 *A Shipwreck'd mariner*," to weep,
It gave my nature such a shock,
    Upon my life, I could not sleep.
To lend you succour I was willing,
And instantly subcrib'd my shilling.[1]
25   But now I find you deal in satire,[2]
It is a very different matter,
I scarcely can believe my eyes,
So wonderful is my surprise,
To think that you, so soft and tender,
30 Should turn out furious as the Witch of Endor.[3]
Oh fye upon you, fye, my dear,
I'm sorry for it, but I fear,
That as you first took up the rod,
You may get whipp'd yourself, by G—.
35 A wasp you know's a little creature,
Famous for crossness and ill nature,
On which no man a thought bestows,
Unless he catch it on his nose,
And then, perhaps, his anger springs,
40 He pinches it, and breaks its wings.
    I, too, myself, can never bear
To hear it buzzing in the air,
Such nasty reptiles teaze and fright me,
I'd rather have a bull-dog bite me.
45   To analyze the matter strictly,
      And scrutinize what you have done,
    Methinks, as FALSTAFF says to QUICKLY,

---

1 The very successful fifth edition of *Elegiac Sonnets* (1789) was published by subscription. For Smith's comments on subscription, see Appendix C1a, pp. 243–44.

2 This appears to be a reference to Smith's creation of an autobiographical character called Mrs. C. Stafford in her novel *Celestina* (1788), who is, like Smith, critical of her estranged husband. For more information on this poem see Claire Knowles, "'Hazarding the Press': Charlotte Smith, the *Morning Post*, and the Perils of Literary Celebrity," *Romanticism* 20.1 (2014): 30–42.

3 According to the Bible, the Witch of Endor was a medium called by Saul to summon the ghost of Samuel (Samuel 1:28).

"There's some one now has set you on."[1]
HAYLEY, perhaps, *protecting Bard!*
50 Who works off verses by the yard,
Spinning them out from day to day,
In one unvarying, wearying lay,
Altho' no human soul can quote
A single line he ever wrote,
55 Because, or may I never thrive,
He is the dullest dog alive.
It must be he, upon my word,
Who made sweet CHARLOTTE so absurd;
For SEWARD would distain such folly,
60 An honest, hearty, buxom Dolly!
Indeed she is the Muse for me,
Handsome, and liberal, and free,
And tho' I love her tuneful clack,
I more should love her lips to smack.
65   Well, let me stop, or folks will think,
That I'm run mad with pen and ink,
And am a cruel Hottentot,
Because eight children you have got,
For every SHE may crack a skull,
70 Who first can prove her nursery full.
Dear precious bantlings! great and small,
May G—— Almighty bless them all!
I would not stain their cheeks with tears,
To live a hundred thousand years;
75 I only wish MAMMA to smile,
And take some drugs to cure her bile,
Then I will praise my charming fair,
Her eyes, and nose, and "raven hair,"
And I will praise her novels fine,
80 Her ETHELINDE, and EMMALINE,[2]
And I will be her flatterer daily,
I'll be—JUST WHAT SHE IS TO HAYLEY.

---

1 This quotation appears to be both incorrectly attributed and misquoted. The
author could be remembering the Duke's observation to Isabella in Shake-
speare's *Measure for Measure*: "Someone has set you on; Confess the truth,
and say by who's advice Thou cams't here to complain" (5.1.116–18).
2 The two novels that "Ticklepitcher" is referring to here are Smith's *Emmeline,
the Orphan of the Castle* (1788) and *Ethelinde, or the Recluse of the Lake* (1789).

5. **"Oberon" [Mary Robinson], "Sonnet to Mrs. Charlotte Smith, on Hearing That Her Son Was Wounded at the Siege of Dunkirk,"** *Oracle,* **17 September 1793. From Judith Pascoe (ed.),** *Mary Robinson: Selected Poems* **(Peterborough, ON: Broadview, 2000), 290**[1]

FULL many an anxious pang, and rending sigh,
Darts, with keen anguish, through a MOTHER's breast;
Full many a graceful TEAR obscures her eye,
While watchful fondness draws her SOUL from rest.

5 The clang of ARMS! Triumphant VALOUR's wreath!
Startle, yet fascinate the glowing mind!
For ah! too oft the crown by FAME entwin'd,
Conceals the desolating lance beneath!

Yet HOPE for THEE shall bend her soothing wings,
10 Steal to thy breast, and check the rising tear,
As to thy polish'd mind rapt Fancy brings
The GALLANT BOY, to BRITAIN's GENIUS dear!
And, while for Him a LAUREL'D Couch SHE strews,
Fair TRUTH shall snatch a Wreath, TO DECK HIS PARENT MUSE!

Sept. 15, 1793.

---

1 For more on Mary Robinson, see Appendix A6.

Appendix F: Tables of Contents for the Volumes of Elegiac Sonnets *Published during Smith's Lifetime*

[*Elegiac Sonnets* was an evolving text. Smith continued to add to it throughout almost her entire writing career. This breakdown of the Tables of Contents of the various editions is designed to give scholars easy access to the publication history of the work, showing in particular how the editions differed and which poems and images were added when. We have also used the titles each edition was given when first published.]

Elegiac Sonnets, and Other Essays (1784)

Elegiac Sonnets, and Other Essays. The Second Edition (1784)

Elegiac Sonnets. The Third Edition. With Twenty Additional Sonnets
(1786)

I.
II. Written at the Close of Spring
III. To a Nightingale
IV. To the Moon
V. To the South Downs
VI. To Hope
VII. On the Departure of the Nightingale
VIII. To Spring
IX.
X. To Mrs. G——
XI. To Sleep
XII. Written on the Sea Shore
XIII. From Petrarch
XIV. From the Same
XV. From the Same
XVI. From the Same
XVII. From the Thirteenth Cantata of Metastasio
XVIII. To the Earl of Egremont
XIX. To Mr. Hayley
XX. To the Countess of A——
XXI. Supposed to be written by Werter
XXII. By the Same
XXIII. By the Same
XXIV. By the Same
XXV. By the Same
XXVI. To the River Arun
XXVII.
XXVIII. To Friendship
XXIX. To Miss C——
XXX. To the River Arun
XXXI. Written in Farm Wood, on the South Downs, May, 1784.
XXXII. To Melancholy. Written on the Banks of the Arun.
XXXIII. To the Naiad of the Arun
XXXIV. To a Friend
XXXV. To Fortitude
XXXVI.

Elegiac Sonnets Fourth Edition (1786)
Same as Edition 3.

Elegiac Sonnets. The Fifth Edition, with Additional Sonnets and Other Poems (1789)
Same as Edition 3, with the addition of:

IV. To The Moon (accompanying image: "Queen of the Silver Bow")
XII. Written on the Sea Shore (accompanying image: "On some rude fragment of the rocky shore")
XXVI. To the River Arun (accompanying image: "For with the infant Otway lingering here")
XXXVI. (accompanying image: "Her pencil sickening fancy throws away")
XXXVII. Sent to the Honorable Mrs. O'Neill, with painted flowers
XXXVIII. From the Novel of Emmeline
XXXIX. To Night. From the same
XL. From the same
XLI. To Tranquillity
XLII. Composed during a walk on the Downs, in November, 1787
XLIII.
XLIV. Written in the church yard at Middleton in Sussex
XLV. On leaving a part of Sussex
XLVI. Written at Penshurst, in Autumn, 1788
XLVII. To Fancy
XLVIII. To Mrs. ★★★★
Ode to Despair. From the novel of Emmeline
Elegy (accompanying image: No Title)
Song. From the French of Cardinal Bernis
The Origin of Flattery

Elegiac Sonnets, The Sixth Edition, with Additional Sonnets and Other Poems (1792)
Same as Edition 5, with the addition of:

XLIX. From the Novel of Celestina
L. From the same
LI. From the same
LII. From the same
LIII. From the same
LIV. The Sleeping Woodman
LV. The Return of the Nightingale
LVI. The Captive escaped in the Wilds of America
LVII. To Dependence
LVIII. The Glow-worm
LIX. Written Sept. 1791, during a remarkable Thunder Storm
Ode to Despair. From the Novel of Emmeline
Elegy
Song. From the French of Cardinal Bernis
The Origin of Flattery
The Peasant of the Alps
Song
Thirty-eight
Verses intended to have been prefixed to the Novel of Emmeline

Elegiac Sonnets, The Seventh Edition, with Additional Sonnets and Other Poems (1795)
Same as the Sixth Edition (including the beginning of the Third Edition)

Elegiac Sonnets, and Other Poems. The Eighth Edition. Vol I (1797)
Same as the Sixth Edition, with the addition of:

New Frontispiece image: "Oh! time has chang'd me"

New Frontispiece image: "Oh! time has chang'd me"
LX. To an amiable Girl
LXI. Supposed to have been written in America
LXII. Written on passing by Moon-light through a village, while the
ground was covered with Snow
LXIII. The Gossamer
LXIV. Written at Bristol in the Summer of 1794
LXV. To Dr. Parry of Bath, with some botanic drawings which had
been made some years
LXVI. Written in a tempestuous Night, on the coast of Sussex
LXVII. On passing over a dreary tract of country, and near the ruins
of a defeated chapel, during a Tempest
LXVIII. Written at Exmouth, Midsummer 1795
LXIX. Written at the same place, on seeing a Seaman return who
had been imprisoned at Rochfort
LXX. On being cautioned against walking on an Headland overlook-
ing the Sea, because it was frequented by a Lunatic (accompany-
ing image: "In moody sadness on the giddy Brink")
LXXI. Written at Weymouth in Winter
LXXII. To the Morning Star. Written near the Sea
LXXIII. To a querulous Acquaintance
LXXIV. The Winter Night
LXXV.
LXXVI. To a Young Man entering the World
LXXVII. To the Insect of the Gossamer
LXXVIII. Snow-drops
LXXIX. To the Goddess of Botany
LXXX. To the Invisible Moon
LXXXI.
LXXXII. To the Shade of Burns
LXXXIII. The Sea View
LXXXIV. To the Muse
The Dead Beggar
The Female Exile (accompanying image: "The gilt fairy Ship")
Occasional Address. Written for the Benefit of a distressed Player,
detained at Brighthelmstone for debt, November 1792
Inscription on a Stone in the Church-Yard at Boreham, in Essex
A descriptive Ode
Verses supposed to have been written in the New Forest, in early
Spring
Song. From the French
Apostrophe to an Old Tree

The Forest Boy (accompanying image: "By the Brook")
Ode to the Poppy. Written by a deceased Friend (accompanying
    image: "Hail lovely Blossom!")
Verses written by the same Lady on seeing her two Sons at play
Verses on the Death of the same Lady, written in September 1794
Fragment, descriptive of the Miseries of War
April
Ode to Death

Elegiac Sonnets, and Other Poems. The Ninth Edition. Vol I (1800)
Same as Volume One of Eighth Edition

Elegiac Sonnets, and Other Poems. Vol II. Second Edition (1800)
Same as Volume Two of Eighth Edition up to LXXXIV, then:

LXXXV.
LXXXVI. Written near a Port on a dark Evening
LXXXVII. Written in October
LXXXVIII. Nepenthe
LXXXIX. To the Sun
XC. To Oblivion
XCI. Reflections on some Drawings of Plants
XCII. Written at Bignor Park in Sussex, in August, 1799
The Dead Beggar
The Female Exile
Occasional Address. Written for the Benefit of a distressed Player,
    detained at Brighthelmstone for debt, November 1792
Inscription on a Stone in the Church-Yard at Boreham, in Essex
A descriptive Ode
Verses supposed to have been written in the New Forest, in early
    Spring
Song. From the French
Apostrophe to an Old Tree
The Forest Boy
Ode to the Poppy. Written by a deceased Friend
Verses written by the same Lady on seeing her two Sons at play
Verses on the Death of the same Lady, written in September 1794
Fragment, descriptive of the Miseries of War
April
Ode to Death
Stanzas from the Novel of the Young Philosopher
To the Winds
To Vesper
Lydia

Works Cited and Further Reading

Primary Sources

Bannerman, Anne. *Poems by Anne Bannerman*. Edinburgh: Mundell & Son, 1800.

Barbauld, Anna Laetitia. *The Poems*. Ed. William McCarthy Kraft and Elizabeth Athens. London: U of Georgia P, 1994.

Bowles, William Lisle. *Sonnets, Written Chiefly on Picturesque Spots, During a Tour*. 2nd ed. Bath: R. Cruttwell, 1789.

Browning, Elizabeth Barrett. *The Letters of Elizabeth Barrett Browning, in Two Volumes*. Ed. Frederick G. Kenyon. London: Smith, Elder and Co., 1897.

[Burney, Frances.] "Brief Reflections Relative to the Emigrant French Clergy: Earnestly Submitted to the Humane Consideration of the Ladies of Great Britain." London: T. Cadell, 1793.

Coleridge, Samuel Taylor. "Introduction to the Sonnets." *Poems*. 2nd ed. London, 1797.

Cowper, William. *The Letters and Prose Works of William Cowper*. Ed. James King and Charles Ryskamp. 5 vols. Oxford: Clarendon, 1984.

———. *The Task, A Poem in Six Books. To which are added, by the same author....* London: J. Johnson, 1785.

———. *The Task and Selected Other Poems*. Ed. James Sambrook. London: Longman, 1994.

Darwin, Erasmus. *The Temple of Nature, or the Origin of Society. A Poem, with Philosophical Notes*. London: J. Johnson, 1803.

Dyce, Alexander. *Specimens of British Poetesses; Selected and Chronologically Arranged*. London: T. Rodd, 1827.

Goethe, Johann Wolfgang von. *The Sorrows of Werter: A German Story*. Trans. ascribed to either Richard Graves or Daniel Malthus. London: J. Dodsley, 1779.

Gray, Thomas. *Poems by Mr. Gray*. Dublin: William Sleater, 1775.

Gray, Thomas, William Collins, and Oliver Goldsmith. *The Poems of Thomas Gray, William Collins and Oliver Goldsmith*. Ed. Roger Lonsdale. London: Longman, 1969.

Keats, John. *Life, Letters and Literary Remains of John Keats*. London: Edward Moxon, 1848.

Milton, John. *The Riverside Milton*. Ed. Roy Flannagan. Boston: Houghton, 1998.

More, Hannah. *A Prefatory Address to the Ladies &c. of Great Britain and Ireland in Behalf of the French Clergy*. 1793. First American Edition. Boston: Weld and Greenough, 1794.

Petrarch, Francesco. *Petrarch's Lyric Poems.* Trans. and ed. Robert M. Durling. Cambridge, MA: Harvard UP, 1976.

Pope, Alexander. *Alexander Pope.* Ed. Pat Rogers. Oxford: Oxford UP, 1993.

Robinson, Mary. *Selected Poems.* Ed. Judith Pascoe. Peterborough, ON: Broadview, 2000.

Seward, Anna. *Letters of Anna Seward written between the years 1784 and 1807. In Six Volumes.* Edinburgh: George Ramsay, 1811.

Shakespeare, William. *The Norton Shakespeare.* Ed. Stephen Greenblatt. 2nd ed. New York: Norton, 1997.

Smith, Charlotte. *The Collected Letters of Charlotte Smith.* Ed. Judith Phillips Stanton. Bloomington and Indianapolis: Indiana UP, 2003.

———. *The Poems of Charlotte Smith.* Ed. Stuart Curran. New York: Oxford UP, 1993.

———. *The Works of Charlotte Smith* Vol. 14. *Elegiac Sonnets Volumes 1 and 2, The Emigrants, Beachy Head: With Other Poems, Uncollected Poems.* Ed. Jacqueline Labbe. London: Pickering and Chatto, 2007.

Thelwall, John. *John Thelwall: Selected Poetry and Poetics.* Ed. Judith Thompson. New York: Palgrave Macmillan, 2015.

Thomson, James. *The Seasons.* 1726–46. Ed. James Sambrook. Oxford: Clarendon, 1981.

West, Jane. *Miscellaneous Poems, and a Tragedy.* York: W. Blanchard, 1791.

Wordsworth, William. *The Prelude, 1798–1799.* Ed. Stephen Parrish. Ithaca, NY: Cornell UP, 1977.

Wordsworth, William, and Samuel Taylor Coleridge. *Lyrical Ballads 1798 and 1800.* Ed. Michael Gamer and Dahlia Porter. Peterborough, ON: Broadview, 2008.

The following electronic databases were used for the sourcing of some texts:

17th and 18th Century Burney Collection Newspapers Online (Gale)
ECCO: Eighteenth-Century Collections Online (Gale)
British Periodicals (Proquest)

Secondary Sources

Anderson, John M. "'*Beachy Head*': The Romantic Fragment Poem as Mosaic." *The Huntington Library Quarterly* 63.4 (2000): 547–74.

Andrews, Kerri. "'Herself [...] Fills the Foreground': Negotiating Autobiography in the *Elegiac Sonnets* and *The Emigrants*." Labbe, *Charlotte Smith in British Romanticism* 13–27.

Backscheider, Paula R. *Eighteenth-Century Women Poets and Their Poetry: Inventing Agency, Inventing Genre*. Baltimore: Johns Hopkins UP, 2005.

Behrendt, Stephen C. *British Women Poets and the Romantic Writing Community*. Baltimore: Johns Hopkins UP, 2009.

——. "Charlotte Smith, Women Poets and the Culture of Celebrity." Labbe, *Charlotte Smith in British Romanticism* 189–202.

Benis, Toby R. *Romantic Diasporas: French Émigrés, British Convicts, and Jews*. New York: Palgrave, 2009.

Blank, Antje. "Charlotte Smith after 200 Years." *Women's Writing* 16.1 (2009): 1–5.

——. "Things as They Were: The Gothic of Real Life in Charlotte Smith's *The Emigrants* and *The Banished Man*." *Women's Writing* 16.1 (2009): 78–93.

Bode, Christopher. "The Subject of Beachy Head." Labbe, *Charlotte Smith in British Romanticism* 57–69.

Boyd, Diane. E. "'Professing Drudge': Charlotte Smith's Negotiation of a Mother-Writer Author Function." *South Atlantic Review* 66.1 (Winter 2001): 145–66.

Brooks, Stella. "The Sonnets of Charlotte Smith." *Critical Survey* 4.1 (1992): 9–21.

Carpenter, Kirsty. *Refugees of the French Revolution: Émigrés in London, 1789–1802*. Basingstoke: Macmillan, 1999.

Cook, Elizabeth Heckendorn. "Charlotte Smith and *The Swallow*: Migration and Romantic Authorship." *Huntington Library Quarterly: Studies in English and American History and Literature* 72.1 (2009): 48–67.

Craciun, Adriana. "Citizens of the World: Emigrés, Romantic Cosmopolitanism, and Charlotte Smith." *Nineteenth-Century Contexts* 29.2–3 (2007): 169–85.

——. "'Empire without End': Charlotte Smith at the Limits of Cosmopolitanism." *Women's Writing* 16.1 (2009): 39–59.

Curran, Stuart. "Introduction." *The Poems of Charlotte Smith*. New York: Oxford UP, 1993.

——. *Poetic Form and British Romanticism*. New York: Oxford UP, 1986.

———. "Romantic Poetry: The I Altered." *Romanticism and Feminism.* Ed. Anne Mellor. Bloomington and Indianapolis: Indiana UP, 1988. 185–207.

Dolan, Elizabeth. *Seeing Suffering in Women's Literature of the Romantic Era.* Aldershot: Ashgate, 2008.

Duckling, Louise. "'Tell My Name to Distant Ages': The Literary Fate of Charlotte Smith." Labbe, *Charlotte Smith in British Romanticism* 203–17.

Ellis, Kate Ferguson. *The Contested Castle: Gothic Novels and the Subversion of Domestic Ideology.* Urbana and Chicago: U of Illinois P, 1989.

Feldman, Paula, and Daniel Robinson. *A Century of Sonnets: The Romantic Era Revival.* Oxford: Oxford UP, 1999.

Fletcher, Loraine. *Charlotte Smith: A Critical Biography.* New York: St Martin's, 1998.

Fry, Carrol L. *Charlotte Smith.* New York: Twayne, 1996.

Garnai, Amy. *Revolutionary Imaginings in the 1790s: Charlotte Smith, Mary Robinson, Elizabeth Inchbald.* Basingstoke: Palgrave, 2009.

George, Jacqueline. "Public Reading and Lyric Pleasure: Eighteenth Century Elocutionary Debates and Poetic Practice." *ELH* 76.2 (2009): 371–97.

Girten, Kristin M. "Charlotte Smith's Tactile Poetics." *Eighteenth Century: Theory and Interpretation* 54.2 (2013): 215–30.

Goodman, Kevis. "Conjectures on Beachy Head: Charlotte Smith's Geological Poetics and the Ground of the Present." *ELH* 81.3 (2014): 983–1006.

Guest, Harriet. *Unbounded Attachment: Sentiment and Politics in the Age of the French Revolution.* Oxford: Oxford UP, 2013.

Gurton-Wachter, Lily. "'An Enemy, I Suppose, That Nature Has Made': Charlotte Smith and the Natural Enemy." *European Romantic Review* 20.2 (2009): 197–205.

Harries, Elizabeth W. "'Out in Left Field': Charlotte Smith's Prefaces, Bourdieu's Categories, and the Public Sphere." *MLQ: A Journal of Literary History* 52.4 (1997): 457–73.

Hart, Monica Smith. "Charlotte Smith's Exilic Persona." *Partial Answers: Journal of Literature and the History of Ideas* 8.2 (2010): 305–23.

Hawley, Judith. "Charlotte Smith's *Elegiac Sonnets*: Losses and Gains." *Women's Poetry in the Enlightenment: The Making of a Canon, 1730–1820.* Ed. Isobel Armstrong and Virginia Blain. London: Macmillan, 1999. 184–98.

Hoeveler, Diane Long. *Gothic Feminism: The Professionalization of Gender from Charlotte Smith to the Brontës.* University Park: Pennsylvania State UP, 1998.

Holt, Kelli M. "Charlotte Smith's *Beachy Head*: Science and the Dual Affliction of Minute Sympathy." *ABO: Interactive Journal for Women in the Arts* 4.1 (2014): Article 3, 13 pages.

Horrocks, Ingrid. *Women Wanderers and the Writing of Mobility, 1784–1814*. Cambridge: Cambridge UP, 2017.

Jon, Bumsoo. "Public Identity, Paratext, and the Aesthetics of Intransparency: Charlotte Smith's *Beachy Head*." *Journal of English Language and Literature* 58.6 (2012): 1167–91.

Kelley, Theresa M. "Romantic Histories: Charlotte Smith and Beachy Head." *Nineteenth-Century Literature* 59.3 (2004): 281–314.

Kennedy, Deborah. "Thorns and Roses: The Sonnets of Charlotte Smith." *Women's Writing* 2.1 (1995): 43–53.

Knowles, Claire. "'Hazarding the Press': Charlotte Smith, the *Morning Post*, and the Perils of Literary Celebrity." *Romanticism* 20:1 (2014): 30–42.

——. *Sensibility and Female Poetic Tradition, 1780–1860: The Legacy of Charlotte Smith*. Farnham: Ashgate, 2009.

Labbe, Jacqueline. "'The absurdity of animals having the passions and faculties of man': Charlotte Smith's Fables (1807)." *European Romantic Review* 19.2 (2008): 157–62.

——, ed. *Charlotte Smith in British Romanticism*. London: Pickering and Chatto, 2008.

——. *Charlotte Smith: Romanticism, Poetry and the Culture of Gender*. Manchester: Manchester UP, 2003.

——. "Selling One's Sorrows: Charlotte Smith, Mary Robinson, and the Marketing of Poetry." *Wordsworth Circle* 25:2 (Spring 1994): 68–71.

——. *Writing Romanticism: Charlotte Smith and William Wordsworth, 1784–1807*. Basingstoke: Palgrave, 2011.

Lokke, Kari. "Charlotte Smith and Literary History: 'Dark Forgetfulness' and the 'Intercession of Saint Monica.'" *Women's Studies* 27.3 (1998): 259–80.

——. "The Figure of the Hermit in Charlotte Smith's *Beachy Head*." *Wordsworth Circle* 39.1–2 (2008): 38–43.

——. "'The Mild Dominion of the Moon': Charlotte Smith and the Politics of Transcendence." *Rebellious Hearts: British Women Writers and the French Revolution*. Ed. Adriana Craciun and Kari E. Lokke. Albany: SUNY P, 2001. 85–106.

McGann, Jerome. *The Poetics of Sensibility: A Revolution in Literary Style*. Oxford: Clarendon, 1996.

Myers, Mary Anne. "Unsexing Petrarch: Charlotte Smith's Lessons in the Sonnet as a Social Medium." *Studies in Romanticism* 53.2 (2014): 239–63.

Özdemir, Erinç. "Charlotte Smith's Poetry as Sentimental Discourse." *Studies in Romanticism* 50.3 (2011): 437–73.

Pinch, Adela. *Strange Fits of Passion: Epistemologies of Emotion, Hume to Austen.* Stanford, CA: Stanford UP, 1996.

Porter, Dahlia. "From Nosegay to Specimen Cabinet: Charlotte Smith and the Labour of Collecting." Labbe, *Charlotte Smith in British Romanticism* 29–44.

Richard, Melissa. "Pastoral Preoccupation and Transformation in Charlotte Smith's *The Emigrants* and *Beachy Head.*" *Turning Points and Transformations: Essays on Language, Literature and Culture.* Ed. J. Page, et al. Newcastle: Cambridge Scholars, 2011. 17–29.

Richey, William. "The Rhetoric of Sympathy in Smith and Wordsworth." *European Romantic Review* 13.4 (2002): 427–43.

Roberts, Bethan. "Literary Past and Present in Charlotte Smith's *Elegiac Sonnets.*" *Studies in English Literature 1500–1900* 54.3 (2014): 649–74.

Robinson, Daniel. "Reviving the Sonnet: Women Romantic Poets and the Sonnet Claim." *European Romantic Review* 6 (Summer 1995): 98–127.

Ruwe, Donelle R. "Charlotte Smith's Sublime: Feminine Poetics, Botany, and *Beachy Head.*" *Prism(s): Essays in Romanticism* 7 (1999): 117–32.

Schor, Esther. *Bearing the Dead: The British Culture of Mourning from the Enlightenment to Victoria.* Princeton, NJ: Princeton UP, 1994.

Sodeman, Melissa. "Charlotte Smith's Literary Exile." *ELH* 76.1 (2009): 131–52.

Stanton, Judith Phillips. "Charlotte Smith's 'Literary Business': Income, Patronage and Indigence." *The Age of Johnson: A Scholarly Annual* 1 (1987): 375–401.

Staves, Susan. *A Literary History of Women's Writing in Britain, 1660–1789.* Cambridge: Cambridge UP, 2006.

Stokes, Christopher. "Lorn Subjects: Haunting, Fracture and Ascesis in Charlotte Smith's *Elegiac Sonnets.*" *Women's Writing* 16.1 (2009): 143–60.

Tayebi, Kandi. "Charlotte Smith and the Quest for the Romantic Prophetic Voice." *Women's Writing* 11.3 (2004): 421–38.

——. "Undermining the Eighteenth-Century Pastoral: Rewriting the Poet's Relationship to Nature in Charlotte Smith's Poetry." *European Romantic Review* 15.1 (March 2004): 131–50.

Terry, Richard. "Sentimental Doubling in Charlotte Smith's *Elegiac Sonnets.*" *ANQ: A Quarterly Journal of Short Articles, Notes, and Reviews* 20.4 (2007): 50–58.

Todd, Janet. *Sensibility: An Introduction.* London and New York: Methuen, 1986.

Wadewitz, Adrianne. "The Politically Engaged Child: Charlotte Smith's Children's Literature and the Discourse of Sensibility." *Beyond Sense and Sensibility: Moral Formation and the Literary Imagination from Johnson to Wordsworth.* Ed. Peggy Thompson. Lewisburg, PA: Bucknell UP, 2015. 91–106.

Wallace, Anne D. "Picturesque Fossils, Sublime Geology? The Crisis of Authority in Charlotte Smith's *Beachy Head.*" *European Romantic Review* 13.1 (2002): 77–93.

White, Daniel E. "Autobiography and Elegy: The Early Romantic Poetics of Thomas Gray and Charlotte Smith." *Early Romantics: Perspectives in Poetry from Pope to Wordsworth.* Ed. Thomas Woodman. London: Macmillan, 1998. 57–69.

Wiley, Michael. *Romantic Migrations: Local, National, and Transnational Dispositions.* New York: Palgrave, 2008.

Wolfson, Susan. *Romantic Interactions: Social Being and the Turns of Literary Action.* Baltimore: Johns Hopkins UP, 2010.

Zimmerman, Sarah M. "'Dost Thou Not Know My Voice?': Charlotte Smith and the Lyric's Audience." *Romanticism and Women Poets: Opening the Doors of Reception.* Ed. Harriet Kramer Linkin and Stephen Behrendt. Lexington: U of Kentucky P, 1999. 101–24.

——. *Romanticism, Lyricism, and History.* New York: SUNY P, 1999.

——. "Varieties of Privacy in Charlotte Smith's Poetry." *European Romantic Review* 18.4 (2007): 483–502.

From the Publisher

A name never says it all, but the word "Broadview" expresses a good deal of the philosophy behind our company. We are open to a broad range of academic approaches and political viewpoints. We pay attention to the broad impact book publishing and book printing has in the wider world; we began using recycled stock more than a decade ago, and for some years now we have used 100% recycled paper for most titles. Our publishing program is internationally oriented and broad-ranging. Our individual titles often appeal to a broad readership too; many are of interest as much to general readers as to academics and students.

Founded in 1985, Broadview remains a fully independent company owned by its shareholders—not an imprint or subsidiary of a larger multinational.

For the most accurate information on our books (including information on pricing, editions, and formats) please visit our website at www.broadviewpress.com. Our print books and ebooks are also available for sale on our site.

On the Broadview website we also offer several goods that are not books—among them the Broadview coffee mug, the Broadview beer stein (inscribed with a line from Geoffrey Chaucer's *Canterbury Tales*), the Broadview fridge magnets (your choice of philosophical or literary), and a range of T-shirts (made from combinations of hemp, bamboo, and/or high-quality pima cotton, with no child labor, sweatshop labor, or environmental degradation involved in their manufacture).

All these goods are available through the "merchandise" section of the Broadview website. When you buy Broadview goods you can support other goods too.

broadview press
www.broadviewpress.com